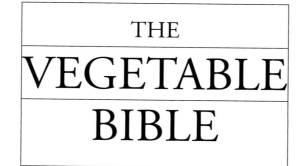

THE
VEGETABLE
BIBLE

THE VEGETABLE BIBLE

Idea and concept: Christian Teubner
Vegetable encyclopedia: Hans-Georg Levin, Elisabeth Lange
Recipes: Andreas Miessmer

whitecap

This edition published in the U.S. and Canada by Whitecap Books. For more information, contact Whitecap Books, 351 Lynn Avenue, North Vancouver, BC, V7J 2C4.

First published by Penguin Studio, an imprint of Penguin Books USA Inc. in 1998.

Original edition published under the title *Das grosse Buch der Gemüse aus aller Welt,* 1991
Copyright © Teubner Edition, Germany, 1991
English language text copyright © Transedition Ltd, England, 1998. All rights reserved.

Note: Kiwano is a registered trademark of J. & S. Morris, Kaukapakapa, New Zealand.
Photographs other than those listed in the Picture Credits: Christian Teubner, Dorothee Gödert
Layout: Susanne Mühldorfer
Origination: PHG-Lithos GmbH, Planegg
Editorial management: Linda Doeser
Design and production: Richard Johnson

ISBN: 1-55285-434-5

Printed & Bound in Dubai
by Emirates Printing Press.

Contents

Vegetables
Their history in the West and in the East

Anyone interested in the history of vegetables should look up the accounts and drawings of medicinal plants made by medieval monks. Roots and herbs were thought to be worth mentioning only for their curative powers. For example, in the Middle Ages, scorzonera or black salsify was reputed to be an antidote to snake venom. Parsnips were thought to be good for treating insomnia, and sorrel was used to cure liver and kidney complaints. Some therapeutic effect was ascribed to almost all domestic vegetables, but the everyday and the simple did not merit attention.

In the fourteenth century, Saint Catherine of Siena, so the story goes, ate nothing but "raw herbs" from the age of 14—what nowadays we would describe as raw fruit and vegetables. Hers was not an unusual story in the history of the Church. A diet rich in vegetables was characteristic of the way of life of early Western monks, since vegetables stood for asceticism. Benedictine and Carthusian

These corn cobs have been harvested when young and are being sold as a vegetable. The Aztecs were raising the golden grain over 5,000 years ago. Market stalls like this one are still seen today in Hungary.

monks were completely vegetarian. The medieval nobility's disdain for "roots and herbs" still exists, to some extent, in the West. Only meat is equated with wealth and those who must eat vegetables are still often thought of as poor or fasting.

The Eastern viewpoint, however, has always been very different. In Asian countries vegetables represent aesthetic and culinary riches. Many Asian cuisines, such as those of China and, later, Japan, resulted from the constraints of poverty, and developed their complexity in spite of, or perhaps precisely because of this. Prepared with great care and sophistication, vegetables formed the dominant part of these culinary traditions. From time immemorial, they have constituted an important component of any meal, second only to grains. The soybean, which has been cultivated in China for over 800 years, still constitutes, together with its products, the focus of Chinese and Japanese cuisine and is esteemed accordingly. To observe the reverence and skill with which a Japanese cook cuts vegetables is like watching a solemn ritual.

The care with which the Chinese vegetable seller has laid out his wares in this old picture (top) shows the importance of vegetables in his culture. This attitude can still be seen throughout Asia, even in a modern Japanese supermarket (above). Here, expensively and hygienically packaged vegetables are laid out for customers to inspect thoroughly before making their selection and purchase. The poverty which throughout history often drove this nation to make use of everything, even seaweed, has led to a reverential treatment of food.

A medieval vegetable garden: The distinction between cultivated and wild plants was blurred and harvests were meager. Even at the beginning of the nineteenth century, one farmer could feed only four town dwellers. Today's farms are vast and high-tech.

Cultivation
Different systems: organic, conventional, and integrated

For centuries, farmers passed their knowledge from generation to generation. Soil fertility and climate, like good or poor harvests, were the will of God, and people just came to terms with them. Then, about 150 years ago, new discoveries in plant nutrition and technology revolutionized agriculture. As a result of nineteenth-century research, soil became more fertile and harvests increased. Labor-saving machines, mineral fertilizers, large-scale cultivation, greenhouses, and chemical pesticides also made impressive increases in yield possible in the twentieth century.

However, even when harvests were good, farmers still had financial problems. Lack of manpower, as villages and small towns decreased in size, together with falling prices, forced further mechanization and the simplification of crop rotation to the point of cultivating a single product. Reliance on chemicals became more and more complete because of a decrease in soil fertility, and crops also became more susceptible to all types of pests. Chemical interference with the delicate biological balance between pests and beneficial predators, and the increasing resistance of insects, molds, and bacteria, caused more and new agricultural chemicals to be used.

This is a brief history of what, until a few years ago, was called "modern," and is now referred to as "conventional," agriculture. People began to criticize this extreme method of production on the grounds that producing surpluses is at the expense of the environment, and it is true that many sins are committed in intensive vegetable cultivation. Cucumbers and tomatoes, for example, are grown in huge plastic tunnels or glasshouses covering many acres. The soil is subjected to radical methods of cultivation with heavy applications of fertilizer and other chemicals.

However, even responsible conventional vegetable growers, who spray against pests only after careful diagnosis, and who observe all the prescribed waiting periods or even exceed them to be entirely sure that their vegetables are residue-

Plastic tunnels large enough for tractors to work in are replacing greenhouses. Here, cucumber plants are being raised.

People have been growing vegetables **under plastic** since the 1970s in order to store heat, provide wind protection, and harvest crops earlier (top). To discourage weeds and pests, the plants are grown under a **polyethylene mulch** stretched out flat (center). With miles of the product being used at a time, people have only begun to come to grips with the problem of disposing of this plastic waste. Better for plants and the environment, but also substantially more expensive, is **paper mulch** (above).

The right variety for the location Here, lollo rosso, romaine, and head lettuces are being grown experimentally in adjacent rows. This allows the grower to determine which variety is best suited to the conditions in this field.

free, may still be criticized by environmentalists. The key word is nitrate. A harmless nutrient, essential for plants, nitrates are washed by rain out of over-fertilized fields and into the groundwater. Bacteria then transform nitrates into nitrites, creating a poison. Nitrites can cause choking attacks in young children, and their metabolic products are reputed to be triggers for some types of adult cancers. It is hardly surprising that many countries have drawn up laws on the maximum concentration of nitrates in drinking water. Even this is not enough because we absorb about 70 percent of the total amount of nitrates from vegetables and salads and only 15–20 percent directly from water. Some governments have now drawn up guidelines for the maximum content of certain nitrate-collecting vegetables.

The so-called alternative farmers, whether they use biodynamic, organic, natural, or ecological methods, are striking a chord with consumers in spite of the higher prices of their produce. Their self-imposed guidelines can be summarized as follows: maintaining and increasing soil fertility, raising healthy crops as far as possible without pesticides, consciously avoiding environmental pollutants, and encouraging species with a high innate resistance to pests. Farmers must achieve these goals, while still adhering to strict rules. For example, chemical and synthetic, highly soluble fertilizers, and the use of herbicides, growth regulators, and desiccants are forbidden. Plant protection is mainly achieved by strengthening the natural defenses of the soil and the plants themselves. Biodynamic and organic vegetable growers take location, crop rotation, plant combinations, time of sowing, and much more just as seriously. As worthwhile as all this sounds, these organic methods mean a larger workforce, lower yields, and a considerable financial risk.

The new "integrated" farming method creates a bridge between ecology and economics. It attempts

Natural predators instead of chemicals: ichneumon fly larvae are used against the tomato pest, whitefly.

Two-thirds of all cultivated land in the world lies in the tropics and subtropics. Water is the limiting factor everywhere, but with good irrigation, three or more harvests a year are possible, as the individual times taken for crops to grow to maturity in hot climates are considerably shorter than in temperate latitudes.

Dutch tomatoes: Ninety percent of tomatoes in Holland are grown with their roots in sterile rock wool. Nutrients are supplied through a small drip tube (top). The advantage of this is a high yield with low use of chemicals. **Sitting down on the job:** The tomatoes are picked from a small wagon and packed immediately into crates (above).

intended to protect both environment and plants. A carefully calculated quantity of fertilizer is applied only after soil tests. Proponents of integrated agriculture consider mineral fertilizers, which are scorned by organic farmers, to be easier to calculate and measure accurately than the organic fertilizers preferred by alternative growers (liquid manure, farmyard manure, or compost), which can also pollute soils, subsequent crops, and the groundwater with an excess of nutrients.

Yet another system of cultivation attempts to come to grips with pressing ecological and economic problems by making use of scientific methods and relying heavily on technology. Vegetable growers in Holland and Belgium, in particular, have evolved into companies with highly rationalized operations. Plants are grown under glass on a massive scale, in order to protect crops from bad weather and environmental pollution. Computers control temperature, watering, lighting, and feeding. A further development has been hydroponically grown crops—those not using soil as a growing medium. Advanced technology has taken the place of traditional knowledge. Plants thrive

These tomatoes are being pollinated in the conventional way by hand. Nowadays, bumblebees once again perform this service for the plants.

to combine environmentally compatible agriculture with modern growing methods. The word "integrated" was first used in connection with plant protection and the use of pesticides. This was tackled by protecting natural predators and taking other steps against pests, planting pest-resistant species, and making use of the most recent biological and biotechnological methods, so that the use of chemicals can remain as low as possible. In contrast to alternative agriculture, chemical pesticides are not completely banned, but are used only where absolutely necessary.

A workable system developed only when environmentally friendly agricultural techniques were also adopted. In addition to other measures, customized applications of mineral fertilizers are

without soil, and are grown in nutrient solutions. Instead of growing in the ground, roots take hold in rock wool (basalt), volcanic granules, or polyurethane or polyethylene foam.

Why go to so much effort? Producers say that yields are higher and up to 85 percent of pesticides are saved, making a switch to organic methods possible. The argument is especially convincing in the case of soils which have been polluted for decades by intensive farming and in water-protection zones, if an increase of nitrate in the soil is to be avoided, since nutrients remain in closed cycles. Nonetheless, experts remain divided on whether the consumer will accept hydroponically grown vegetables in the long term. Many also wonder what will happen to the normal coexistence of vegetables with the fungi, bacteria, and microbes that populate the soil if the roots of plants are kept germ-free. Scientists can only shrug their shoulders in answer to this question. The few trials which have been carried out so far reveal little about the changes in the complicated metabolic systems.

Which then is the best system for growing vegetables? Even experts are reluctant to pronounce on this. Agriculture is undergoing a learning process, where yesterday's cast-iron certainties have sometimes been proved false and brand-new methods may be obsolete by tomorrow. Genetic engineering may even make pesticides superfluous.

"Baby" vegetables—celebrity chefs love the little ones

Growing them pays dividends because, depending on the type, miniature vegetables sell for two to three times as much as comparable normal-size ones. One wonders why these tiny cabbages, carrots, fennel bulbs, and leeks are worth so much. Perhaps it is simply an in-built preference for the young and tender. Besides, miniature vegetables give the impression that they are even more delicate than the most tender, young vegetable of normal size. Unlike fruit, there is no direct correlation in vegetables between ripeness and optimum nutrients. Even when very young, vegetables have just about all of the constituents which are to be found in larger specimens. Thus, carrots, leeks, cauliflowers, cabbages, and zucchini, when sown more densely and harvested much earlier, result in miniature editions. On the other hand, dwarf species are selected for mini cucumbers, pattypan squash, and eggplants, for which a longer growing period would not mean that they became any larger. Mini artichokes, for example, come from dwarf species, which are also picked early.

Storing vegetables
It pays to be careful as you can avoid deterioration

Most vegetables lose their freshness quickly at room temperature. Water is lost within hours, causing the vegetable to wilt. At the same time, vitamins sensitive to air and light are lost. Fungi and bacteria spread and quality is significantly reduced. This is because natural metabolic processes continue after vegetables have been harvested. The plant is no longer providing nutrients, so constituents are constantly being broken down and transformed. Storage at low temperatures delays these processes. Large companies have cool rooms for this purpose, where both temperature and humidity can be controlled. Smaller companies and ordinary homes must content themselves with refrigerators with separate storage zones with temperatures ranging from 32–34°F, 41–45°F, and 50–54°F. Even then, the vegetables must sorted according to type and covered in plastic wrap to create the required level of humidity. This is especially important for sensitive salad greens and leafy vegetables, which dry out incredibly quickly, spoiling the flavor.

A refrigerator with three storage zones, ideal for all types of vegetables: lettuces and leafy vegetables are stored at 32–34°F, potatoes at 41°F, and fruits that are used like vegetables (tomatoes, bell peppers, etc.), which are sensitive to the cold, at 50–54°F.

Storage times for fresh vegetables				
Vegetable	Temperature in °F	Rel. humidity %	Storage time	
			Months	Weeks
Asparagus	34–36	92–95		2
Beets	32–34	92–95	6	
Belgian endive	32–34	90		4
Bell peppers	46–48	90–93		3
Broccoli	32–34	95		1–2
Brussels sprouts	28	92–95	2–3	
Cabbage, green	28	92–95	2–3	
Cabbage, red and white	32–34	92–95	5–8	
Cabbage, Savoy	30	92–95	max. 3	
Carrots	34	95	5–6	
Cauliflower	32–34	95		2–4
Celery	32–34	92–95		4
Celery root	32–34	92–95	5–6	
Chinese cabbage	34	92–95	2–3	
Corn	32–34	92–95		max. 1
Cucumbers	45–46	92–95		1–2
Eggplants	50	92–95		3
Endive	32–34	92–95		3
Fava beans	32–34	92–95		3
Fennel	34	92–95	3	
Garlic	32–34	65–75	6–7	
Head lettuce	32–34	95		1–2
Horseradish	28–30	92–95	12–18	
Kohlrabi, with tops	32–34	92–95		2
Kohlrabi, without tops	32–34	92–95		3
Leeks	30–32	95	2	
Mâche (corn salad)	34	95		3
Onions	30	70–75	8	
Parsley root	28–30	95		up to 8
Peas in pods	30	92–95		1
Potatoes	39–41	92–95	8	
Pumpkin	50–54	60–70	3	
Radishes	32–34	92–95		1
Rhubarb	32–34	92–95		3
Scallions	32–34	95		1
Spinach	32–34	92–95		max. 1
String beans	45–46	92–95		1–2
Tomatoes, ripe	46–50	80–85		1
Tomatoes, semi-ripe	54	85–90		max. 3
Winter radishes	32–34	92–95	3–5	

Source: Deutsche Gesellschaft für Hauswirtschaft EV (Publ.), *Lebensmittelverarbeitung im Haushalt* ("Processing of food in the home"), Stuttgart (Ulmer Verlag) 1984

Healthy eating in today's world
Enjoying the pleasures of the table with a clear conscience

Our ancestors usually had just one dietary problem—not enough food. Even at the beginning of the twentieth century, many people in the Western world suffered from hunger and so were more susceptible to illness and disease, often dying in childhood. Eating too much was a problem found only among a small class of the rich; a fashionable figure was curvaceous and, implicitly, well fed. Those times are long past. Today, it is not in style to be voluptuous and is certainly no longer an indication of social success and high income. Nowadays, we are at pains to cope with a surplus of food, and many fight the battle of the bulge.

Basic nutrients
An important trio

Carbohydrate, protein, and fat form the basis of the human diet. These fundamental nutrients ensure that we have enough energy for all our bodily functions and energy for work and leisure: without them, nothing runs properly. In addition, proteins provide the building blocks for muscles and other organs, fats act as a cushion and provide basic substances for all our cells. The foods we eat are mixtures of the three basic nutrients combined in different proportions. Sugar consists almost entirely of carbohydrate, vegetable oil of fat, and lean meat primarily supplies protein. The illustration overleaf shows at a glance which foods are the main providers of protein, fat, and carbohydrate.

Our bodies need different amounts of the three basic nutrients, but scientists disagree over the exact proportions. In the 1960s, they argued the case for as much **protein** as possible, but we have since learned that there is no advantage in consuming excessive quantities. We know from sports medicine, in particular, that metabolism is delayed when excess protein is consumed, and that the body reacts with a reduced performance. The recommendation nowadays is approximately 0.8 gram protein per kilogram of body weight per day. For children, pregnant women, and nursing mothers, this should be increased to 2–2.3 grams. More important than the quantity, however, is the quality. A source of protein is ideal for humans only if plenty of bodily protein can be created from the constituents (amino acids). Experts call this the "biological value" of the food and have assigned reference figures to individual sources of protein. A hen's egg was used as the reference point, with a value of 100.

Sources of protein

Protein source	Biological value
Animal:	
Hen's egg	100
Beef	92
Milk	90
Vegetable:	
Potato	99
Soy	85
Legumes	73

The biological value can be increased by combining animal and plant proteins. This is very important because an excess of animal products can adversely affect the metabolism because of their high content of fat and cholesterol. Perhaps this sounds rather complicated, but we put it into practice every day when we prepare a meal: potatoes with fried eggs, for example, have a biological value of 136. The value is thus higher than the egg (100) or the potatoes (99) alone. The combination of potatoes with dairy products, meat, or fish is nearly as good. Legumes provide a good source of protein when eaten with grains. A typical example from South American cuisine is beans and corn tortillas. In predominantly vegetarian India, lentils (dhal) with rice or bread are eaten daily, providing the poor with sufficient protein to stay healthy. Dishes based on beans with bean curd and seeds are also ideal.

Protein content of vegetables

Vegetables, according to type	1–5%
Legumes	about 25%
Soybeans	35–40%
Potatoes	2–3%

As with protein, researchers have only recently been able to agree on recommendations for **fat** consumption. Here, the argument was less about the recommended quantities than about the different types of fat. Nowadays, almost all scientists advise us to consume more vegetable than animal fats. This is because cholesterol, known as a risk factor in cardiovascular diseases, is present mainly in animal fats. Vegetable oils, however, are usually rich in unsaturated fatty acids, which have a regulatory effect on cholesterol levels in the blood. More important for health than the type of fat is the amount consumed; in the Western world our total fat consumption is usually far too high. A reduced diet is the right idea in most cases.

Researchers have also made new discoveries about **carbohydrates**. Proponents of wholefood diets wrote off the most popular carbohydrate provider, sugar, as harmful. In fact, it has been proved harmful only to teeth and body weight. Nonetheless, the unequivocal opinion of nutritionists is that complex (starch-containing) sources of carbohydrates, such as potatoes, legumes, and bread, should constitute the largest part of our consumption. Sugar passes immediately into the bloodstream, but complex or starch-containing carbohydrates stay in the stomach longer and are absorbed by the body more slowly, but also more continuously. The advantages of this are enormous: fewer fluctuations in blood sugar level and fewer cravings for yet more sweet foods.

Our bodies need a certain amount of basic nutrients and tolerate a large range of variation from day to day. If, however, we eat exclusively too much or too little over a long period, we pay the price, even if the day of reckoning is a long way off.

Extensive choice from the market stall: preparing fresh vegetables as soon as possible after purchase and without using too much fat goes a long way toward ensuring your good health.

Nutrient density
Highest for vegetables

Most of us spend our days sitting: in the car, at the desk, in front of the computer screen or the television. During the last 20 years, the proportion of people in jobs requiring hard physical labor has shrunk dramatically. Even in the home, machines now perform almost all tasks that once required physical effort. As a result, even when we eat apparently normally, we may consume more energy—calories—than our bodies can use. Simply reducing the amount we eat does not solve the problem, as this also reduces the quantities of vitamins, minerals, trace elements, and fiber, and impairs our performance. What is more, we cannot ignore our instincts for any length of time without paying the price. Those who keep themselves on a tight rein, eating only half their fill in order to stay or become slim, must reckon on eventual ravenous hunger, cravings, and uncontrolled bingeing. What we need, then, are foods that satisfy, but contain fewer calories and plenty of nutrients. Experts refer to such foods as having high nutrient density. Unlike candy or fatty meat with a low nutrient density, all vegetables fulfill this demand of modern nutritional science. They contribute a great deal to our physical maintenance, providing the following daily average percentages in a normal diet.

Different types of bean curd: the protein-rich blocks of soybean curd are as much a part of Asian cuisine as different sorts of meat are of Western cooking.

0%	Cholesterol
1%	Fat
7%	Protein
10%	Calories
12%	Potassium
15%	Iron
20%	Vitamins Niacin and B$_1$
25%	Magnesium and vitamin A
35%	Vitamin B$_6$
40%	Vitamin C

The favorable ratio of calories to nutrients is easy to see. From artichokes to zucchini, vegetables are unlikely to make you fat, unless you eat huge quantities. Even starchy potatoes and legumes are low in calories in relation to how filling they are. They only become fattening when they are served with a lot of fat and meat. The results of a major study on the health of vegetarians astonished even the experts. People whose diets center on vegetables are seldom troubled with the typical illnesses of Western society. Although the vegetarians in the study ate as much as the meat-eating control group, very few of them were overweight and their cholesterol counts and blood pressure were considerably lower.

60 percent carbohydrate is ideal. We can eat our fill of starchy foods, such as potatoes, vegetables, grains, rice, and pasta, which provide the right sort of carbohydrates. Sugary foods should be eaten in moderation. Although rich in carbohydrates, they offer little of use besides concentrated calories.

Eating habits
Why we like what we like

In the course of our lives, we swallow between 30 and 40 tons of food, and on a global scale most of this consists of vegetables, legumes, and grains. The composition of the foods we eat has a bearing on our health and life expectancy. Eating is of such central importance for our survival that our bodies cannot leave decisions on this matter to our minds alone. Our habits show clearly how strong a role is played by the subconscious and by instinct. Disgust protects us from eating foods that have gone off. Hunger, appetite, and feelings of fullness are controlled by internal signals in healthy people, but culture and upbringing also color our behavior.

A child becomes accustomed to the cooking of his native country as automatically as he learns his mother tongue. In South America, he will eat beans and corn daily, in Japan, seaweed and soy products, and in Italy, pasta and various sauces. These early experiences influence us so profoundly that the eating habits established in childhood and youth usually remain the same throughout life. We tend to approach unknown foods and dishes with caution, or try them only with great suspicion. Just how deep our mistrust is can be seen in the following tragic example. Many thousands of children have died from the effects of malnutrition in the African state of Zambia, although plenty of nutritious soybeans are grown there. These were exported rather than eaten, however, as nobody had helped the people to become familiar with an unaccustomed food. Only after an aid worker showed mothers that dishes prepared with soy products taste good did child mortality figures fall.

This behavior is not limited to people from particular cultures or countries. Despite repeated famines, Frederick the Great of Prussia had to trick the rural populace into eating potatoes, which were still considered an exotic vegetable in the seventeenth century. He ordered his soldiers to guard a potato field as diligently as if they were protecting a great treasure. This aroused curiosity and finally persuaded the farmers to try the nutritious tubers and gradually accept them as food. This process of acceptance has followed a similar course in recent years with quite a number of now familiar vegetables, such as eggplant, bok choi, and zucchini. It was only when they became fashionable, and others had tried them without coming to any harm that conservative eaters accepted them. What we choose depends very much on the influence of our environment.

15 percent protein: Milk and dairy products, eggs, an occasional piece of meat, fish once a week, or a slice of cheese, sausage, or salami with bread, provides the body with ample animal protein. Plant protein as a necessary supplement comes from potatoes, pulses, grains, and other plant foods.

30 percent fat maximum: Our diet should contain only moderate amounts of fat. It really pays to make savings here. Although fat improves the flavor of food and is indispensable in cooking, it is hidden in many foods, and we often greatly exceed our ideal allowances. It is best to use more vegetable fats and fewer animal fats.

Fiber
Boost the immune system and regulate cholesterol levels

It was comparatively recently that nutritionists recognized the importance of fiber in our diets. Once known as roughage, it used to be considered superfluous ballast that weakened the body by placing additional demands on the digestive system. This was one reason why coarse vegetables, such as legumes and cabbage, were dismissed as poor man's food. After British researchers established a connection between highly refined food and some of the diseases of modern civilization in the 1970s, dieticians began to address the subject. The advantages of a fiber-rich diet have now been scientifically verified: it contains fewer animal products, less fat, less cholesterol, and fewer calories, and it satisfies hunger for longer.

Even now, opinions differ as to what fiber actually is. One thing is certain—it is present only in plant foods. Most types of fiber belong to the carbohydrates group, but their composition varies so greatly that their actions on the human body cannot be classed together. Their main functions can be explained using the example of cellulose, which is present in large quantities in both grains and vegetables. Our gastric juices cannot break down these large molecules, but cellulose absorbs water in the intestine, swelling up, and increasing the bulk of the broken-down food. As a result, digestive juices flow more freely. In the intestine, the cellulose "ties up" matter which is irritating to the mucosa or indigestible—possibly even poisonous—and conveys it quickly out of the body.

The word "fiber" normally evokes images of whole-wheat bread and wheat bran. Indeed, the indigestible constituents of the grain husk are among the most effective of this group and have been extensively researched. The functions of fiber in vegetables have not been so well examined.

This may be because the proportion of fiber is lower in vegetables. As a result of their high water content, green and root vegetables contain only 1–5 percent fiber. Legumes, however, provide up to 20 percent, twice as much fiber as whole-wheat. In addition to the main constituents of pectin and cellulose, many types of vegetables contain fiber in the form of indigestible mucilages and protein constituents, vegetable gums, and complex sugars. Although present in relatively small quantities, these are extremely helpful. Of no nutritional value for the body, they act as a sort of bacteria fodder, improving the gut flora (bacteria present in the

It makes a big difference to the body whether vegetables are eaten raw or finely chopped and cooked. Nutrients enter the bloodstream more slowly from coarsely grated raw food than from cooked, puréed vegetables. This is particularly important for diabetics and overweight people, since both are often prone to fluctuations in blood-sugar levels.

Fiber may produce flatulence, but this is not inevitable. The gas-producing effect of cabbage, for example, is well known. Its fiber content, however, is in the middle of the range, lower than that of whole-wheat bread. Over 90 percent of the fiber in cabbage is broken down in the intestine by the bacteria present there. It is these which produce the unpleasant intestinal gases. Certain spices, such as caraway and fennel seeds, can help to alleviate these annoying side effects.

intestine that are essential for digestion). This may result in embarrassing gas from time to time, but ensures a healthy intestine.

The intestine is important as the main location of the body's immune system. The intestinal mucosa are colonized by up to 500 microorganisms. By means of a complex mechanism, fiber, particularly that from raw vegetables, prevents the wrong sorts of bacteria from taking hold. In addition, a well-filled intestine stimulates circulation, providing the immune cells established there with ample oxygen and nutrients. If the intestine is in good shape through the consumption of plenty of vegetables, infectious illnesses can be fought off more easily and environmental pollution coped with better.

Pectin also has a beneficial effect. Present in many vegetables and fruits, it is well known to cooks as a gelling agent. Average daily consumption is about 3 grams, so it is not very important in terms of quantity, but its effect is impressive. It indirectly regulates cholesterol levels by binding acids secreted by the gall bladder. The body requires cholesterol to replace these acids, so cholesterol levels fall as pectin consumption increases.

Vitamins and minerals
Small amounts, large effects

During metabolism, thousands of substances are created and broken down every minute. Most of these are synthesized by the body itself, but a few must be provided regularly through the food we eat. This is the case with vitamins, whose functions are chiefly regulatory. Minerals and trace elements are also essential to enable a multitude of building and conversion processes to take place in the body. Like vitamins, they ensure that these processes take place without a hitch. If vitamins or minerals are in short supply, the body attempts to adjust to the emergency, turning the heat down a notch, so to speak. With any deficiency, the initial consequences are identical: reduced performance and a feeling of being slightly indisposed that is often hardly noticeable. If vitamins or minerals are lacking over a relatively long period, deficiency diseases arise. A well-known example of vitamin C deficiency is scurvy; in the past, sailors on journeys lasting several months without fresh fruit or vegetables used to die from this.

Such severe deficiency conditions now rarely occur in Europe and North America, and in the Third World almost always go hand in hand with general and extreme malnutrition. In spite of this, the matter should not be taken lightly. Vitamin and mineral supplements are not necessary, but an optimal intake through diet delays symptoms of wear and tear and degenerative diseases. There are even indications of a connection between inadequate vitamin intake and cancer. If you include fresh vegetables in your daily menu, you can leave pocket calculators and vitamin tables behind. All vegetables are good-to-excellent providers of vital vitamins and minerals. Listing quantities in milligrams or micrograms is of no use in an everyday context because it is impossible to judge your current daily requirement. All kinds of circumstances, such as your general state of health, what other things you are eating, the climate, the season, psychological pressures, and much else, play too large a role, and make for major fluctuations in requirements. Besides, even the researchers do not know the answer right down to the last microgram.

The vitamin content—how many vitamins or minerals a particular vegetable on the plate contains at a particular moment—is no more certain than any one person's daily requirement. Plants grown in the same field can vary widely. Even within the same tomato, one side of the fruit (the one turned toward the sun) often has more vitamins than the other. No one can quantify losses during storage and transportation. Moreover, just how many nutrients sensitive to light, air, water, and heat fall by the wayside during the trimming, washing, cutting up, and cooking of vegetables could be determined only by expensive and time-consuming laboratory tests. The figures listed in nutrient tables are only statistical averages. They provide guidelines to whether the daily diet contains enough vital nutrients, but are not a great deal of use to the layman in day-to-day life.

It is much more important for the ordinary person to take care that as few vitamins and minerals as possible are lost during preparation. Vitamin C, for example, is destroyed by oxygen and heat. Minerals are flushed out and vitamins A, B$_2$, and B$_6$ break down with exposure to light. These disadvantages can easily be minimized when preparing and cooking vegetables. Always wash them before cutting them up, otherwise too many vitamins and minerals end up down the drain. Never leave trimmed or sliced vegetables soaking in water or their minerals will leach out. It is best to prepare all vegetables just before use, since the greater the surface area exposed, the more susceptible the vitamins. If it is absolutely necessary to store prepared vegetables, sprinkle them with a little vinegar or lemon juice, cover with plastic

Bell peppers are among the vegetables richest in vitamin C. Red bell peppers contain 150 mg of vitamin C, but green bell peppers contain only 139 mg. Yellow bell peppers contain as much as 293 mg. The side of the vegetable facing the sun often contains more vitamins than the opposite one.

wrap, and refrigerate, or store in a cool, dark place. Cooking is also an important consideration. Most vitamins are destroyed in the heating-up phase by the vegetable's own enzymes. These are neutralized at temperatures of 140–158°F; the longer it takes to reach this temperature, the greater the damage. When blanching vegetables, bring a large saucepan of water to a rolling boil and add only small quantities of vegetables at one time, so that the water temperature does not drop too much.

Beneficial vegetables
A medicine chest on the plate

Hundreds of biologically active substances are present in vegetables. Some of their effects on the human body are completely unknown. Just as nature produces indigestible substances and toxins, it also produces vegetables with healing properties. Although research is still in its infancy, some vegetables have been thoroughly investigated. Among these are garlic, onions, and leeks. All contain natural antibiotics, called phytocides. Of the three, leeks have the least effect and garlic the greatest. It contains a substance called allicin, which is even effective against some bacteria and fungi immune to common medicines. In addition, onions and garlic protect the heart and vascular system, regulate blood lipid and cholesterol levels, and protect against thrombosis. This might sound like magic, but it has been proved scientifically. On the other hand, just how many cloves of garlic and onions must be included in the individual diet to achieve this effect is still being debated.

Several members of the *Cruciferae* family, such as cabbage, radish, horseradish, cress, and watercress, are being researched, as there are indications that they contain substances that neutralize carcinogens. Winter radish is recognized by researchers as being helpful in the prevention and treatment of liver and gall bladder complaints, although the active constituents have not yet been isolated. Horseradish, cress, and watercress are effective remedies for otherwise stubborn fungal infections because of the mustard oils they contain, and eating 2 ounces of cress per day is said to increase the body's resistance to influenza.

From the *Apiaceae* family, carrots are valued for treating worms in children, as well as for having an overall regulatory effect on the bowels. Celery has a slight tranquilizing effect, and fennel is prized for soothing stomach cramps. Fennel oil is also an expectorant and helps relieve coughs and colds.

Many members of the *Compositae* family contain bitter constituents that, for centuries, have been considered therapeutic. This may even be the origin of the belief that medicine must taste nasty to do you any good. In modern medicine, these naturally occurring bitter constituents had fallen into oblivion until recently. However, they are worth notice since they act as an appetite stimulant and also aid digestion. The bitter substances contained in the salad greens endive, Belgian endive, and some lettuces have a calming effect on the nervous system and were once used as a soporific. A serving of salad in the evening is certainly a mild sedative, free of side effects and especially suitable for children. The constituents of other members of the *Compositae* family, such as dandelion and artichokes, stimulate the secretion of bile, essential for the digestion of fats, and are thought to have a detoxifying effect on the liver. Eating these vegetables is an effective preventive measure where there is a predisposition to gallstones. The bitter substance cynarine from the artichoke has recently been more thoroughly investigated. It is thought to help regulate blood lipid levels indirectly by causing increased excretion of cholesterol.

Even this brief summary of the medicinally active constituents of well-known vegetables suggests that this is a broad and important research area just waiting to be investigated more fully. One interesting result is already clear: many claims of folk medicine can be scientifically verified. The boundary between vegetables as food and as therapeutic plants is obviously a blurred one.

Fennel—medicinal herb, spice, and vegetable: In some European countries, a children's drink, good for stomach upsets and gas, is brewed from the seeds of the plant. The therapeutic effect comes from volatile oils, which also give the vegetable its intense flavor. The bulb of the plant, however, contains only one-tenth the active ingredient.

Toxins in vegetables
Harmful by nature

The more natural, the healthier! Ideally, vegetables should be eaten raw and in as unprocessed a state as possible. This is the opinion of many laymen and even a few experts. It is a simple theory and many people believe it, but this does not automatically make it correct. Evolution has ensured that each group of plants has developed special survival features, but does not take into account whether humans might want to eat them. Many vegetables contain substances which, while useful to the plant, are harmful to people. We have to make the right choices and find ways of removing these substances from the plants or of rendering them harmless.

Alkaloids: These harmful nitrogen compounds are found in the nightshade family. Potatoes, tomatoes, eggplants, and bell peppers contain relatively large amounts of these neurotoxins. Until recently, only potatoes had been thoroughly researched, as they are a staple food in many countries. Depending on type and origin, the green parts of these plants contain considerable quantities of the alkaloid solanine. Potato tubers contain only harmless quantities of 0.002–0.1 percent, but the content increases when the potatoes are not stored properly. Light turns potatoes green, and the percentage of the toxin increases a hundredfold. These quantities cause nausea, diarrhea with vomiting, and headaches, and, in the worst case, even unconsciousness and convulsions to the point of respiratory paralysis. Potatoes should always be stored in the dark, and small green spots should be cut out. Very green potatoes should always be thrown away, since cooking does not destroy the toxin. Small quantities of solanine pass into the cooking water even from blemish-free potatoes. It is safer to discard cooking water, rather than reuse it.

The alkaloid tomatine, found in tomatoes, is similar to solanine. Again, it occurs mainly in the green parts of the fruit. Unripe, green tomatoes are not suitable for eating, even in chutney or pickles. This is also true of underripe eggplants.

Capsaicin, a burning-hot alkaloid, is found in the hotter members of the capsicum family. Chiles, for example, contain up to 1 percent capsaicin. Eaten in excess, chiles can damage mucous membranes or even "burn" the gastrointestinal tract. In small amounts, however, capsaicin promotes circulation and stimulates the sense of taste.

Substances containing hydrogen cyanide: These are primarily found in cassava and, to a lesser

Green tomatoes: consume with caution. Like potatoes and other members of the nightshade family, unripe tomatoes contain an alkaloid which can cause damage to the nervous system.

Bacteria and fungi
Friend or foe?

Yeast causes bread and cakes to rise. Bacteria and yeasts turn fresh juice into wine and, in turn, wine into vinegar. Cheese, yogurt, and kefir could not be made without the help of these single-celled organisms. Air-cured meats, such as salami, ripen only with the aid of microorganisms, and it takes lactic bacteria to turn white cabbage into sauerkraut. We can put these tiny organisms to work wherever they are useful to us. This is only true, however, when we are dealing with cultivated strains, where we know just what they need to flourish and exactly what effect they have on specific foodstuffs. Other bacteria, yeasts, and fungi, on the other hand, are seldom useful in foods and are quite frequently dangerous.

Although the public tends to get worked up over environmental pollution and the residues in foods, a far greater danger is posed to individuals by food poisoning. It can take hold more quickly and have more serious consequences in children, the elderly, and invalids than in strong and healthy people. There are quite possibly tens of thousands of unreported cases of food poisoning a year.

What exactly is food poisoning?

The World Health Organization defines one kind of food poisoning in terms of infections—illnesses caused by bacteria, such as salmonella. Nausea, fever, pain, diarrhea, or vomiting occur a few hours after eating contaminated food. Similar symptoms also occur from infection with other pathogens and are generally treated with antibiotics.

Genuine poisoning, the second form, is caused by toxins formed by microorganisms. Botulism is particularly feared, as it is often deadly. The poison of the bacterium *Clostridium botulinum* can lead to blindness and respiratory paralysis within the space of 12–48 hours. Some yeasts and molds produce toxic substances, the best known of which are aflatoxins, which are carcinogenic. Unlike bacterial toxins, fungal toxins take effect slowly.

Although microorganisms are present everywhere, it is not difficult to prevent infections and food poisoning. Hygiene is the watchword. Aim to provide microbes with the worst possible conditions for multiplying. The same basic rules for preparing food must be followed in the home and in commercial kitchens. Fortunately, the dangers when handling vegetables are far smaller than when preparing animal foods, but this is only true as long

extent, in unripe bamboo shoots, yams, and sweet potatoes. During preparation, enzymes contained in the plants themselves may release hydrogen cyanide, which can cause paralysis, choking attacks, goiter, and nervous disorders. However, cooks in the countries where these vegetables grow have developed methods of preparation that either neutralize the toxin or remove it almost completely. These vegetables are never eaten raw. The toxin disappears with thorough rinsing, repeatedly changing the cooking water, or roasting the vegetables.

Toxins in legumes: Although legumes are an important staple for millions of people, several toxic substances occur in kidney beans, garbanzo beans, peas, and lentils, among others. They can all be rendered harmless by soaking, where appropriate, and vigorously boiling the legumes. Raw legumes, especially when consumed in relatively large quantities or on a regular basis, are very harmful.

Oxalic acid: Spinach, rhubarb, sorrel, and Swiss chard contain this. It is easily detected in the mouth because it sets the teeth on edge and causes a slight numbness of the tongue. It inhibits the absorption of calcium and iron and encourages the formation of kidney stones. Some of it is destroyed by cooking the food in plenty of water or by blanching it, but there is always some left. It is wise to avoid feeding children these otherwise nutritious vegetables too often and in excessive quantities.

Not all cooks are scrupulous about hygiene. This Italian farmer's wife has simply spread out puréed tomatoes on a wooden board in the sun so that the liquid can evaporate, without regard for the many potentially harmful environmental influences.

as vegetables are processed on their own. Many dishes mix meat, eggs, and dairy products as well as vegetables. In these cases, stringent safety measures apply. A potato salad, for example, could become a breeding ground for salmonella because of the raw egg yolk in the mayonnaise. Equally, a combination of poultry and vegetables must be handled with scrupulous attention to hygiene.

By following a few simple measures, you can keep troublesome germs in check. First, wash fresh vegetables thoroughly; most bacteria and fungi on their surfaces can be rinsed off. Do not leave just-cooked vegetables standing at room temperature or microbes will multiply exponentially. When reheating foods, make sure that everything is piping hot to render germs harmless. If you are in any doubt about storage conditions or how long food has been standing, it is better to throw it away. Vegetables keep best and have limited protection against bacteria when they are stored, whole and unwashed, in a cool place. Never pack them in airtight containers, since all vegetables "breathe," even after they have been picked. If they are starting to wilt, wither or, worse, go off, or if they are musty or show traces of mold, throw them away.

Take care when preserving!

Preserving and bottling need mentioning. Since the majority of pathogens do not multiply in acid preparations, vegetables preserved in vinegar are not a problem. Traditional brining, which starts lactic fermentation, used to make sauerkraut, is a safe method. When vegetables such as beans, peas, carrots, spinach, and asparagus are bottled at home, some of the microorganisms or their spores may survive preserving temperatures and multiply during storage. Spoilage is usually easy to detect: gas formation causes the lids of the jars to bulge and the contents smell revoltingly sour or foul. It is less easy to detect spoilage caused by organisms that do not form gases. This occasionally occurs with beans and root vegetables. It is recognizable by a slightly sour smell and by the cloudy liquid. Throw the vegetables away.

The greatest hazard is posed by bottling beans, carrots, and asparagus at home, since the spores of *Clostridium botulinum* could survive the preserving process and breed rapidly as they are heated. Great care must be taken. Although only very few cases of illness and even fewer deaths occur each year as a result of this sort of poisoning, it is wiser to use only commercially canned beans, carrots, and asparagus. An alternative method of preserving these vegetables at home would be to freeze them.

Wash thoroughly. Some of the bacteria on the surface of vegetables can simply be washed off. Even more important, however, is cleaning kitchen counters and utensils, especially if they have been used to prepare meat, which can easily cross-contaminate vegetable dishes with its dangerous germs.

Cool quickly. Do not leave foods standing for long periods in warm rooms, since bacteria grow at breakneck speed at temperatures of 68–86°F. Cool freshly cooked foods quickly, cover, and refrigerate (most pathogens cannot multiply at temperatures under 41°F).

Reheat ready-prepared dishes until thoroughly hot.
Around half of all cases of food poisoning could be avoided by bringing previously prepared dishes to a rolling boil before eating, rather than simply warming them up to a pleasant eating temperature. Almost all germs are killed at temperatures of about 176–194°F.

Preserving vegetables: Bottling home-grown produce is very satisfying, but make sure all equipment is thoroughly sterilized. Even then, some germs may survive the high temperatures.

Energy and nutritional content of important vegetables
per 3½ ounces (100 grams) edible content

Vegetable	kJ	kcal	Total fiber (g)	Potassium (mg)	Calcium (mg)	Phosphorus (mg)	Iron (mg)	Vitamin A (µg)	Vitamin B₁ (mg)	Vitamin B₂ (mg)	Vitamin C (mg)
Artichoke	230	55	-	350	53	130	1.5	17	0.14	0.05	8
Asparagus	109	26	1.5	220	22	46	1.0	50	0.14	0.16	28
Beets	184	44	2.2	335	16	33	0.7	2	0.03	0.05	10
Belgian endive	67	16	1.1	192	26	26	0.7	216	0.05	0.03	10
Bell peppers	100	24	1.8	213	10	26	0.7	100	0.07	0.07	140
Broccoli	138	33	3.2	410	113	78	1.3	316	0.10	0.20	110
Brussels sprouts	218	52	2.5	390	36	80	1.5	55	0.10	0.16	102
Cabbage (green)	238	57	4.8	436	230	90	2.7	833	0.20	0.20	140
Cabbage (red)	126	30	2.4	267	38	32	0.5	5	0.07	0.05	50
Cabbage (Savoy)	126	30	2.4	275	57	55	0.9	12	0.05	0.07	50
Cabbage (white)	105	25	2.1	233	49	29	0.4	10	0.05	0.05	47
Carrots	172	41	2.3	341	37	36	0.7	110	0.06	0.05	8
Cauliflower	113	27	2.3	311	22	72	1.1	21	0.10	0.11	69
Celery root	167	40	-	310	55	105	0.5	3	0.06	0.06	10
Chinese cabbage	67	16	0.9	202	40	30	0.6	13	0.03	0.04	36
Chives	227	54	-	434	167	75	1.3	50	0.14	0.15	47
Corn	431	103	-	300	7	116	0.5	120	0.15	0.12	12
Cress	192	46	-	550	214	38	2.9	365	0.15	0.19	60
Cucumber	54	13	0.7	141	15	23	0.5	28	0.02	0.03	+
Eggplant	234	56	1.7	273	53	101	1.2	15	0.12	0.04	6
Endive	80	19	1.9	320	68	54	1.6	333	0.06	0.10	10
Fennel	209	50	1.3	492	107	54	2.7	781	0.22	0.11	93
Garlic	569	136	-	-	38	134	1.4	-	0.20	0.08	14
Head lettuce	71	17	1.4	194	23	31	0.7	150	0.06	0.08	10
Horseradish	314	75	-	554	105	65	1.4	4	0.14	0.11	114
Kohlrabi	130	31	1.6	372	41	51	0.5	2	0.06	0.04	66
Leeks	113	27	2.8	260	120	34	2.0	333	0.12	0.06	25
Mâche (corn salad)	88	21	1.6	420	32	49	2.0	650	0.07	0.08	26
Onion	167	40	1.6	157	27	36	0.5	33	0.03	0.04	10
Parsley	252	60	-	1,000	245	128	8.0	1207	0.14	0.30	166
Parsley root	138	33	-	880	190	80	3.2	5	0.10	0.10	41
Parsnips	285	68	-	469	51	73	0.6	4	0.08	0.13	18
Peas	331	79	5.3	316	26	116	1.9	63	0.35	0.14	27
Pumpkin	113	27	-	383	22	44	0.8	100	0.05	0.07	9
Radishes	84	20	0.8	242	35	28	1.2	4	0.04	0.04	27
Rhubarb	75	18	0.8	270	52	24	0.5	12	0.02	0.03	10
Sauerkraut, raw	103	25	2.2	228	48	43	0.6	20	0.03	0.05	20
Scorzonera (black salsify)	326	78	-	320	58	76	3.3	3	0.15	0.03	4
Spinach	126	30	1.7	470	93	51	3.1	816	0.10	0.20	51
String beans	146	35	3.6	243	56	44	0.8	60	0.08	0.11	19
Swiss chard	96	23	-	376	103	39	2.7	583	0.10	0.20	39
Tomatoes	88	21	1.4	270	13	27	0.05	1.33	0.06	0.04	24
Winter radish	80	19	2.7	322	32	30	0.9	+	0.03	0.03	29
Zucchini	117	28	0.8	200	30	25	0.5	58	0.05	0.09	16

Abbreviations and symbols:: kJ = kilojoule, kcal = kilocalorie (1 kcal = 4184 kJ), g = gram, mg = milligram (1 mg = 0.001 g), µg = microgram (1 µg = 0.001 mg), + = constituent only present in trace quantities; - = no data available.
Source: Auswertungs- und Informationsdienst für Ernährung, Landwirtschaft und Forsten (German Evaluation and Information Service for Nutrition, Agriculture, and Forests) (AID) e.V.

Preparing vegetables

Vegetable	Loss from trimming %	Equipment	Min.–max. time(minutes)	Quantity	Method
Arugula	10	Hands	10–20	2 lb	Sort through, pull off thick stalks, wash
Asparagus	30	Asparagus peeler, string, asparagus knife	8–15	2 lb	see page 110
Avocado pear	25	Knife, spoon	1–2	1	see page 88
Bamboo shoots	65	Knife	10–20	2 lb	see page 87
Beet	20	Knife	5–10	2 lb	Wash and scrub, remove leaves; peel after boiling
Bell peppers	25	Knife	4–10	2 lb	see page 122
Bok choi	20	Knife	6–10	2 lb	Cut off hard root ends, separate into leaves
Broccoli	40	Knife	2–5	2 lb	see page 58
Broccoli rabe	45	Knife	8–12	2 lb	Separate stalk and flowerets
Brussels sprouts	18	Knife	10–25	2 lb	Remove withered leaves, cut off stalk and cut cross in bottom
Cabbage (red/white)	22	Knife, mandolin grater	5–15	1 head	see page 150
Cabbage (Savoy)	28	Knife	5–10	1 head	Cut out stalk,cut up or quarter and slice
Cauliflower					
Celery	35	Knife, peeler if necessary	6–12	2 lb	Cut off leaves and root, string individual stalks with the knife, peel thick stalks if necessary
Celery root	27	Knife	4–15	1 lb	see page 147
Chinese mustard cabbage	25	Knife	4–8	2 lb	see page 52
Cucumber	12–20	Knife, peeler, mandolin	3–8	2 lb	Cut off ends, peel; if wished, halve, remove seeds with melon grater, melon baller, slice
Dandelion	20	Knife	10–20	2 lb	Remove root, cut off bitter stalks, wash
Eggplant	5–10	Knife, peeler if necessary	5–15	2 lb	Wash, cut off calyx, see page 151
Fennel	8	Knife	5–10	2 lb	see page 140
Globe artichokes (large)	50–75	Thread, knife, scissors, serrated knife	whole 2–5	1	Remove stalk and outer leaves, tie (50% loss); ditto, remove hearts, trim (75% loss), see page 46
Globe artichokes, (small)	30	Spoon or melon baller	2–4	1	see page 46
Head lettuce	30	Knife, colander, salad spinner	2–5	1 head	see pages 33, 146
Horseradish	35	Knife, mandolin or grater	5–10	1	Wash, peel, slice on mandolin or grate
Japanese burdock	40	Knife, swivel peeler	10–25	2 lb	see page 47
Jerusalem artichokes	20	Knife	10–20	2 lb	see page 49
Kohlrabi	32	Knife	6–15	2 lb	see page 147
Leeks	50	Knife	3–8	2 lb	Cut off dark green leaf ends, cut off roots, halve, wash and slice
Lotus root	10	Knife	4–10	2 lb	see page 115
Okra	15	Knife	10–20	2 lb	see page 112
Parsley roots	35	Knife, peeler	6–12	2 lb	Wash, peel, slice, cut off hard root ends
Peas in pods	60	Hands	8–20	2 lb	Shell and strip from pods
Potatoes	30	Swivel peeler, knife	5–10	2 lb	Wash, scrub, peel, cut up or cut out decoratively
Radicchio	25	Knife	5–10	2 lb	see page 39
Scallions	30	Knife	3–8	2 lb	Trim dark green stalk ends, cut off root
Scorzonera (black salsify)	44	Knife, peeler	10–25	2 lb	see page 47
Spinach leaf and root	10 and 35, resp.	Hands	20–40	2 lb	Remove damaged bits, roots and stalks (stems can be left on young spinach), wash
String beans	7	Knife	6–12	2 lb	Top and tail, string if necessary
Sugar snap peas	5	Hands, knife	10–20	2 lb	Top, tail and string
Swiss chard	15	Knife	6–15	2 lb	see page 146
Turnips	25	Knife, swivel peeler	8–15	2 lb	Cut off leaves and root, peel and cut up
Water chestnuts	25	Knife	15–25	2 lb	see page 82
Yam	30	Knife, peeler	5–10	2 lb	Wash, peel, slice
Winter radishes	10	Knife, swivel peeler	3–10	2 lb	Peel, top and tail
Zucchini	17	Knife	6–10	2 lb	Top, tail and slice; core large zucchini if necessary

Vegetable encyclopedia

The culinary landscape has been changing. In addition to the well-known influences of *haute cuisine*, which have percolated downward, so to speak, from the perfectionist celebrity chef to the home cook, a second trend has traveled upward from ordinary people. Wholefoods and vegetarianism, as a sort of alternative *nouvelle cuisine*, have also changed the cooking habits of professional chefs, and moved the side dish of vegetables to the very center of the plate. Consumption of vegetables has risen, and as far as health is concerned, vegetables beat all other foods to first place in people's awareness. It is hardly surprising that vegetable specialties from tropical and subtropical countries now arrive fresh in our markets. Many transportation and organizational problems have been overcome, and lack of ripeness, often a problem with imported fruit, is less of a concern with vegetables. Highly specialized fine-food transporters even convey small quantities of exotic leaves, roots, fruits, and tubers all over the world.

In addition, some vegetables which were once considered exotic are now grown on a large scale in countries where they are not indigenous. Dutch vegetable growers, for example, through their close contact with the people of their former colonies, have learned to appreciate the vegetables of Southeast Asia and now cultivate them in greenhouses, not just for the Asian community in the Netherlands, but also for customers in many other countries. There is now a vast variety of vegetables for us to choose from and the time is ripe for an encyclopedia of all the major vegetables of the world, classified according to their botanical families, illustrated with detailed photographs and clearly explained.

New Zealand spinach used to be a popular summer substitute for common spinach, which has a tendency to bolt quickly. Now, it is one of the "forgotten" vegetables, grown only in home gardens and vegetable plots. The thick-fleshed leaves and shoots of this "cut-and-come-again" vegetable can be picked throughout the summer.

Ice plant is a desert plant that owes its name to the eye-catching salt crystals on its stems and leaves which resemble frozen dewdrops. When picked regularly, new leaves keep growing. This specialty is not widely cultivated.

Chinese spinach, with the unmistakable dark veining of its leaves, is one of many vegetables known as callaloo in the Caribbean. Some varieties have purple leaves. It can be harvested only 20–30 days after sowing.

Amaranthus dubius is widely distributed in West Africa, the Caribbean, and on the island of Java, and is thought to be the only species of leaf amaranth. The tender, dark green leaves and the young shoots should be prepared as soon as possible after harvesting, as they are highly perishable.

Aizoaceae **(Ice plant family).** This family contains some 2,500 species. Its botanical name is derived from the Greek *aizoon* ("to live eternally") and was probably chosen because many of these plants flourish under unfavorable climatic conditions in steppes and deserts. Their thick-fleshed, succulent, moisture-storing leaves developed to defy drought. **New Zealand spinach** (*Tetragonia tetragonioides*). This grows wild in New Zealand, on the Australian coast, and in Polynesia and Japan, but is also cultivated. Although not related to ordinary spinach, it is prepared in a similar way, boiled briefly or eaten raw in salads. **Ice plant** (*Mesembryanthemum cristallinum*). Indigenous to the coasts of South Africa, where it is known as a medicinal herb, it is cultivated today in Central and Southern Europe, India, California, and Australia. It needs plenty of warmth, and in temperate climates grows almost exclusively in greenhouses. Used for decoration, raw as a salad ingredient, or cooked like spinach.

Amaranthaceae **(Amaranth family).** The amaranth family is native to the tropics and subtropics of America, Africa, and Asia. The genus *amaranthus* includes about 60 species, which are classified according to their uses as grain amaranths, leaf amaranths, and dual-purpose amaranths. **Amaranth, leaf amaranth** (*Amaranthus tricolor*). **Chinese spinach** (var. *gangeticus*), *Amaranthus dubius*, *hybridus* and *cruentus* belongs to the family of leaf amaranths. It is one of the most useful vegetables in the Third World, as the leaves provide plenty of protein, minerals, and considerable quantities of vitamin C. It is not exported because it is highly perishable, although it can be found in large cities in the United States. In its countries of origin, its leaves and shoots are cooked like spinach.

Araceae **(Arum family).** With over 100 genera and 1,500 species, the arum family grows mainly in the tropics. **Taro** (*Colocasia esculenta*). The most important varieties are **dasheen** (var. *esculenta*) and **eddo** (var. *antiquorum*). The taro resembles the yam in appearance and should be peeled, sliced, and boiled like potatoes. The smaller eddo is popular in Caribbean and West African cooking. Wear gloves when peeling it, as it can irritate the skin, then bake or boil. **Tannia, tania, (yellow) yautia, coco yam** (*Xanthosoma sagittifolium*). The starchy tubers, as well as the leaves and shoots, of the taro and tannia are important staple foods in tropical marshlands. They are very similar in terms of nutritional content and preparation. The smaller daughter tubers of the tannia plant are eaten; the large mother tuber is used for animal fodder.

Taro is grown on the Hawaiian island of Kauai on large, flooded fields. Harvesting is still carried out by hand.

Taro and Tannia
TWO FILLING, STARCHY TUBERS

Not exactly a taste sensation, but still versatile, filling, and cheap: this description fits the starchy taro and tannia tubers. The white to light gray flesh of the tubers is prepared like potatoes: boiled in salted water, roasted, deep-fried, or baked. Long cooking times and changing the cooking water are important, however, since the calcium oxalate crystals contained in the vegetables are irritating to the lining of the intestine. Its valuable nutrients make taro one of the most important cultivated plants of the tropics and subtropics. In India and Southeast Asia, these undemanding swamp plants also flourish wild. Tannia, like taro, requires tropical heat, but the plants can tolerate less water and so are grown where it is not humid enough for taro.

The tubers of the eddo form a relatively small main tuber with numerous little oval tubers on the stem. The dasheen (not illustrated) possesses a large main tuber with just a few subsidiary ones. The dasheen contains fewer calcium oxalate crystals. Both have a shaggy, dark mahogany skin and resemble the yam in appearance.

Only as many tannia tubers as are needed at one time are harvested, since they spoil quickly once lifted, but remain fresh in the soil. It is difficult to tell tannia and taro tubers apart, as they are closely related. Tannia tubers have a slightly higher starch content, but otherwise the nutritional value is the same.

The leaves—or more precisely, the place where the leaf is attached to the stem—are the surest way of telling tannia and taro apart. The tannia stalk (above) starts at the base of the leaf blade, while the taro stalk starts further toward the center of the leaf.

Malabar spinach is also called Indian spinach after its country of origin. Its leaves, which are usually round or oval and dark green in color, grow on succulent shoots up to 20 feet long.

Ceylon spinach, a red-stemmed variety of Malabar spinach, comes from East Asia. As it does not keep well, it is hardly ever exported, but is grown in a few greenhouses in Holland. Stems and leaves regrow continuously after picking, and in the tropics can be harvested for up to 180 days.

The vegetable papaya, also known as raw or green papaya, is a fruit that is harvested while still unripe. It cannot be eaten raw, but must be cooked before it is eaten.

Papaya and Mango
FRUIT AND VEGETABLE

Fully ripened, both are eaten throughout most of the world as fruits. Green, unripe fruit, on the other hand, is prepared as a vegetable, mainly in its native tropical countries. A green mango, harvested while still unripe (left) is used, like a vegetable papaya, as a cooking vegetable, but can also be eaten raw like an apple. On Java and in the Philippines, they even stew and eat the young, tender leaves of the mango tree.

Anacardiaceae. The green, unripe **mango** (*Mangifera indica*), is one of the members of this family that are used as vegetables. However, most mangoes are nearly ripe when exported, intended to be eaten as fruit. From time to time, vegetable mangoes do come on the market and they are often available in Asian foodstores. These are usually the long, smaller varieties. They are most commonly used for making mango chutney, but are also suitable for eating raw, seasoned with salt and Worcestershire sauce.

Basellaceae. This family contains only a few genera and species, which are native to Asia and the tropics of America. All the plants of this family are herbaceous, with a creeping or climbing habit, and with fleshy stalks and leaves. Only the species of the following three genera are cultivated as vegetables. **Ulluco** (*Ullucus tuberosus*). This tuber, similar to a potato and native to the Andes, is eaten boiled or dried; the leaves are sometimes also eaten as a vegetable. **Madeira vine** (*Boussingaultia cordifolia*). Yields the basell potato; the leaves are sometimes eaten like spinach. This plant has become naturalized in Southern and Southeastern Europe. **Malabar spinach, vine spinach, slippery vegetable** (*Basella alba*). This genus is more important than the other two, as the succulent shoots and leaves are rich in protein, vitamins, and minerals. The taste is mild and pleasant, but Westerners often find the slimy consistency of the cooked vegetable off-putting.

Caricaceae.(Papaya family). This family, which is indigenous to tropical Africa and South America, includes, among others, the **papaya** or **pawpaw** (*Carica papaya*) and the **babaco** (*Carica pentagona*) (not illustrated). Both tend to be exported as fully ripened, aromatic fruits, but are popular in their countries of origin as cooked vegetables when the skin is still green and the flesh still white. At this stage, they are a particularly rich source of the enzyme papain, although their vitamin content is considerably lower than in ripe fruits. Unripe papaya makes an excellent meat tenderizer in marinades. Peeled, seeded papayas and babacos can be boiled, stuffed and baked, or shredded in a salad.

Chenopodiaceae (Goosefoot family). Most of the plants in this family are herbaceous annuals or perennials with showy, often succulent, leaves sometimes covered in a waxy bloom. Many members of this family have deep tap roots, so they can grow in salty soils. *Beta* is the most important genus, and includes the vegetable beet and chard, as well as the useful agricultural crop plants sugar beet and fodder beet. **Beet** (*Beta vulgaris* ssp. *vulgaris* var. *conditiva*). This biennial, deep-rooting plant is

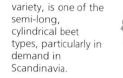

Formanova, a late variety, is one of the semi-long, cylindrical beet types, particularly in demand in Scandinavia.

Chioggia is a round, sweet, smooth-skinned beet. It is bright red on the outside with a bold pattern of red and white rings inside. It is cultivated and sold primarily in Italy, where beet juice, incidentally, is used to color pasta: a few drops of the intense liquid dye is enough to give a beautiful shade of red.

Beets
THE HEALTHY ROOT THAT IS HARD TO BEAT

Beets were an important natural remedy in times past because of their high iron content, and today they owe their popularity to their pleasant taste, as well as their nutritional value. In addition to sugars, protein, fat, and organic acids, they contain calcium, potassium, magnesium, phosphorous, sodium, sulfur, iodine, and many B vitamins. The vitamin C content, at about 10 percent, is also relatively high. Unfortunately, beets, which are known as "nitrogen collectors," are also the vegetable with the highest nitrate content. This is probably not too important, however, since the consumption of beets is not very high in any case. Fresh beets are available year round. They take a fairly long time to prepare and must be handled carefully. Wash, but do not peel them, then cook in boiling salted water or roast for about an hour. Drain and peel when cool enough to handle. A beet salad is very tasty. So, too, are cooked beets flavored with red wine, onions, salt, and sugar, served with a pan-fried entreé. The vegetable may be best known when it is pickled; many varieties are available.

Burpee's Golden, in spite of having no red pigment, has a typical beet taste. Yellow beets are of commercial importance only for their pigment. For food, they are grown almost exclusively by enthusiastic home gardeners and by specialty farmers. The same is true for white-fleshed beets.

Beets are best known when pickled or bottled. It can be rather complicated and time-consuming to preserve them at home, but it is worth the effort. The tubers should be cooked first, as they are then easier to peel. In addition, they lose less juice when skinned after cooking. The beets can then be sliced with a crinkle-cut knife for a decorative effect.

Beets are available year round. In May, the old beets from the stored winter crop are replaced by the new harvest, which is grown under glass or plastic and remains on sale until July, usually in bunches with 3–5 vegetables with their greens still attached. These nutritious leaves can also be eaten and may be prepared in the same way as spinach.

Garden orach, here a red-stemmed form, is a decorative annual requiring a lot of sunshine. It can grow up to 6½ feet high.

Green garden orach (top) provides a tasty vegetable from May to October. This relatively undemanding plant is easy to grow in home gardens. The leaves have a mild taste and can be prepared in the same way as spinach. **Quinoa** (above) is an important food staple in its native South America. Although it is possible to use it as a leaf vegetable, this takes second place to the use of the nutritious seeds.

Good King Henry was once an esteemed medicinal plant because of its blood purifying and laxative effects. Today it is gathered as a wild vegetable or occasionally cultivated by home gardeners.

Horenso is a variety of spinach from Japan. The arrow-shaped leaves, which taper to a point, have a slightly sweet flavor. This specialty is best prepared like young spinach. Short cooking times keep the taste and the delicate leaf structure intact. Blanching reduces the high nitrate content of all types of spinach by up to 70 percent.

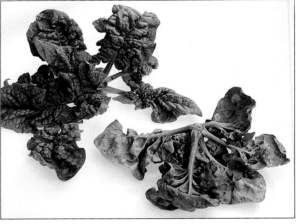

Spring spinach or young spinach (top) has especially fine, delicate leaves and is excellent in salads. The boundary between summer spinach and **fall spinach** (center) is blurred. Both types can be eaten raw, but the latter's leaves are tougher than those of spring spinach. The most robust and strongest-tasting are the leaves of **winter spinach** (bottom), which dominates the market from late fall to early spring. Its leaves are coarser, and often curly. Only about 15 percent of the crop is sold fresh—the vast majority is processed by the frozen foods industry.

grown in most countries with temperate climates. The red color of the tubers, which weigh 4 ounces–1¼ pounds, is caused by high concentrations of betanin and some anthocyanin. There are also white, yellow, and multicolored types. **Orach(e), garden orach(e)** (*Atriplex hortensis*). From the Middle Ages until the beginning of the nineteenth century, this robust weed, known as the spinach plant or mountain spinach, was widespread throughout Central and Southern Europe. Now, only an insignificant quantity is cultivated and it is of negligible commercial importance. It is closely related to spinach, which has increasingly replaced it, but contains three times as much vitamin C. There are green-, yellow-, and red-leafed, as well as variegated types. The last two are less common. **Good King Henry, wild spinach** (*Chenopodium bonus-henricus*). Indigenous to Europe, Good King Henry was once an important leaf vegetable. It has now been supplanted by its cultivated relative, spinach, despite containing substantially more nutrients. It can be eaten cooked or raw. Fat Hen is a closely related member of the goosefoot family with a milder taste. Once cultivated, nowadays it only grows wild. **Quinoa, pigweed** (*Chenopodium quinoa*). Like amaranth, quinoa is one of the group of pseudocereals: starchy seeds that are not actually grains. Quinoa flourishes at high altitudes, where cereals cannot ripen. This, together with its high protein, fat, and mineral content makes it an important staple in the Andes. Quinoa seed is used like a grain and, in countries where it is cultivated, the leaves are prepared like spinach. **Spinach** (*Spinacia oleracea*). Indigenous to Central Asia, spinach is cultivated throughout the world, with the exception of the tropics. It is not classified by variety, but according to the sowing time (spring, summer, and winter spinach) and the harvesting method (leaf spinach is harvested by hand; and root spinach is mechanically harvested). Its iron content (3 mg per 100 g) falls far short of what it was once thought to be, and because of the way it is biochemically "locked" in the plant, only small quantities can be absorbed by the human body. It is nonetheless rich in other important minerals, proteins, and vitamins, including calcium and potassium and vitamins A, B, and C. **Horenso** is a variety of spinach with a milder, sweeter taste. **Swiss chard, chard, spinach beet, leaf beet, perpetual spinach** ("leaf" or "cutting" chard) (*Beta vulgaris* var. *vulgaris*), and ("stalk" or "rib" chard) (*Beta vulgaris* var. *flavescens*). Coming into fashion again after long neglect, this vegetable is popular and widely grown in Italy, France, Spain, Holland,

The bright red color of broad red-stalked chard regrettably changes to a rather gray shade when the chard is cooked.

Stalk chard (top) in this form is the most commonly available. Individual varieties differ mainly in leaf color (lighter or darker) and stalk width. **Red-stalked leaf or cutting chard** (center) is especially attractive because of its color. **Cutting chard** (above) is eaten in Italy and the United States like spinach, but because it does not keep well it is generally not exported. Its leaves grow to a relatively large size. Very large chard leaves taste pungent and bitter, so the best time to harvest and eat them is when they are just a little larger than spinach leaves.

Samphire is sometimes misleadingly sold as a seaweed, but it is actually a marsh plant native to the coastal areas of Northwest Europe. Samphire is usually gathered and only very seldom cultivated. Only young plants are suitable for eating. It is quite salty with a crisp texture and a flavor reminiscent of the sea.

The sea aster, a typical example of seaside and salt-marsh flora, is a coastal plant which grows wild. Only the young leaves are gathered, from April to June in the period prior to flowering. Flowering makes the vegetable turn tough and tasteless. The sea aster is beginning to be cultivated on a small scale in some European countries.

The salad chrysanthemum is a popular vegetable in East and Southeast Asia. In Japan, the flowers are also eaten Otherwise, only the young leaves and shoots are consumed, raw or cooked.

Switzerland, and the United States. Leaf chard develops relatively small, broad leaves and narrow leaf stalks. Stalk chard has large leaves and fleshy stalks up to 4 inches across. Both varieties may have white or red stalks and are particularly rich in protein and minerals. They are mainly on the market from spring to fall. Chard leaves are prepared like spinach or stuffed. The stalks are strung, sliced, and steamed. **Samphire, marsh samphire, glasswort, sea asparagus** (*Salicornia europaea*). This leafless plant, with its dark-green or reddish branching stalks, both looks and tastes like seaweed, but is actually a plant that grows in shallow marshes and on salty mudflats throughout Europe and North America. Young plants can be eaten raw or cooked. Its season is quite short, usually from late summer to early fall. Rock samphire, also known as sea fennel, grows on rocky shores and is often confused with marsh samphire although they are unrelated species.

***Compositae (Asteraceae)* (Composites).** With over 1,000 genera and 20,000 species, the composites, worldwide in distribution, are the largest family of dicotyledonous plants. They are characterized by basket-like flower clusters composed of tongue-and-groove flowers (Latin *compositus*). The composites vary greatly as to which parts are used: leaves (salad greens, dandelion, sea aster), flowerheads (artichoke), leaf stalks (cardoon), roots (scorzonera, salsify), tubers (Jerusalem artichoke), and forced shoots (Belgian endive, dandelion). In addition to the popular vegetable varieties, many are also grown or gathered as medicinal plants, such as camomile, wormwood, and arnica. **Sea aster** (*Aster tripolium*). This perennial reaches a height of 8–39 inches and grows wild in coastal areas, from Europe via North Africa to Central Asia and Japan. Its narrow, fleshy leaves are gathered between April and June and are served as a vegetable side dish, particularly as an accompaniment to mussels and oysters. **Garland chrysanthemum** (*Chrysanthemum coronarium*). This aromatic, fast-growing plant is one of the most popular vegetables in East and Southeast Asia. Leaves and shoots are added to soups or cooked and served as a side dish. Their distinctively hot, flowery taste is shown off to best advantage when they are used raw in salads or as a garnish. **Head lettuce, roundhead lettuce, cabbage lettuce, butterhead lettuce** (*Lactuca sativa* var. *capitata*). This familiar salad green is probably descended from wild lettuce (*Lactuca serriola*), and was known in Greek and Roman times for the gentle calming or sedative effect of the sap it contains (*Lactuca*, from the Latin *lac*, "milk"). Head lettuce is one of

Red head lettuce is becoming more and more popular, since its leaves have a more delicate texture and better flavor than green-leaf varieties.

Head lettuces
THE EPITOME OF FRESHNESS

Everyone recognizes it—strong green outer leaves surrounding a light yellow heart with a juicy, mild, almost neutral taste. Today, it is number one in the "most popular leaf vegetable" stakes. Soon, all this could change, though. Newer varieties, such as lollo rosso, oakleaf lettuce, and frisée, or rediscoveries such as romaine, are becoming increasingly available. In particular, the decorative red varieties will soon be giving the familiar green lettuces a run for their money, to the benefit of the consumer. The red color is caused by anthocyanin, a water soluble pigment occurring as a metabolic product. The brightness of the red is also affected to a certain extent by the environment. Lower or greatly fluctuating temperatures, together with intense light, lead to optimal coloring. Equally, the intensity of the coloring is reduced by low exposure to sunlight and high temperatures over a relatively long period. Differences in color between the individual varieties of lettuce, however, are mainly to do with type, and can be controlled by environmental factors only to a limited extent. Conversely, it can be said that certain varieties color well, even in adverse weather conditions.

The hearts of large, strong crisphead lettuce grown outdoors are so firm that they are difficult to tear apart. It is better to halve them and cut out the core, then quarter, and shred.

Insufficient "head formation," or hearting, is a typical problem in winter, when greenhouse lettuces often fail to develop firm heads owing to a lack of adequate light or warmth. The lettuce is often only held together by its plastic bag.

the most cultivated vegetables. Just why it is far and away the most popular of all lettuce varieties is hard to explain, since its refreshing but neutral flavor hardly differs from that of long or cut lettuces. Perhaps it is particularly attractive simply because it is just the right size for a family meal. Lettuces cultivated outside can weigh as much as 1 pound, while those grown under glass are sold at weights of about 4 ounces upward. It is worth noting that lack of light and insufficient warmth often prevent complete formation of the head in greenhouse lettuces in winter. The lettuce then consists of fairly loose leaves hanging together on the stalk and it withers more quickly. This is why greenhouse produce is sometimes sold in plastic bags to prevent excessive evaporation. A further disadvantage is that in the winter, head lettuce often contains undesirably high levels of nitrates, which amass in the plant particularly when there is too little light during growth. Head lettuce loses freshness quickly, especially when it is stored unwrapped and in warm conditions. It is also very sensitive to ethylene, a gas given off by ripe fruit, including vegetable fruits, during storage. Ethylene causes reddish-brown spots to appear on the leaf ribs and speeds up spoilage, so lettuce should be stored separately from fruits, including tomatoes. Red-leafed varieties are gaining in commercial importance. They are even more delicate and sensitive than the green-leafed types and must be transported quickly and kept quite cool to ensure they arrive fresh at the consumer's table. Well-known varieties include Continuity, Four Seasons, and Rougette de Montpellier from France. In addition to the butterhead lettuces, crisphead and iceberg lettuces, as well as the new crosses of these, belong to the same group. **Batavia.** This crisphead lettuce was developed in France. Today, it is also grown outdoors in Italy and Western Switzerland, and in greenhouses in Holland and Germany. A new Dutch cross between crisphead and butterhead lettuce is marketed in Europe under the name **curly lettuce. Iceberg lettuce.** This variety forms large, tightly closed heads and weighs up to three times as much as butterhead lettuce. Its leaves are crisp, fleshy, shiny, and coarse-veined, and it is much more densely packed and considerably crunchier than butterhead lettuce. Depending on the type, leaf color is light or dark green; there are also red types. Far less perishable than butterhead lettuce, it can be stored, wrapped in plastic, in the refrigerator for two weeks; once cut, it will stay crisp for up to a week longer.

   Romaine lettuce, Cos lettuce (*Lactuca sativa* var. *longifolia*) belongs to the group known as Long lettuce. Romaine grows everywhere that round

Rougette de Montpellier is an extremely small red-leaf variety of roundhead lettuce developed in France. The red color shades into reddish-brown, but the heart is always green.

Batavia lettuce is one of the head-forming varieties. It is a head lettuce, a little like iceberg in appearance, size, and taste, although it has a less crunchy texture. Its slightly curly, thick-fleshed leaves can shade from a dark reddish brown (top) to light green with red edges (above).

Curly lettuce a Dutch, cross-bred variety, forms large, loose heads. It is mild and slightly sweet in flavor.

Little Gem, known as "sucrine" in France, is a small head lettuce similar to romaine, with compact, slightly sweet-tasting hearts, which are generally sold without the outside leaves.

Crisphead lettuces may have very diverse leaf structure and head formation, depending on their origin and type. **Crispsalat** (top) was once only grown in Holland, always under glass. It has three or more wrapping leaves and a spherical heart. It is sold from November to March at a minimum weight of 11 ounces. The firm heads of **green crisphead lettuce** (second) are generally sold, wrapping leaves still on, at farmers' markets. In Switzerland, this variety is called "Krachsalat." **Red crisphead lettuce** (third) has only recently been cultivated in any significant quantity, but its commercial importance is still insignificant in comparison with the green variety. This is a superb specimen with its wrapping leaves still on. **Iceberg lettuce** (bottom) is the best-known crisphead variety: very firm, pale green to yellowish green lettuce hearts without wrapping leaves, generally packed in plastic to protect against transpiration. The cut head shows the highly compact structure with the typical crooked midribs.

Tearing up iceberg lettuce: First remove the loose leaves, then bring the lettuce with its core down sharply on a firm counter or the edge of a table. The core can now be twisted out effortlessly, and the leaves pulled off.

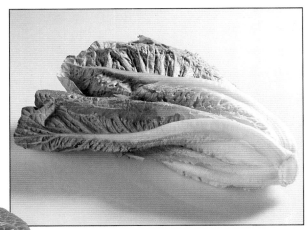

Romaine lettuce grows upright to a height of 14–16 inches and has elongated leaves with rounded tips. The outer leaves are dark green, the inner leaves delicate and blanched light yellow owing to head formation. Older varieties had to be tied together to blanch the inner part. New types are self-closing. The heads can be rounder or more oval in shape, depending on variety.

The dark red lollo rosso (top) and the yellowish green **lollo biondo** (above) actually belong to the cutting or looseleaf lettuce family, but their tightly crimped, tender leaves form such a compact, hemispherical rosette that they give the impression of a head. They taste the same, with a slightly nutty note.

Stem lettuce is grown first and foremost for its thickened, fleshy stem which provides an asparagus-like vegetable. The stems, which grow ¾–1¼ inches thick and up to 4 feet long, are harvested in the summer and early fall.

Looseleaf lettuce, for example, the "Grand Rapids" variety shown here, is available in pots in many European countries. The lettuces, together with their root balls, are planted in small pots and loosely wrapped with plastic. In this way, when kept at the appropriate temperature in the refrigerator, they stay fresh for about 10 days, providing fresh salad greens as needed.

This halved romaine clearly shows the typical golden yellow heart. The pale color is a result of light exclusion.

lettuce flourishes. It is usually harvested in September and October, at a weight of about 11 ounces. It is also imported at other times of year. Owing to its slightly coarser and firmer leaves, it keeps better than head lettuce—for two to three days under refrigeration. Unlike other lettuces, it is not only eaten raw, but also cooked as a vegetable. Prepared in this way, the stalks taste a little like asparagus. The variety **Little Gem**, which has been known for some time, but has only been in demand again in recent years, is particularly popular in Great Britain. The small heads, weighing only 3–4 ounces, are usually sold without the outside leaves and keep fresh in the refrigerator for up to about a week. Winter Density is another small, Romaine-type lettuce. **Cutting lettuce, looseleaf lettuce, curled lettuce** (*Lactuca sativa* var. *crispa*). This group contains all the non-hearting types of lettuce, so there is great variation in color and shape. Leaves may be round or elongated, indented or with unbroken margins, and the plants range from low and bushy to upright. The fully grown leaves are either cut or picked individually, making a number of harvests possible. The entire plant may be cut; this is usually the method with commercial cultivation. The Italian varieties **lollo rosso**, also known as red lollo, and **lollo biondo**, also known as green lollo, can be treated as a "cut-and-come-again" crop throughout the summer, or the whole plant may be cut, making just one crop possible. Both varieties taste pleasantly strong and slightly bitter. **Oakleaf lettuce, feuille de chêne, red salad bowl lettuce** is grown chiefly outdoors and harvested throughout the summer. Oakleaf lettuce is not only tempting because of its attractive leaves, which resemble oak foliage, but also because of its nutty flavor. It is highly perishable, so it should be used as soon as possible after purchase. Refrigerated, it stays fresh for a day at most. **Stem lettuce, asparagus lettuce, celtuce** (*Lactuca sativa* var. *angustana*). Stem lettuce is very closely related to wild lettuce (*Lactuca serriola*). Native to China, it is mainly cultivated there. An American seed company brought this variety to the West under the name "celtuce" (combined from celery and lettuce) in 1942. In Europe it is still a little-known specialty, grown primarily in gardens rather than commercially. The stems can be eaten raw or cooked and the tender young leaves used for salad. **Indian lettuce** (*Lactuca indica*). Despite its common name, this variety is originally from China. An upright-growing perennial, it reaches a height of up to 4¼ feet. It is grown for its leaves, which are picked as required and cooked as a vegetable. The primitive form of **endive** was used by the Ancient

Green oakleaf lettuce, here the variety "Salad Bowl," with yellowish green leaves, is the second most important variety of oakleaf lettuce.

Red oakleaf lettuce or feuille de chêne—here the variety "Red Salad Bowl" (top)—is the most commonly grown type of oakleaf lettuce. Harlekin, ("Harlequin"), here the variety "Carnival" (above), is also referred to in the Frankfurt area of Germany as "Schnabelsalat" ("duck-bill lettuce") on account of its highly chiseled leaves. It, too, is available in both green- and red-leaf varieties. Neither of these looseleaf lettuces can be stored for long, because their leaves are too delicate.

Indian lettuce, as the name implies, comes originally from Asia—from China, actually—but it is now cultivated in Malaysia, Indonesia, Japan, the Philippines, and Taiwan. This upright-growing perennial vegetable is largely unknown in the West.

Only small-headed varieties of frisée can be displayed like this in wooden crates, with the yellow heart showing. Normally, curly endives are packed heart-downward.

Escarole (top) forms a large, flat rosette of broad, unsplit leaves with unbroken margins and thick ribs. The green leaves form a semi-closed, more or less full head, with a yellow or green heart. The leaves stay fresh for longer than the jagged, highly chiseled leaves of the frisée. **Frisée** forms a compact, usually hemispherical leaf rosette. The fullness of the inner leaves makes the heart slightly yellowish. According to type, some have gold hearts (center) and some are green throughout (above). As with escarole, the yellow-hearted variety is the more delicate. At least one third of the plants cultivated commercially are of this sort. The outer leaves, even in otherwise perfect heads, sometimes have dried edges, but are generally not eaten in any case. Common to all three is a slightly bitter taste.

Egyptians as a vegetable. It did not reached Central and Northern Europe until the thirteenth century, however, and the earliest mention of it in North America was in 1803. It is now widely cultivated in southern regions and enjoys the same sort of popularity as head lettuce. Botanically, it is related to Belgian endive, rather than to lettuce species of the genus *Lactuca*. **Escarole, broad-leafed endive** (*Cichorium endivia* var. *latifolium*). Intybin, a bitter substance in the leaves, acts as a mild appetite stimulant and digestive, so it is particularly appealing in hors d'oeuvre salads. Escarole is the least bitter member of the chicory family. It is mainly available during the colder half of the year, but it is marketed on a smaller scale in the summer months as well. **Frisée, curly endive** (*Cichorium endivia* var. *crispum*). Even a few years ago this variety was seldom planted extensively, as farmers considered it to be too temperamental and too sensitive to the cold; its traditional growing areas are in southern Europe. As frisée has now become so popular, growing it under glass in cooler regions is worthwhile. The ancestor of the **Chicory family** is wild chicory (*Cichorium intybus*), which still grows wild in Europe and North Africa, and as far East as Siberia. The Ancient Greeks and Romans were familiar with it as both a medicinal plant and a vegetable. The cultivated varieties descended from wild chicory—root chicory (*Cichorium intybus* var. *sativum*) and salad chicory (*Cichorium intybus* var. *foliosum*), have been known in Europe since the Middle Ages. The former was initially used as animal fodder, and later as the basis for ersatz coffee. Salad chicory can in turn be subdivided into five groups: radicchio, sugarloaf, large-leafed chicory, cutting or leaf chicory, and Belgian endive or witloof chicory. **Radicchio, red chicory** (*Cichorium intybus* var. *foliosum*). The dark to wine-red, occasionally greenish yellow, salad plant with its shiny white leaf ribs is mainly cultivated in Italy, chiefly in the province of Veneto. The largest growing and marketing center lies right on the Adriatic in Chioggia. Since the mid-1980s, Italian radicchio has been available almost year round in many other countries. It is now increasingly being cultivated elsewhere, including the United States. In fact, radicchio has become so popular in the last two decades that its name has been "de-Italianized." (In Italy it is pronounced with a hard "k" rather than a soft "ch.") Radicchio heads are usually harvested with a small root stub attached, so that the leaves or heads hold their shape better. Depending on type, radicchio may form small heads or open leaf-rosettes. Treviso and Castelfranco are two especially popular varieties. The former is

Preparing radicchio: It is best to cut compact radicchio heads through the center, removing any unappetizing outer leaves first, if necessary. Cut out the white core inside the head if you do not like its bitter taste; otherwise, slice it finely and add to the salad.

Radicchio
A VARIETY OF GROWING METHODS AND TYPES

There are two types of radicchio, classified according to their growing methods. The first is sown or planted in the spring or summer and harvested up until the first fall frosts (Palla rossa, Chioggia). The second is sown or planted in summer, overwinters in the field, and is harvested in the spring. The predominantly green leaves die off in the fall and the plant develops new leaves with the arrival of warmer weather and forms either a head or just a leaf rosette (Veronese types). These plants contain less of the bitter substances, as they are broken down by frost. However, losses with this method of cultivation are larger. A relatively rare method of cultivation is to force the plants lifted in the fall and planted in earth or water like Belgian endive, in order to produce a leaf rosette (Radicchio di Treviso).

Radicchio di Treviso is easy to distinguish from other varieties; its narrow, elongated leaves with their thick, white midribs do not form a solid head. Its taste is very strong and more bitter than that of other varieties.

The best-known varieties at a glance: Radicchio di Chioggia forms round heads and is one of the most commonly available varieties, especially the red types (1); however, there are also greenish yellow (2) and reddish white (5) types. **Rossa di Verona** (3) is small, rather mild-tasting and intensely colored. **Radicchio di Treviso** (4) can be recognized by its elongated shape and white central vein.

Green cicorino, here the variety "A grumolo verde," is a rosette chicory from Italy, which comes on the market as a winter chicory very early in spring.

Red cicorino is more popular than the green type and much more bitter in taste than Belgian endive. Like the green variety, it is sown in June or July and cut back to the heart leaves at the end of October. When properly protected in winter, the plant produces rosettes from February to April. Traditionally, it is cultivated in northern Italy and Switzerland.

especially popular for cooked dishes, as it does not release any bitter substances that might spoil them. The latter, usually eaten raw, is especially decorative with red-streaked green leaves and a red and white heart. The noticeably bitter taste of radicchio—and of all chicory varieties, for that matter—is the result of the bitter substance intybin, contained in the leaf ribs and reputed to be a metabolic stimulant. Radicchio may be eaten raw in a salad, mixed with milder-tasting lettuces, and it is also good stir-fried or poached as a side dish, or topped with mozzarella cheese and broiled. It is popular in risottos and as a stuffing for ravioli in Italy. The leaves lose their decorative color when they are cooked, becoming a brownish green. **Sugarloaf** chicory was originally from the South of France, Italy, and southern Switzerland. It is only cultivated commercially in a few other places, but has acquired some popularity with amateur gardeners. Harvested from September to the end of November, it is tolerant of light frosts. The bitter leaves are seldom seen on sale, although it is a very nutritious salad green for the winter months, and can be stored for a long period. Although related to the vegetable chicories, sugarloaf is more like romaine lettuce or Chinese cabbage in appearance. It forms large, firm yellowish green, tightly closed heads, weighing up to 4 pounds. The most important variety is actually called Sugarloaf because of its shape rather than its flavor. It tastes nutty, with the typical bitter flavor of Belgian endive. This bitterness becomes milder as it ripens (as a result of the effect of frost), and can also be minimized by soaking it briefly in lukewarm water. It may used as a salad green and it also delicious served au gratin or boiled. **Large-leafed chicory** originated in Italy, where it is still most widely cultivated. It is also grown in the United States, Spain, and France. It develops dandelion-like, dark green leaves up to 2 feet long, which are held together in a thick bunch by a short stalk and do not form a head. They resemble an upright-growing dandelion plant. Large-leafed chicory is more bitter than the other chicory varieties, but it is precisely its high intybin content, with its beneficial effect on the digestion and blood vessels, which is appreciated by connoisseurs. It is also quite high in vitamins and minerals. Although the plants are not winter-hardy, they are highly disease-resistant. It is harvested about three months after sowing. The various types differ mainly in the shape of their leaves, which may be slit or toothed. The most important variety is Catalogna, an Italian variety with long, narrow and often heavily slit leaves. The delicate heart is ideal made into a salad, and it is

Sugarloaf chicory owes its name to its shape, not at all to its rather bitter taste. It is an important variety of chicory, although in appearance it is more like romaine lettuce or Chinese cabbage. Unlike these, however, it stays fresh for many weeks and is a useful salad for the fall and winter months.

Catalogna di Galatina (below) is an Italian specialty, in which the somewhat bizarre-looking, crunchy shoots grow from the inside of the plant during the course of the winter. The shoots are very tasty eaten raw or cooked. This **Catalogna selection** (far below) has particularly strongly serrated leaves.

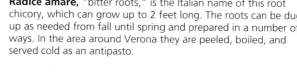

Soncino is an Italian root chicory, which is dug up as needed from fall to spring and prepared in various ways. The white roots are rather bitter tasting, but very healthy.

Radice amare, "bitter roots," is the Italian name of this root chicory, which can grow up to 2 feet long. The roots can be dug up as needed from fall until spring and prepared in a number of ways. In the area around Verona they are peeled, boiled, and served cold as an antipasto.

Catalogna is the the most important Italian variety of large-leaf chicory. The dandelion-like leaves, which may be slightly or even extremely serrated, are characteristic of this variety.

Shoulder to shoulder, the roots stand in 2 inches of water warmed to 64°F. The pale shoots grow in complete darkness. Here, in the light of the flashlight beam, they glow red.

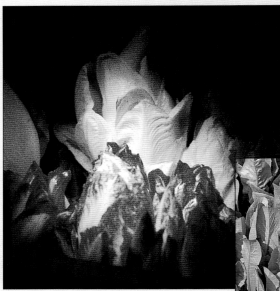

Sown in May (here, plants in the field), the Belgian endive roots are lifted in late fall for forcing to produce the white heads.

Roots lifted from the garden need three weeks on average to produce heads ready for harvesting. Shown, from left to right: a young shoot which has just appeared, then further development of the shoot after one, two, and three weeks, respectively.

Red Belgian endive, here the variety "Carla," is a 1990s cross between white Belgian endive and radicchio rosso. It is mainly available in February and March.

Belgian endive
THE CRUNCHY DELICACY THAT GROWS IN THE DARK

White Belgian endive with its tightly closed head. The more it shades into green, the more bitter the taste!

Belgian endive was discovered by a happy coincidence: A century ago, after an exceptionally bountiful harvest, Belgian farmers planted the roots deep in the soil. These put forth delicate shoots during the winter. To this day, the Belgians are the biggest exporters of this crunchy variety. This delicate, bitter salad vegetable still needs absolute darkness to preserve its appetizing white color.

Cutting up Belgian endive:

Wash the Belgian endive under cold running water. Remove and discard any discolored or wilted leaves. Make a conical cut and remove the inside of the lower part of the stalk.

The cone, which contains most of the bitter substances, can now be pulled out with the fingertips and discarded. With newer varieties, the bitterness has been reduced to such an extent that the entire shoot can be used.

also good cooked with garlic in oil. **Belgian endive, witloof chicory, Brussels chicory, French endive** (*Cichorium intybus* var. *foliosum*). Belgian endive has gained in importance over the past hundred years. The main growing countries are Belgium, France, Holland, and Germany. Cultivation can be divided into two stages: growing the roots and forcing the leaves. Roots are mainly grown by agricultural companies which use the leaves as animal fodder. They are stored temporarily after harvesting from September onward, since thorough cooling causes shoots to be produced more readily. For forcing, they are placed shoulder to shoulder in crates, containers, or pits, or on screens in cellars or darkened forcing rooms. There are three different forcing methods: in soil with a covering of soil (dredging the roots in moist sand or peat, then covering them loosely with soil); in soil without a covering of soil (the dredged roots are covered with opaque plastic); and in water without covering. The third method is becoming prevalent because it reduces effort and expense. Belgian endive is harvested by hand; the heads are broken or cut off just above the root, then washed and trimmed, and packed in lightproof cardboard boxes. They should not be exposed to light for more than a short period, because even a small amount of light causes the outer leaves to turn yellow or green, making them bitter and impairing their quality. Even after purchase, Belgian endive must be stored away from light, ideally in the refrigerator vegetable compartment, where it will stay fresh for several days. This is also true of red Belgian endive, a cross between radicchio and Belgian endive, which has been on the market since the mid 1980s. It loses its attractive red color when cooked. Belgian endive is not sold according to variety; rather, each forcing method has first early, second early, mid-season, and maincrop varieties. Belgian endive is delicious in mixed, and sweet salads or au gratin with ham, Parmesan cheese, or béchamel sauce. It is also good cooked whole, made into a soup, or au gratin with a ground meat stuffing. **Dandelion, lion's tooth** (*Taraxacum officinale*). Known in the Middle Ages as a medicinal plant, dandelions grow wild all over America, Europe, and Asia, but they are also cultivated, chiefly in France. The leaves of cultivated varieties differ in color, size, and degree of dentation. The green, sometimes even reddish, leaves taste spicy. The blanched dandelion, grown in darkened rooms, contains far smaller quantities of bitter substances than its wild relative. It is good in salads or mixed with herbs and creamy or cottage cheese. It can also be prepared like spinach or cooked in vegetable soups.

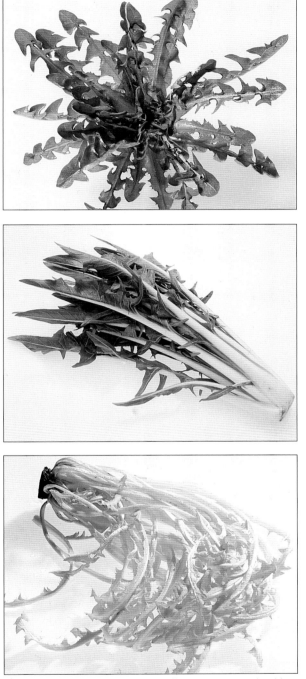

Wild dandelion (top) has an especially savory taste. It should never be picked near busy streets and factories, however, because of exhaust fumes. **The typical dandelion** of the varieties cultivated now (center) can be recognized by its leaves, which taper to a point, are upright-growing, and only moderately toothed. Do not confuse it with large-leaf chicory or Catalogna. **Blanched dandelion** (above) is achieved by excluding light. The pale yellow color and the greatly reduced leaf surface, which consists almost entirely of the rib, are typical.

Large-headed French globe artichokes: "Camus de Bretagne" ("Brittany snub-nose") is the most important French variety, so named on account of its truncated spherical shape (left). This relatively new purple variety (right) also comes from Brittany.

Medium-large Italian globe artichokes: "Romanesco" (left), Italy's most important export artichoke, is available from March to June. "Catanese" (right) has green outer leaves shading into violet.

Purple varieties from Italy: "Violetto di Toscana" is deep violet on the outside and tinged green on the inside (left). There are also more elongated varieties which are a slightly less deep shade of violet (right).

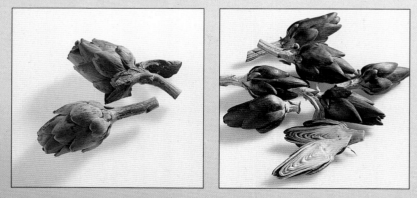

Small varieties: "Tudela," an elongated, green variety, comes from Spain (left). These elongate violet specimens (right), like all other small artichokes, are so tender that they can be cooked whole.

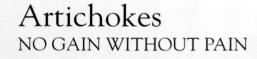

Medium-large, green-leaf varieties of artichokes.

Artichokes
NO GAIN WITHOUT PAIN

It takes some patience and effort to reach the tender heart of this edible relative of the thistle. For those who shun the work, there are always ready-to-eat artichoke hearts, conveniently frozen or preserved in jars or cans. The small trouble taken in preparing and eating them fresh, however, is amply rewarded. The artichoke heart, hidden under a great many leaves and the choke, is distinguished by a particularly fine flavor that is best complemented by sauces such as vinaigrette, hollandaise, or lemon mayonnaise. Although the artichoke is too time-consuming and too expensive to serve as a main course—after all, only about 20 percent of each leaf is actually eaten—this fine vegetable is always a delight as an hors d'oeuvre.

Artichoke, globe artichoke (*Cynara scolymus*). The original home of this thistle-like plant is not known precisely, but it is thought to be native to Arabia, the Mediterranean, Iran, and Turkey. As early as 500 B.C., it was known in Egypt and Rome as an expensive specialty, and in eighteenth-century France it still constituted a culinary privilege of the aristocracy. Today, by contrast, in the countries where it is grown it is an everyday, affordable vegetable. Highly sensitive to frost, the artichoke is cultivated in the temperate and southern latitudes, especially around the Mediterranean. Major producing countries are France, Italy, Spain, Egypt, Israel, Algeria, Morocco, and Turkey. Miniature artichokes are a specialty from California and Provence. Thanks to the different harvest times in the various countries, artichokes are available practically all year round, but they are especially plentiful in late fall and early summer. Artichokes are generally sold individually; only very small types are occasionally sold by weight. The edible part of this plant, which may grow up to 6½ feet tall, is the flower bud or globe. Developing over the course of the summer from the leaf rosettes, the globes are a little like pine cones in appearance. Round or cylindrical in shape, they measure 2¾–5 inches in length and weigh 5 ounces–2¼ pounds. The globes are harvested before the blossoms open to ensure fine flavor. Artichokes owe their delicate, tangy taste to the bitter substance cynarin. They also contain substantial quantities of the carbohydrate inulin, calcium, protein, iron, provitamin A, and vitamin B_1. The edible parts of the artichoke are small: the *fond* or heart of the flower bud, and the tender, fleshy portions of the leaf sections. Numerous varieties, differing in size, shape, and color, are cultivated in the growing countries. In France, the varieties are categorized into three groups: Brittany artichokes with large, green heads (Camus de Bretagne, Camerys, Caribou), Midi (South of France) artichokes with violet leaves (Violet de Provence, Violet de Hyères, Violet du Gapeau), and secondary varieties classified between Camus and the purple varieties (Blanc Hyerois). Italian artichokes come chiefly from the provinces of Puglia, Sicily, Sardinia, and Tuscany. The four main varieties are Catanese (medium-large, cylindrical, closed head with outer leaves green, shading into violet), Romanesco (large, spherical, closed head with a characteristic opening at the top, with green leaves under an opaque reddish violet color), Spinoso Sardo (medium-large, conical, closed head with violet-green leaves, tapering to a point, with a large thorn), and Violetto di Toscana (medium-large, elliptical,

Balancing on long stalks, the still unopened globes, ripe for harvesting, tower above the plants in the field (top). The thorny variety "Spinoso Sardo" (above) is cultivated chiefly on the Italian island of Sardinia.

Small artichokes are a standard item in southern European markets—the smaller, the more appealing—and are increasingly popular in the United States and Britain.

Very young artichokes can be eaten whole because they are so tender. In some parts of Italy and France they are sometimes sold already cooked.

Preparing artichoke hearts:

Wash the globe (flower bud), then break off the stem or cut it off with a sharp knife. Breaking the stem detaches the hard fibers from the base.

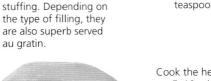

Artichokes are harvested by hand and gathered in large panniers. This is one of the reasons for their relatively high cost.

Rub some lemon juice into the base of the globe to prevent it from turning brown through exposure to the air. Vinegar may be used instead of lemon juice, if desired.

If you require only the artichoke hearts, cut away about two thirds of the outside leaves using a heavy, sharp knife.

The remaining outside leaves can now be easily removed from around the base of the bud with the knife, exposing the fibrous choke.

Lastly, pare the artichoke hearts: use a small sharp vegetable knife to remove any traces of leaf buds and hard spots from the underside of the artichoke base.

Tender artichoke hearts with their natural hollow are very well suited to stuffing. Depending on the type of filling, they are also superb served au gratin.

Remove the fibrous, inedible choke with a melon baller or teaspoon and discard.

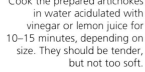

Cook the hearts for about 5–10 minutes in water acidulated with lemon juice or vinegar. Drain thoroughly and use as desired.

Cooking whole young globe artichokes:

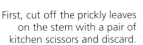

First, cut off the prickly leaves on the stem with a pair of kitchen scissors and discard.

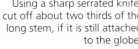

Using a sharp serrated knife, cut off about two thirds of the long stem, if it is still attached to the globe.

Trim the pointed, prickly, and rather bitter leaf tips with kitchen scissors.

The outside leaves are usually too tough to eat. Remove them until the tender, pale inner leaves are revealed.

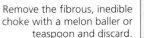

Next, cut off the leaves from the top of the artichoke with a sharp serrated knife; their toughness will spoil the dish.

The remaining portion of the flower stalk is tender and good to eat, provided that it is peeled with a vegetable knife.

Cook the prepared artichokes in water acidulated with vinegar or lemon juice for 10–15 minutes, depending on size. They should be tender, but not too soft.

After briefly cooling the artichokes or rinsing them in cold water, halve them, remove the choke with a spoon, and proceed with your recipe.

closed head with violet leaves with dark green shading). There are also countless local varieties which are seldom exported. In Spain, cultivation for export is limited mainly to the province of Valencia; the main artichoke variety is the green Tudela. The variety Green Globe comprises nearly 90 percent of Californian-grown artichokes, and other varieties include Magnifico, Imperial Star, and Emerald. The globe artichoke is superb boiled and served with warm or cold sauces, and the hearts are delicious filled with cheese, meat, or ham, or in salads. The hearts are also good as a side dish with poultry and pan-fried meats, as a pizza topping, as a garnish for cold platters, and mixed with other vegetables. It is not suitable for eating raw, except for really young artichokes. **Scorzonera, black salsify** (*Scorzonera hispanica*). Scorzonera ("black root") has been cultivated as a vegetable since the seventeenth century; before that, it was used solely as a medicinal plant. As time went on, it increasingly supplanted white-skinned salsify. Belgium is the most important producer and exporter of this vegetable, followed by France and Holland. While very popular in continental Europe, it is less common in the United States and Britain. Scorzonera is a winter-hardy perennial; its narrow, tapering leaves with unbroken margins reach a height of 2–4 feet. Although only the roots are sold, the leaf stalks, buds, and flowers can be used in salads. Commercially cultivated scorzonera is harvested in October, as soon as the leaves wither. The fragile roots must be carefully lifted from the soil with a garden fork. Scorzonera appears on the market from October to April. The roots should be straight, as thick as possible, undamaged, and free from forking or subsidiary roots. They should also be white-fleshed, and not fibrous or woody. The nutritional value of scorzonera is only surpassed by that of peas and beans, making it a highly useful winter vegetable. It is almost always cooked by boiling. **Edible burdock** (*Arctium lappa* var. *edule*). The large burdock (*Arctium lappa*) grows wild and is not eaten, but the edible burdock originated in China and was being cultivated in Japan over 1,000 years ago, and there it is still a traditional, low-calorie foodstuff, prized for its high fiber content. It is little known in the West, found only occasionally in Asian supermarkets. The roots of the cultivated Japanese varieties reach lengths of up to 3 feet. Edible burdock is a vigorous, herbaceous, highly branched plant with large, broad, mostly oval, and unsplit leaves growing on bare stalks. Although the young leaf stalks can be eaten, the portion of the plant which is of greatest interest to the cook is the long, fleshy root, which resembles

With a diameter of just ¾–1½ inches, **scorzonera** reaches a length of 12–20 inches. Dowel- or slightly spindle-shaped, it has a brownish black skin that may be velvety thick or corky. The inside is fleshy, soft, white, and juicy. Take care, as it can cause annoying stains. Its nutty, delicate, and slightly spicy taste is mildly reminiscent of asparagus.

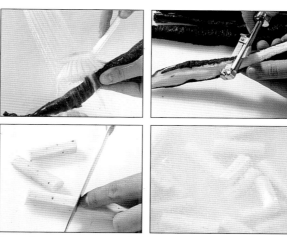

Preparing scorzonera: Scrub thoroughly under cold running water. Using a vegetable peeler or sharp knife, peel thinly from end to tip. Next, cut the root into small pieces. Add these immediately to a bowl of water into which you have stirred a little flour and vinegar. This stops the juices, which leak from the root when it is cut, from turning the flesh brown.

Preparing burdock: Wash the burdock roots if necessary, and peel thinly with a knife or vegetable peeler. Cut into pieces and place in water to keep fresh until required. Burdock can be prepared according to recipes for scorzonera. In Japan, the main country of consumption, it is seasoned with *konnyaku*, a gelatinous substance produced from the starchy tuber of *Amorphophallus konjac* and sesame seeds.

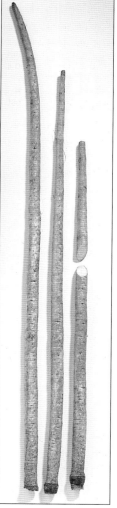

At only ¾–1½ inches thick, **edible burdock** can reach an impressive length of over 3 feet. The wild variety, on the other hand, only grows to about 16 inches long.

Cardoon stalks are blanched, cut back to about 16–20 inches, and packed in crates before being sold. Prickly and thorn-free, wide-ribbed and full-ribbed, and green and reddish varieties are cultivated. However, they are all usually sold as "cardoon" plain and simple, rather than by variety name. When buying, look for firm, crunchy leaf stalks and fresh leaves.

Salsify can be distinguished from scorzonera by its pale, substantially shorter roots and its narrow, leek-like leaves.

Preparing cardoons: First cut off the leaf stalk end with a sharp knife, then remove the remains of the leaves, as well as prickly edges. Pull off the tough, inedible strings. Then cut the prepared leaf stalks into finger-length pieces and place immediately in water acidulated with vinegar, so that they do not turn black. Cook the sliced cardoon in salted water for 25–30 minutes. Drain thoroughly and string the stalks once more before serving, if necessary.

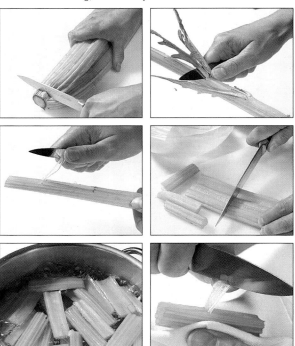

scorzonera. It is also prepared and cooked like scorzonera. **Salsify, oyster plant, vegetable oyster** (*Tragopogon porrifolium* ssp. *porrifolium*). This was known even in ancient times as a vegetable, and was esteemed in central Europe until the end of the sixteenth century. It was then almost entirely superseded by scorzonera because its core was frequently woody and because it sometimes bloomed in the first year, which rendered its roots worthless. Only in Britain, southern Europe, and southern Germany is it still marginally important as a decorative and useful plant, although it is also grown in the United States. Salsify is very similar to scorzonera. It can be distinguished by its narrower leaves and reddish violet flowers, whereas scorzonera produces yellow flowers. The root is yellowish white, much shorter than the scorzonera root, and has numerous subsidiary roots. In taste, too, it is reminiscent of scorzonera, and can be prepared in the same way. **Cardoon, prickly artichoke** (*Cynara cardunculus*). Indigenous to the Mediterranean and North Africa, cardoon was still a very popular vegetable in several countries in the nineteenth century. Now, it is looked on almost as "exotic," and is only of regional importance in Spain, the South of France, and Italy. It is from Italy that small imports of cardoon, thought to be the ancestor of the artichoke, arrive on the market in the fall. Canned cardoon, while not common, is available all year. The leaf stalks, which taste similar to artichokes, are reminiscent of celery in appearance, and can also be prepared like it. Unlike the artichoke, the flower buds are not eaten. **Jerusalem artichoke** (*Helianthus tuberosus*). This tuber, indigenous to North America, was taken by seafarers to France at the beginning of the seventeenth century. These carbohydrate-rich tubers were an important food until the potato gained ascendancy in the mid-eighteenth century. Today, the Jerusalem artichoke is cultivated on a significant scale only in certain regions. A frost-hardy plant, which produces yellow flowers in the fall, it resembles the sunflower, to which it is related, the "Jerusalem" of the name being a corruption of the Italian for sunflower (*girasole*). Between 24 and 36 small-to-medium tubers form on the roots, like the potato. They vary from pear- to apple-shaped, depending upon variety, Also depending on the variety, the color of the skin ranges from light brown to violet, but the flesh is always white to cream colored. Jerusalem artichokes are available from October to May. They are good served raw, grated, and mixed with lemon juice, as well as steamed, roasted, or baked. They are also excellent puréed, in gratins, and added to soups.

Jerusalem artichokes
A former staple that is coming back into fashion

Before the overwhelming shift to the potato in the eighteenth century, these peculiarly shaped tubers, known also as "sunchokes" were an important vegetable because of their high nutritional value. In some places, they have remained popular, but in other countries they have been almost totally overlooked and are, these days, considered almost exotic. The Jerusalem artichoke is also grown for animal fodder. Fresh Jerusalem artichokes are available and some of the crop also finds its way into the food-processing industry, since the high sugar content of the tubers makes them the ideal raw material for the production of fructose, syrup, alcohol, and spirits. Roasted, Jerusalem artichoke has also been used as a coffee substitute. The fresh tubers have a delicate taste are delicious boiled and puréed, baked, sautéed, roasted, or parboiled and then dipped in a light batter and deep-fried.

Thorough washing of the tubers is important, as Jerusalem artichokes are best cooked with their skins on to preserve their flavor.

Jerusalem artichoke tubers vary greatly in color and shape: from spindle-shaped, pink-skinned varieties like "Violettes Rennes" from France (below), which resemble sweet potatoes, all the way to small, violet tubers which taper to a point, like the variety "Rote Zonenkugel" (bottom). Regardless of the shape and skin color of the tubers, their flesh is always white to cream and pleasantly sweet in taste.

Preparing Jerusalem artichokes:

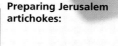

After rinsing thoroughly, scrub the tubers with a clean, vegetable brush under cold running water to remove soil and sand residues.

If you wish to peel Jerusalem artichokes, you can blanch the tubers for a few minutes in boiling water and then rinse under cold water, as for potatoes boiled in their skins.

Jerusalem artichoke tubers are often very awkwardly shaped, which makes peeling a chore. However, they can also be eaten with their skins on.

The skin can now be peeled off easily with a sharp kitchen knife. Jerusalem artichokes can be cooked, whole or sliced, in a wide variety of ways.

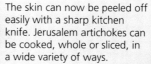

This sweet potato with its spindle-shaped, red-skinned tubers and salmon-pink flesh contains more carotene than white-fleshed varieties, and is more nutritious. This is also true of yellow-fleshed tubers.

Sweet potato varieties with red to violet skin and white flesh are the ones most frequently cultivated worldwide (below). Their shapes vary between oval and elongated spindle-shaped. Light-brown-skinned sweet potatoes with white flesh (bottom) are popular chiefly in Italy. Although prepared in a similar manner to potatoes, they are not related species.

Convolvulaceae **(Morning glory family).** Around 1,600 species, which are mostly indigenous to the tropics and subtropics, belong to this family. A few species are also found in more northerly latitudes. (*Calystegia* sp.). These are twining plants and seldom grow upright, but grow along the ground. **Sweet potato** (*Ipomoea batatas*). Indigenous to Central and South America, the sweet potato is now cultivated in the tropics and subtropics, as well as in the warmer lands of the temperate latitudes. It ranks fifth on the list of the world's most important food staples, after rice, wheat, corn, and cassava, as it constitutes a substantial source of carbohydrate and carotene. Sweet potatoes are cultivated year round, but can be stored for only a limited period because of their high water content. The spindle-shaped, fleshy rhizomes thicken into potato-like tubers, but they are not related to the potato. Differences in flavor depend on the sugar content of the tubers. Breeders are trying to develop the sugar/starch ratio in favor of starch, in order to encourage acceptance as a staple food. **Chinese water spinach, swamp cabbage, ung choy** (*Ipomoea aquatica*). Chinese water spinach is indigenous to the tropics of Asia and is now often grown in the United States for sale in Asian communities.

Cruciferae (Brassicaceae) **(Crucifers).** This family comprises 380 genera with around 3,000 species. Cruciferous plants are most widespread in the northern temperate zones. Of importance in addition to rape, turnips, and mustard are the many varieties of cabbage (*Brassica*), radishes and daikon (*Raphanus*), horseradish (*Armoracia*), and cress (*Lepidium*), as well as watercress (*Nasturtium*). **Broccoli rabe, cima di rapa** (*Brassica rapa* var. *cymosa*). The little flowers of this loose-leafed cabbage are eaten, as well as the leaves. They tend to tone down the strong flavor. Cook like other varieties of cabbage. It is especially good steamed. **Turnip greens, turnip tops** (*Brassica rapa* var. *rapa*). Turnip greens are the leafy parts obtained from all May or fall varieties of turnips. They are excellent chopped and added to a salad, or cooked briefly as a side dish in the same way as other greens. **Mustard greens, leaf mustard, Indian mustard, Chinese mustard cabbage, gai choy, swatow mustard** (*Brassica juncea* ssp. *integrifolia*). This relative of Sarepta mustard (*Brassica juncea* ssp. *juncea*) is cultivated primarily in Southeast Asia as a vegetable. The leaves vary greatly in shape; some are curly and some types form firm heads with considerably thickened leaf stalks. Mustard greens should always be briefly blanched or boiled on account of their pungent, bitter taste. In China, mustard cabbage is preserved like sauerkraut.

Broccoli rabe resembles both turnip and broccoli in appearance. Descended from a wild herb which grows in the Mediterranean, today it is cultivated there, in the Italian provinces of Campania and Puglia, and in the United States. It is rarely available elsewhere.

Turnip greens, as their name implies, belong to the turnip family, being nothing other than the leaves of May and fall turnips. Those with simple leaves with an unbroken margin (below) are produced from the white May turnip. Turnip greens of the variety "Namenia" have serrated leaves (bottom).

These two varieties of Chinese water spinach show how greatly it can vary in appearance. Water spinach is cultivated in the tropics of Asia year round, but is not exported because it does not keep well. For this reason, it is almost completely unknown in many Western countries, although it is cultivated under glass in some places, such as Britain and Holland, and is grown in the United States. It can be eaten raw, but is usually prepared like spinach, which it slightly resembles in taste. It is used for flavoring in soups in China.

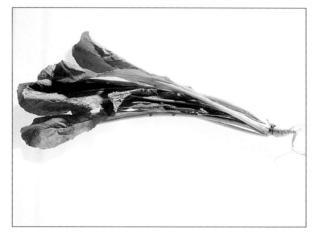

Recently, **mustard greens** (amsoi) have also been cultivated in this form on a limited scale under glass.

Leaf rape, which is hardly grown now, is considered to be a specialty in East Frisia in northern Europe. It is ideal for garden plots, since it is quick and easy to grow, and is frost-hardy. The young leaves and stalks are harvested when 6–8 inches in length, before the plant flowers. Pleasantly mild in taste, it can be prepared like spinach.

Mustard greens pickled in lactic acid, in a similar way to sauerkraut, are highly regarded by the Chinese. The lactic acid takes the edge off the bitter substances contained in the greens, while simultaneously adding a spicy taste.

Cutting up mustard greens:

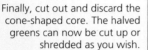

Cut off the thick stalks at the base of the head with a sharp kitchen knife. These need to cook longer than the leaves.

Cut the greens in half lengthwise, using a large, heavy knife.

Finally, cut out and discard the cone-shaped core. The halved greens can now be cut up or shredded as you wish.

Mustard greens
HOT AS MUSTARD, TENDER AS SPINACH

The delicate leaves with their spicy, bitter taste are rich in vitamin C and calcium, while being very low in calories. As one of their alternative names—Chinese mustard cabbage—implies, they are especially popular in Chinese cuisine.

Turnip (*Brassica rapa* var. *rapa*). This cultivated plant was well known in antiquity. Before the spread of the potato, turnips, with their high nutritional value, were among the most important staple foods for man and beast. Today, by contrast, the turnip is of only slight importance although quite large areas are given over to its cultivation in the United States, southern Europe, and Asia. **Teltow turnips** (*Brassica rapa* subvar. *pygmaea*) and **May turnips** (*Brassica rapa* subvar. *majalis*) are the finest turnip varieties. Teltow turnips flourish in a sandy soil and, depending on the time of sowing, come on the market from May to August, as well as from October to December or January. As its name implies, the fine, white May turnip is only available from May to June. It is good boiled or glazed, in vegetable stews, or served raw in a salad. The **fall turnip** (*Brassica rapa* subvar. *rapifera*) is often sown in the summer in the stubble and harvested in October and November. It is excellent boiled and puréed, and also good in casseroles or stews. The fall turnip is unsuitable for eating raw. **Leaf rape** (*Brassica napus* var. *pabularia*). This is a cabbage, that is botanically very closely related to rape, being a leafy form of it. **Rutabaga, swede, (yellow) turnip** (*Brassica napus* var. *napobrassica*). Rutabaga is thought to be a cross between the fall turnip and kohlrabi. Cultivated worldwide in all temperate zones, the main harvest time is October and November. The white-fleshed varieties of this least demanding of root vegetables generally provide animal fodder. The orange-fleshed ones are very healthy vegetables, high in nutrients and low in calories. Rutabagas grow for the most part above ground, and reach 3–3½ pounds in weight. The leaves are always blue-green, in contrast to the grass-green leaves of the very similar turnip. It can be prepared and cooked like the fall turnip. **Kohlrabi, turnip-cabbage** (*Brassica oleracea* convar. *acephala* var. *gongylodes*). The origins of kohlrabi are disputed. Germany, where it was first mentioned in 1558, harvests 40,000 tons a year, and is both the world's largest producer and consumer. It is quite popular in some other parts of continental Europe, but less so in the United States and Britain. It is also extensively grown in Kashmir. Although it belongs to the brassicas, it is also classified as a stalk vegetable: it develops, not from the leaves or the flowers, but from the lower part of the stem just above the soil line. The bulbs are shaped like flattened spheres and reach a diameter of up to 8 inches. Their color varies from whitish, to green, or reddish to deep purple. The leaves are very rich in carotene, protein, and minerals, so the heart leaves are a particularly healthy addition to the diet.

Fall turnips—here a variety with the graphic name "Round white red-headed" (top)—are white-fleshed with green or red heads. May turnips (above) are smaller, spherical, and also white-fleshed, but more delicately flavored than fall turnips. The fine leaves of the May turnip can be prepared like spinach.

All kohlrabi is the same in terms of taste and nutritional value, whether one of the reddish-violet (top) or green varieties (above). Red varieties are preferred for their decorative color, but this is not shown off to best advantage after peeling, since the crisp, juicy flesh of this vegetable is always white.

Teltow turnips are a dwarf form of the white turnip. These mild, sweet vegetables are named after the only area where they were cultivated before World War II, around Teltow, Germany. Gourmets consider them a delicacy.

Kabu or Japanese turnip is a variety that is almost identical in appearance to the May turnip. They are also quite similar in flavor, although kabu is noticeably hotter and more like a radish.

Rutabaga, here a yellow-fleshed variety, is among the lowest in calories of root vegetables, and very valuable from a nutritional standpoint. Often unjustly neglected, this vegetable is slowly being rediscovered.

Shanghai bok choi is a smaller variety. The light green leaf stalks and leaves are typical of this variety, which is cultivated only in China, and even there only on a very small scale.

Bok choi, is a white-stalked cabbage with dark green leaves. Because it does not travel well, it is seldom exported by the countries in Asia where it is widely grown, but it is now cultivated on an increasing scale in the West.

Mustard spinach or tendergreen, here the variety "Komatsuna," was probably produced by crossing Chinese cabbage and bok choi with the turnip. The leaves are gray-green and smooth, with an unbroken margin. Like spinach, it can be briefly boiled, eaten raw, or served au gratin. In Japan, the turnip- to tuber-shaped roots are also eaten.

Depending on the variety, **Chinese cabbage** has yellow to dark green outer leaves with broad white ribs. The inner leaves are yellow to golden yellow. Chinese cabbage may be one of three shapes: oval (above right), very oval (right), and long or cylindrical (below). Depending on shape and size, the heads can weigh up to 4½ pounds.

Chinese broccoli (top) is cultivated first and foremost for its fleshy stems, although both the young leaves and the flowers, provided they have not yet opened, can also be eaten. The leaves are coarse, blue-green and coated with a waxy bloom. The flowers are white. Chinese broccoli is harvested either by cutting the plant level with the soil, or by allowing it to continue growing and harvesting just the side shoots. **Choy sum** (above) is a tropical leaf cabbage with green oval leaves and small yellow flowers. Either the shoot tips, including the edible flowers, are harvested, or the entire plant is picked. Both are prepared in a similar fashion to broccoli.

Bok choi, pak choi, spoon cabbage, Chinese celery cabbage, Chinese white cabbage, mustard cabbage (*Brassica chinensis*). This delicate leaf-stalk vegetable is mainly cultivated in China, Korea, Japan, and the United States. The plants, 16–20 inches tall, are ready for harvest after just two months. Bok choi does not form a closed head, and resembles Swiss chard in appearance and taste. Its nutritional value is twice that of white cabbage, with the leaf-ribs being highest in nutrients. It is delicious steamed, stir-fried, or eaten raw. It is unsuitable for dishes with a long cooking time.

Chinese cabbage, Chinese leaves, Napa cabbage, Peking cabbage, celery cabbage, po tsai (*Brassica pekinensis*). Chinese cabbage is a cross between turnip and bok choi. Unlike the latter, it forms large, loose heads. It differs from the other heading cabbage types in its complete lack of stalk—the leaves close by themselves—as well as in its digestibility. The Japanese have been successful in breeding new hybrid varieties: a cabbage that grows faster, with a better flavor and a more uniform size. This "Japanese cabbage," however, is still marketed as Chinese cabbage. It is ideal in sweet and savory salads, steamed, or stir-fried. The leaves are also good as wrappers for stuffed cabbage dishes. It is unsuitable for dishes with a long cooking time.

Chinese kale, Chinese broccoli, white flowering broccoli, early kailaan, gaai laan (*Brassica alboglabra*). This brassica, which grows up to 3 feet high, is non-heading, but forms strong stems and flowers like broccoli. It is an everyday vegetable throughout Asia, and is cultivated on a large scale there. It is also available in the West. **Chinese flowering cabbage, flowering white cabbage, choy sum, mock pak choi** (*Brassica chinensis* var. *parachinensis*). This tropical leaf cabbage is indigenous to East and Southeast Asia, but is also cultivated in West Africa and South America.

Tendergreen, mustard spinach, spinach mustard (*Brassica perviridis*). Originally from and mostly cultivated in Northern China, Japan, and Korea, this leaf cabbage has also been cultivated on a small scale in the American South for the last 50 years or so. It does not keep well. **Kale, curly kale, green cabbage** (*Brassica oleracea* convar. *acephala* var. *sabellica*). Curly kale, the most widely available type, has the highest carbohydrate and protein content of all the cabbage varieties. There are conspicuous differences in stalk heights (low, semi-high, and high growth habits) as well as in shape, color, and curliness of the leaves. There is hardly any difference between varieties in terms of flavor. **Black cabbage, kale, borecole** (*Brassica oleracea* convar. *acephala* var. *viridis*). This variety of kale can

Preparing kale: First remove the stalk with a sharp knife and peel off the individual leaves. Next, cut out the midribs and cut the washed leaves into strips. Sauté in a little oil or butter, add stock, and braise for about 45 minutes.

Cavolo nero ("black cabbage") is a hearty, spicy, long-leaf borecole, so called on account of its extremely dark color (top). Like its close relative, **curly kale** (above), it is suitable for serving with hearty, winter dishes. It tastes best after the first night frosts, which convert its starch into sugar and make it more digestible. The heads, which are actually leaf rosettes, survive freezing temperatures unharmed.

Cutting up cauliflower:

Cut off the tough stalk at the base of the curd with a sharp kitchen knife. A large, stable cook's knife is particularly suitable for this purpose.

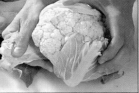

The leaves that are very tightly clustered around the head of a fresh cauliflower can be easily peeled off. Remove the small inside leaves also.

If the cauliflower is to be cooked whole, make a crosswise incision in the base of the stalk. Otherwise, cut off the stalk completely to make it easier to break into flowerets.

Break or cut the cauliflower into flowerets, rinse under cold running water, and proceed with your recipe.

be prepared in the same way as green curly kale. **Cauliflower** (*Brassica oleracea* convar. *botrytis* var. *botrytis*). Cauliflower is especially popular because of its mild cabbage flavor. The largest producers (China with 1 million and India with 0.7 million tons, respectively) consume all of their record harvests at home. It is widely available and a major export crop from France and Italy. Cauliflower owes its name to the undeveloped inflorescence, also known as a "flower" or "curd." The heads should be harvested when they are free from buds, firm, and closed. Its snow-white color is achieved by a simple trick: the large green leaves are either bent or tied together over the head. Since the curd cannot make any chlorophyll, the green coloring in plants, because of the lack of light, it remains white. New varieties are being bred so that the leaves automatically serve as protection from the sun. Colorful cauliflower heads are becoming popular, and the curd is deliberately exposed to sunlight—the more sunlight, the stronger the color. Romanesco is one of the green cauliflower varieties that are now fashionable. **Green cauliflower** not only makes a visual impact, it is also substantially richer in vitamin C, protein, and minerals than white cauliflower. Purple varieties are also cultivated. Anthocyanins are responsible for the red coloration, with direct sunlight and cool temperatures promoting depth of color. High temperatures explain the sometimes irregular appearance of some Italian purple varieties. It is important to distinguish between type-determined yellow and purple varieties, and the tendency of white cauliflowers to turn yellow or brown after harvesting because of exposure to sunlight, which impairs quality. **Mini-cauliflower**, a specialty as rare as it is expensive, is cultivated chiefly in France and California for the restaurant trade, but is also grown elsewhere. Like full-size cauliflowers, these decorative miniatures come in shades of white, green, and purple. Cauliflower grown under glass needs only a quick wash. Summer cauliflower grown outdoors, however, should be placed head down in cold water acidulated with vinegar for up to 15 minutes, since beetles and other insects may lurk among the flowerets. One of the most versatile of vegetables, cauliflower can be prepared in a great variety of ways: boiled or steamed whole or broken into flowerets, stir-fried, served au gratin with a béchamel sauce, in a casserole, or in vegetable soups. It is also good raw, puréed as a base for creamy soups, cooked, in salads, battered and fried, or divided into flowerets and braised with other ingredients in meat or fish curries. It is ruined by overcooking, becoming soggy, gray, and unpleasant.

Cauliflower in the field: the large, inward-turning heart leaves keep the sun off, so that the curds remain white. After harvesting, these leaves are trimmed back and the heads are packed in crates.

Romanesco is the generic term for chartreuse-colored varieties of cauliflower, notable for their minaret- or turret-like structure (top). In fact, this decorative vegetable is sometimes known as minaret cabbage. It is shown off to best advantage when cooked and served whole. **Purple cauliflower** (above), a southern Italian specialty, ranges from a reddish to a deep purple shade, according to variety. With longer cooking times, however, it loses its color, turning green.

Green cauliflower is not only considered to be more aromatic, it also contains more nutrients and less nitrate than the white varieties. The best known and most widely cultivated green variety is "Alverda," shown here. Green cauliflower differs in appearance from its white relative only in color; their heads are shaped the same.

Cauliflower
AN OLD FAVORITE SHOWS ITS STARTLING NEW COLORS

Although mentioned as far back as 1,500 years ago, cauliflower has been naturalized for only 500 years. Today, it is a cultivated vegetable in the truest sense of the word and is grown around the world. Correspondingly, there are numerous and varied recipes from the four corners of the world for this most delicate of the Brassicas. Cauliflower is well suited to both Northern and Southern European cooking, as well as Arab and Asian dishes, since its subtle cabbage flavor means that it is delicious boiled, braised, baked, fried, or au gratin—in practically any way imaginable. From the point of view of flavor, it really does not matter whether the cauliflower is white or of a different color.

Broccoli, calabrese, sprouting broccoli (*Brassica oleracea* convar. *botrytis* var. *italica*). Broccoli is one of the few vegetables, particularly of the brassica family, to have undergone a meteoric rise in popularity over the past few years. It is cultivated throughout Europe, particularly in Italy and Spain, as well as in the United States. This market expansion is occurring at the expense of other brassicas, to the detriment of cauliflower in particular. Like cauliflower, to which it is closely related, broccoli also consists mainly of flowering stems and buds, with the leaves being only of secondary importance. However, unlike cauliflower, broccoli does not form a closed flower or curd. Its head consists of clearly differentiated, glossy green to bluish flowering buds on top of fleshy stems with numerous side shoots. There are purple, yellow, and even white varieties of broccoli, although these are less common. Broccoli is far superior to cauliflower in nutritional content, with a 60 percent higher vitamin C content and 60 times more carotene. It can be prepared like cauliflower and is also good braised in tomato sauce, or cooked in butter. It is less suitable for eating raw. **Brussels sprouts** (*Brassica oleracea* convar. *fruticosa* var. *gemmifera*). This vegetable was first cultivated in the area around the Belgian capital, hence its name. Today, Brussels sprouts are widely grown in the United States, Britain, France, and Holland. Harvest time lasts from the end of August into December. The "sprouts" are miniature cabbage heads, buds which grow in the angle between the leaf bases and the stem. Depending on the variety, the plant, which grows up to 3 feet in height, can produce sprouts of over 1½ inches in diameter. Their color ranges from light green through dark green to red. They are excellent briefly steamed, boiled, or stir-fried, and are also good au gratin with béchamel sauce or cheese, as the basis of a soup, in stews or slowly braised in the oven. They are unsuitable for eating raw. **Savoy cabbage** (*Brassica oleracea* convar. *capitata* var. *sabauda*). Savoy cabbage, together with white and red cabbage, is one of the most important and popular kinds of cabbage. It has a mild flavor and is particularly tender. The crimped or curly leaves form loose, round, oval, or tapering heads. Varieties are classified as early, midseason, fall, and winter types. Early Savoy cabbage, on the market from May, always has a pale, tender heart and needs only very brief cooking. Late varieties have dark green, robust leaves and a very pronounced cabbage flavor. Early varieties are ideal quartered and lightly boiled, steamed, or stir-fried. Late varieties are good in vegetable soups, stews, or casseroles. Savoy is less suitable for eating raw than other types of cabbage.

A broccoli plant in the field, with the little "heads" clearly recognizable. If only the main head is harvested, smaller side shoots are sent out.

Green broccoli still dominates the market. According to variety, the range of colors varies from medium green, through dark green to blue-green (top). **Purple broccoli** is very popular in Italy and among professional cooks elsewhere. It is easily confused with purple cauliflower (above).

Preparing broccoli: First remove the lower stalk end and cut off the side shoots. Peel the stalks and finely chop them, together with the leaves. Cook the stalks briefly on their own first, then add the flowerets, and, finally, the leaves.

Brussels sprouts are often sold with their outer leaves already trimmed. The higher price of trimmed sprouts is offset by the saving in time and the fact that little is wasted. When buying, look for smooth, unblemished, small heads. Brussels sprouts with spots or signs of withering have been stored too long, will taste slightly musty, and contain fewer nutrients.

Brussels sprouts in the field: the buds grow close together between the long-stalked leaves.

Red Brussels sprouts, also known as "Rubine" Brussels sprouts, are purple only on the outside, being green on the inside. The attractive red color is unfortunately lost in cooking. Red Brussels sprouts come on the market infrequently and are of no commercial importance, as they provide only about 30 percent of the yield of the green type.

Fall Savoy cabbage, also known as storing Savoy, can be recognized by its large, closed head, thick, very crimped leaves, and its large wrapping leaves. It comes on the market from late summer onward.

A typical summer Savoy cabbage (top): the head is loose, the leaves are delicate and moderately crinkly. **Curly Early Savoy** has a relatively small, almost flower-shaped open head with delicate golden yellow leaves on the inside (center). Early and midcrop Savoy should be cooked briefly to preserve both nutrients and flavor—15 minutes maximum. **Violet-green Savoy cabbage** (bottom), a less common variety, is very widely grown in the area around Verona, Italy.

Typical green summer cabbages are on sale in a vegetable market.

White cabbage is harvested by hand, which takes place year-round. The cabbage head is cut, trimmed, and individually packed for sale, or placed in large crates for storage. Mechanical harvesters are not commonly used, since they can cause damage to the cabbages, making them unsuitable for storage.

Green summer cabbage is available from May into late fall. This variety has a firmer head and thicker leaves than the very early spring cabbages.

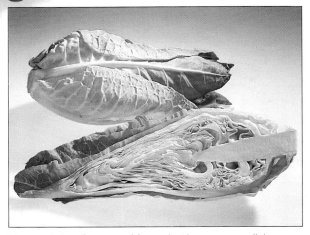

Many varieties of **green cabbage**, but by no means all, have this typical tapering shape. The "Filderkraut" cabbage, grown in the area of the same name near Stuttgart, Germany, is used almost exclusively for making sauerkraut.

White cabbage (*Brassica oleracea* convar. *capitata* var. *capitata* f. *alba*). Known even to the ancient Romans, the white cabbage is the most important of all head cabbage species. Despite its ubiquity, it is often considered to be typically German and East European. Although Germany is, in fact, one of the leading producers, the United States, Holland, Russia, France, Poland, Denmark, China, Korea, and many other countries cultivate white cabbage on a large scale. Botanically, the ovoid, spherical, or pointed head of the white cabbage is the compressed shoot of the plant. Whitish green to green in color, it is formed from the smooth, glossy leaves, which are covered with a waxy layer. White cabbage is classified into early, midseason, late, and winter varieties. It is perfect for stuffed cabbage, in a stew, grated raw (in coleslaw), and also good in soups and specialties. Various kinds of pickled white cabbage are popular in both the East and West. *Kimchee* is a Korean specialty, for example, and the result of fermenting cabbage in lactic acid, is sauerkraut. **Green cabbage** is available in an immense number of varieties. The earliest cabbages, available from the end of March, are considered a particular delicacy. It is distinguished by its tender leaves, its very subtle cabbage flavor and the pointed shape of the head with its upward-growing leaves. Depending on the time of harvest, a distinction is drawn between early and summer green cabbages. Summer types are usually less tender. **Collard greens, spring greens** are non-hearting, green cabbages and, in spite of the British name "spring greens," are available year round. Green cabbage is also grown in the tropics and marketed as collard greens. These are not usually as heavy and do not have well-formed heads because of excessively high temperatures that make them mature too quickly. Collard greens have the same nutritional value as other green cabbages and a pleasant flavor. Cook like cabbage or braise with meat. **Red cabbage** (*Brassica oleracea* convar. *capitata* var. *capitata* f. *rubra*). Red cabbage is just another form within the same species and so has much in common with green and white cabbage. In addition to the purplish violet color, its main distinguishing features are the smaller, very firm head and the slightly sweetish taste. Like other cabbages, the head shapes of red cabbage range from round with a flat top, through spherical, to balloon-shaped and oval. The main growing areas, with the exception of China, are the same as for the white cabbage. Red cabbage, too, is classified according to early, midcrop, fall, and winter types. It contains less carotene than other types of cabbage, but it is particularly rich in vitamin C.

This cut red cabbage perfectly illustrates the crimped leaves which, packed in tight layers, form the head.

Green, white, and red cabbage
POPULAR AND GOOD VALUE

Nutritionists recommend that we should eat our greens with gusto—and our whites and reds, too, in the case of cabbage. Although worldwide acreage given over to the cultivation of cabbages has decreased, these weighty heads are still one of our favorite vegetables. Hardly surprising, since green, red, or white, cabbage is extremely versatile, rich in vitamin C and minerals, and to top it off, as keenly priced a vegetable as you will ever find. Moreover, cabbages are available year round, although they are especially popular in the winter. The strong taste of cabbage traditionally belongs to the cold season and hearty cooking. The high fiber content ensures a pleasant, long-lasting feeling of satisfaction. Although cabbage was not made for delicate, light dishes, Chinese methods of preparation—with their short cooking times and generous seasoning—are well suited to this vegetable. Made into coleslaw, it is not exactly haute cuisine, but is nonetheless marvelously crunchy and spicy. White and red cabbage are prepared in the same manner for cooking. Halve the head, cut out the hard stalk, and wash the halves. Then, depending on your taste or your recipe, cut the cabbage coarsely into strips, grate finely or shred in a food processor. Stuffed cabbage leaves are the exception to the rule. To make these, first remove the outer leaves and then peel off leaves which are large enough to stuff and roll and are about the same size. Blanch briefly in boiling water, then cut the leaf ribs smooth with a sharp knife. Finally, place the filling on the leaves, roll up, secure with toothpicks or tie with string, and braise or steam according to taste.

These flattened spherical white cabbages illustrate just one of the great variety of shapes in which cabbages come. In Asia, white cabbage is referred to simply as "flat cabbage."

Collard greens, are really just non-hearting cabbages and, although known in Britain as spring greens, are available year round.

Arugula (top) produces seeds which are pressed for their oil, especially in India, where it is known as yamba oil. Otherwise, the aromatic, pleasantly hot leaves, which are either smooth or serrated like dandelion leaves, are used as a seasoning herb or a salad plant. Wild arugula is rarer than the cultivated type, and can be recognized by its more highly serrated leaves and its intense, bitter, peppery taste (above).

The leaves of the fully grown sea kale grow up to 1 foot long. Blue-green in color, they are slightly wavy, waxy, oval and feather-like. They are borne on bare stalks ¾–1-inch thick.

These sea kale shoots are approximately 8 inches long, with barely opened leaves. They are produced in the third year after planting by forcing, combined with light exclusion (plants are covered with peat or an inverted pail). The stalks taste similar to kohlrabi, and the small, frilly leaves have a strong cabbage flavor. Commercial cultivation is limited almost exclusively to Britain and France.

Arugula, rugola, (garden) rocket, Mediterranean rocket, salad rocket, Roman rocket, Italian cress, roquette, rucola (*Eruca vesicaria* ssp. *sativa*). This annual herb with its hot-tasting leaves and red or white flowers is indigenous to Southern Europe and the Mediterranean countries, its range extending as far as Afghanistan and Turkistan. Today, arugula is cultivated in the Mediterranean, the Middle East, Northern and Central India, and Brazil. In the Middle Ages it was esteemed not only as a diuretic and a digestive, but also as a culinary herb. It is only since the early 1980s that the example set by haute cuisine has brought about a new surge in its popularity in the United States and Britain, although it has remained consistently popular in both France and Italy. It goes well with mild varieties of salad greens and is also good cooked quickly in olive oil. **Sea kale, silver kale** (*Crambe maritima*). This sturdy, open, leafy cabbage grows wild in the coastal areas of Northern and Western Europe. In some places, wild sea kale is a legally protected species, although not an endangered one. Only the blanched shoots of the cultivated plant are sold. Rich in vitamin C, this vegetable is on the market from December to April, but exports are scant. **Cress, garden cress** (*Lepidium sativum* ssp. *sativum*). Cress is the most important of around 80 different species of the genus *Lepidium*. In Denmark, Belgium, Holland, France, and England there are enormous horticultural centers specializing exclusively in its year-round cultivation. The fast-growing plant is never allowed to grow to its full height of 1–2 feet, but is always harvested two to three days after germination. **Watercress** (*Nasturtium officinale*). Although indigenous to Europe, watercress is nowadays found throughout the world. This herbaceous aquatic plant sends out shoots which creep along the bottom of ponds and springs. Its hollow stems grow up over the water's surface and bear dark green, highly nutritious leaves. It is delicious in salads or as a seasoning herb for salads, egg, and creamy or cottage cheese dishes, and for flavoring compound butters. **Land cress** or **American cress** is a useful substitute. **Spoonwort, scurvy grass, scorbute grass** (*Cochlearia officinalis*). This salad plant is frequently found growing wild in the coastal regions of Northern and Western Europe. It is used like watercress. **Wintercress, common wintercress, yellow rocket** (*Barbarea vulgaris*). Wintercress is a winter-hardy wild plant with simple or slightly feather-like leaves. It grows in Southwestern Europe, Asia, and North Africa on roadsides and in moist clay soils. It has been cultivated on a small scale only in France and North America.

Spoonwort has shiny, spoon-shaped, fleshy dark green leaves with a very peppery flavor. In many areas of Germany, England, and France it is referred to as "scurvy grass," owing to its high vitamin C content and its former use as a preventative against the deficiency disease.

Wintercress has a rather pungent taste, but it is worth including a little in salad mixtures for its extraordinarily high vitamin C content.

Cress
HOT PICK-ME-UP

The large cress family is composed virtually of "adopted children." Although several salad plants bear the name cress, they all belong to different genera. The fact that they are always mentioned in the same breath is probably because they have two things in common: first, a more or less bitter, slightly hot taste, and second, volatile mustard oils with invigorating properties. In Europe, the most widely available and frequently used variety is garden cress, whose sprouts lend a piquant flavor to salads, egg, and cottage cheese dishes, and vegetable soups. As a rule, therefore, when cress is mentioned in European cookbooks, it is these small, slender sprouting plants—most easily harvested with kitchen scissors—which are meant. The distant relatives of garden cress are always referred to by their proper names (watercress, spoonwort, wintercress).

Watercress is seldom marketed in the West with its long root system—which adapts it well to growing in streams—still attached (right). More usually just the mineral-rich, aromatic leaves and stems are sold (below). In Asia, the entire plant, including the roots, is cooked as a vegetable.

Horseradish is mechanically washed before it is delivered for commercial processing. After undergoing a rough peeling process, followed by trimming if necessary, the roots are put in a grating drum, and grated to a pulp.

Wearing a protective mask is absolutely essential during the processing of horseradish. As the roots are broken up, mustard oils are released which would literally move the workers to tears by irritating their mucous membranes.

Horseradish
SOME LIKE IT HOT

This unprepossessing yellowish brown root really packs a punch. Its heat and characteristic flavor result from high concentrations of sulfurous mustard oils. It tastes strongest freshly grated; after a short while, the volatile oils evaporate and the flavor fades.

Horseradish as it ought to look: the skin intact, the flesh white and firm.

Wasabi the Japanese cousin of Western horseradish. The rhizomes, and less commonly the leaf stalks of the plant, provide a hot condiment for Japanese dishes. It is used grated raw or reconstituted from its dried, powdered form.

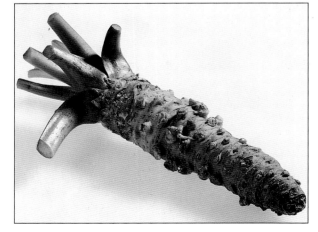

Horseradish (*Armoracia rusticana*). These hot-tasting roots are native to Eastern and Southeastern Europe, where they are still of great importance, and to parts of Asia. Horseradish is grown first and foremost for the food processing industry. Only small quantities are available in fresh-produce markets. Just where the light brown, white-fleshed roots get their name is debatable. Usually, when "horse" is used as a prefix for plant names, as in horse parsley, it denotes coarseness and vigor, and undoubtedly these large, knobby roots are very difficult to pull up and handle. What is certain, however, is that horseradish has been valued as a medicinal plant and condiment since the twelfth century, owing to its high content of volatile oils and antibiotic properties. A herbaceous perennial, it grows to a height of about 3 feet; its root, which reaches deep down into the soil, is the part that is used. Although there are different varieties of horseradish, the only commercial classification is according to origin. Horseradish is frost-hardy and so is well suited to storing. It is harvested in the fall, winter, and spring. Freshly grated, it is an excellent accompaniment to roast beef, sausages, salads, and smoked fish, and it is also good in warm and cold sauces and with hard-cooked eggs. It is not used as a cooked vegetable, as cooking destroys its flavor.

Wasabi, Japanese horseradish (*Eutrema wasabi*). Wasabi is known to have been cultivated for over 1,000 years. It grows wild on the islands of Japan, except on Hokkaido. It is cultivated in Japan almost exclusively on Honshu, generally over small areas and for preference along or in the (often terraced) mountain watercourses. In the West, it is usually available only in powdered form. **Winter radish, black radish** (*Raphanus sativus* var. *niger*). The winter or black radish, originally indigenous to the Middle East, is one of the most ancient cultivated plants known. The builders of the Egyptian pyramids fortified themselves with this vegetable. It ultimately reached Northern Europe in the baggage of a Roman soldier. It has been known as a vegetable and medicinal plant since the thirteenth century, long before the small radish (*Raphanus sativus* var. *sativus*). The main areas of cultivation are East Asia, China, Japan, and Korea. Consumption in the West is of comparatively minor commercial importance, whereas the Japanese eat over 28 pounds per head per year, and the Koreans an incredible 66 pounds. The tuber of this biennial plant is formed from the basal part of the main shoot and a portion of the root. Depending on variety, it can be round, bung-shaped, spindle-shaped, cylindrical, or oval. Its length ranges between 4 inches and 1 foot,

Semi-long red or white winter radishes appear on the market as early as May. They are sold in bunches with their greens still attached. They do not need to be peeled, just washed and trimmed. Their color has no bearing on their taste.

White, Red, and Black
POPULAR ACROSS THE WORLD

Winter radishes come in a wide variety of shapes and colors: from white, through pink, red, brown, and purple to black. Winter radishes are not just tasty: their wealth of minerals and mustard oil also make them healthy. In medieval times, they were even used as medicinal plants to cure gall-bladder and liver complaints. On an international scale, Japan and, above all, Korea are the leading consumers.

White radish, daikon, or mooli are shown here on sale in a covered European market in late summer. The mild, pleasant taste of these vegetables, which grow up to 20 inches long, has attracted a loyal following in the West.

Some winter or black radishes are carrot-shaped. These taste exactly the same as the round black varieties.

Black radishes or winter radishes, are suitable for storage and can withstand temperatures as low as 14°F even in the field. Their flesh is particularly firm. They should always be peeled, as their skin is hard to digest.

White radish or daikon in its original form: a blunt-tipped, 1-foot long root, tapering toward the base of the leaves. In China, winter radishes are used chiefly as cooking vegetables and are of great nutritional importance.

Daikon cress is grown from the seeds of the white radish or daikon. It tastes like the more familiar garden cress and is used in the same way. It is usually marketed in plastic baskets. If misted regularly with cold water, it can be kept for about a week in the refrigerator.

A white winter radish (below) of average length does not turn woody so easily as extremely long radishes. It does not need peeling; thorough washing normally suffices. **Daikon** or mooli (bottom) is a Japanese hybrid radish, now widely cultivated in the West. Its long, slender shape distinguishes it clearly from European and American varieties. It has very mild flavor and a high vitamin C content.

The red winter radish is preferred by many people because of its attractive color, although it is otherwise no different from its white relative. It loses its red color when heated.

Münchner weißer Treib und Setz ("Munich White Sprout and Plant") is a German variety of winter radish particularly suited to greenhouse or early outdoor cultivation. It is characterized by its short, squat shape and its aromatic taste.

sometimes even exceeding this. Skin color can be white, pink, red, brown, and purple to black, as well as red and white. In addition to many nutrients, the winter radish contains mustard oils, which account for its intense heat. Spring radishes are milder, whereas black fall and winter radishes can be eye-wateringly sharp. Sprinkling salt over the radish slices or heating them takes the edge off. They are best raw on buttered bread or in salads, or with cold meat platters. They make a good snack with beer, and, when cooked briefly, are a delicious accompaniment to pan-fried meats. **White radish, daikon, mooli, Chinese/Japanese/Oriental radish, winter radish** (*Raphanus sativus* var. *longipinnatus*). In East Asia these Japanese hybrid radishes are one of the most important vegetable types. They may grow up to 3 feet in length and tip the scales at about 44 pounds. Generally speaking, however, the white radish reaches a weight of "only" 4¼ pounds. **Daikon cress.** This sprouting vegetable is raised from the seeds of the daikon. Resembling garden cress in taste, it is prepared in a similar manner, giving rise to its arbitrary name. A recent arrival on the market, it is quite difficult to obtain. Daikon cress should never be cooked. **Radish, small radish** (*Raphanus sativus* var. *sativus*). Just where the familiar small radish originated is not known for certain: wild forms have been found in China and the Middle East. In ancient times small radishes were cultivated in Japanese and Chinese gardens as decorative plants, but the mild to hot rootlets have only been in the West for about 400 years. Today small radishes are cultivated worldwide, both under glass and outdoors. Tolerant of a wide range of climates and soils, they can be grown and harvested year round. The names of different types of radish can be confusing, particularly as the term "winter radish" is often applied in a nonspecific way. The small radish (*Raphanus sativus* var. *sativus*) might be mistaken for a dwarf form of the black or winter radish (*Raphanus sativus* var. *niger*). In fact, they are different varieties of the same species. The tuber of the small radish develops from the hypocotyl, the zone between the root and the cotyledon. Usually round, it can also be ovoid, cylindrical, or turnip-like in shape. In addition to the familiar red radishes, there are also white, pink, purple, and red-and-white skinned varieties; the flesh is always white. Again, mustard oils are responsible for the taste of small radishes, with outdoor varieties containing a greater concentration of them than produce grown under glass. Radishes are delicious in salads, sliced on bread, or as a garnish for cold platters and salads. They may also be gently cooked and served in a light sauce.

There are many types of two-toned small radish varieties. They differ from one another in the shape of the tubers and the extent of the white portion.

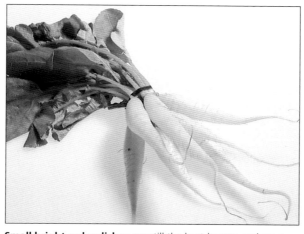

Small bright red radishes are still the best-known and most popular variety with the consumer, while the small, round white ones are less in demand and less often available (top). **Red radishes with white tips** are particularly popular in France (center). The variety Blanche Transparente ("Transparent white"), a long, small white radish, is of regional importance only (above). Its similarity to the winter radish (*Raphanus sativus* var. *niger*) is not limited to its appearance: in taste, too, it has more in common than with small round radishes.

The Palatinate Giant Radish is one of the large-growing varieties. No different from its smaller relatives in taste, it does save time in trimming and cutting.

A bitter gourd on the vine: The light green fruits of the long bitter gourd, with their almost smooth surfaces, grow up to a length of 1 foot on shoots 10–33 feet long, which are trained to grow over trellises or frames.

A market in Singapore: Displayed here and throughout Asia, in all imaginable shapes, colors, and sizes, are the popular fruiting vegetables that are the tropical members of the gourd family.

Long bitter gourds are harvested before they are ripe. At this stage, the fruits are light green and the seeds, which are embedded in the white, cottony flesh, are still light brown. The seed covering tastes pleasantly sweet.

Gourds and squashes
A FAMILY WITH MANY EXOTIC RELATIVES

The extensive gourd family has a venerable pedigree: The original form is a winter squash cultivated in America as long as 8,000 years ago by the native peoples. The descendants of this plant are numerous and varied. Over the millennia, many species, subspecies, and varieties have evolved. Among the members of the gourd family known to us today are pumpkins, winter squash, pattypan squash, spaghetti squash, ornamental gourds, zucchini, and cucumbers. The majority of the 850 or so known species—including melons, which are chiefly eaten as a fruit—are not only exotic in appearance and taste, but also the overwhelming proportion of these long or short, club-shaped or spherical fruits with their smooth or rough skin are also indigenous to foreign lands. The main areas of cultivation are the Asian tropics and Africa, where gourds are a staple of the daily diet. In addition, the fully ripe bottle gourd serves an equally important role as a provider of useful domestic items, such as bottles, vases, storage containers, and bowls, since its shell is watertight. In India, the fully grown, hollowed-out bottle gourd traditionally provides the body of a musical instrument, the sitar. Now and closer to home, however, it is primarily our diets which are enriched by the large gourd family with its variety of flavors, shapes, and colors.

***Cucurbitaceae* (Gourd family).** This large family comprises around 100 genera with about 850 species. Mostly creeping vines and bushes, they are chiefly indigenous to the tropics, subtropics, and the moderately warm latitudes. Few members of the gourd family occur in the wild in temperate zones. The fruit of the species which are most familiar as vegetables or fruit mostly belong to the genera *Cucumis*, *Cucurbita*, and *Citrullus*. In the tropics, fruits from the genera *Lagenaria*, *Luffa*, *Momordica*, *Sechium*, and *Trichosanthes* are also cultivated. The fruit of all species are used in the human diet. Their weight can range from just a few ounces to more than 100 pounds. **Karela, bitter gourd, bitter melon, bitter cucumber, balsam pear** (*Momordica charantia*). This vegetable takes many of its names from its high concentration of bitter constituents. Relatively unusual in the West, it is an important vegetable in India, Indonesia, Sri Lanka, Malaysia, China, the Philippines, and the Caribbean. Small quantities are exported from Thailand, India, and Kenya. The Dutch have been cultivating it under glass, mainly to cater for immigrants from the former Dutch colonies, and it is also grown in the United States. The fruits vary in size, shape, color, texture and degree of bitterness. The Indian karela is darker and thinner than the Chinese, while the Thai karela is white when immature. Ripe bitter melons are yellow to reddish orange in color and have pale, firm flesh. If left on the plant to ripen completely, the fruit bursts open. It is a good vegetable to hollow out and fill. It is also delicious in curries, and good pickled, stir-fried in Chinese rice dishes, and in salads. It is a good idea to blanch it before using. It is unsuitable for eating raw. **Dudi, bottle gourd, calabash, white-flowered gourd, hairy gourd, doohdi, lokhi, woo lo gwa** (*Lagenaria siceraria*). One of the oldest cultivated plants in the world, the dudi has an almost legendary past. The seeds are said to have been borne by ocean currents from tropical Africa to South America. Archeological finds suggest that it was already to be found in Peru 12,000 years ago. Today, it is cultivated in all tropical and subtropical regions. There are numerous varieties, differing greatly in shape and size: bottle gourds can reach lengths of between 4 inches and 3 feet, and weights of over 2¼ pounds. Only young, unripe, small fruits with soft rinds are eaten. The firm, white flesh is very mild-tasting and slightly reminiscent of cucumber. The very tough, watertight shell of the fully mature pot-bellied forms serve as eating and storage utensils. Dudi is good stuffed with ground meat and braised or baked and can be prepared in the same way as summer squash. It is not suitable for eating

Preparing karela for stuffing: Wash the fruit and cut iut in half with a sharp knife. Remove the flesh and seeds with a teaspoon. Finely chop the flesh, mix it with the other filling ingredients, and use to stuff the two half shells.

This deeply furrowed, spiny fruit is the second and more common form of the bitter gourd. They are either short (about 4 inches) and spindle-shaped (top), or reach lengths of up to 1 foot (above). The latter type, however, whose yellow coloring is already indicative of an advanced stage of ripeness, is seldom eaten as a vegetable, since its flesh turns spongy and soft and the bitter taste becomes much more pronounced. The seeds can be used as a condiment.

Dudi or calabash gourds are slender, light green edible bottle gourds whose close relationship to zucchini is revealed by their appearance and taste. This variety, which is exported by India, is prepared with the skin on (above). Dudis can be diced, sliced, or halved and hollowed out. In Sicily too, especially long varieties of the edible bottle gourd are sold (right).

In the countries where it is grown, the **tindola** or ivy gourd is picked when underripe, and eaten fresh or pickled. In India, fruits harvested before they are ripe are popular as a cooking vegetable. The leaves and shoots are also cooked.

Tinda or round melon is an apple-size, light green fruit, which is eaten cooked, pickled, or candied. The seeds are good roasted and eaten as a nibble.

Snake gourds reach the enormous length of up to 6½ feet with a diameter of only 1½–4 inches. They owe their name to their typical shape, which is sometimes twisted like a piece of string. Weights are often placed on top of snake gourds while they are growing to make them straighter. In Asia, Africa, and their native India, this slightly sweetish gourd is enjoyed as a cooked vegetable or a substantial addition to soup.

The kiwano is one of the largest and tastiest of the African wild cucumbers. When the fruit is completely ripe, the peel is orange-yellow, the flesh is bright green and gelatinous.

raw. **Snake gourd, club gourd, long tomato** (*Trichosanthes cucumerina* var. *anguina*). These extremely long fruits are only distantly related to the more familiar cucumber. Snake gourds are cultivated in Southeast Asia, China, Japan, West Africa, Latin America, and the Caribbean, as well as tropical Australia. **Tindoori, tindola, ivy gourd, small gourd, scarlet gourd** (*Coccinia grandis*). These elongated oval fruits, measuring only about 4 inches in length, are mainly of local importance in the countries in which they are cultivated (India, Indonesia, Malaysia, and Central Africa), but some are exported. Their mild-flavored juicy flesh is reminiscent of the cucumber in taste. Ripe tindooris are red, but only the unripe, green fruits are eaten, even though they may sometimes be bitter. **Tinda, round melon, squash melon, round gourd** (*Praecitrullus fistulosus*). These small fruits come from India, and are only cultivated there and in neighboring Pakistan. They are equally esteemed as a vegetable, as animal fodder, and as a medicinal plant. **Kiwano, horned cucumber, jelly melon,** (*Cucumis metuliferus*). This is a sort of halfway-house between a vegetable and fruit, since it cannot be properly classified as one or the other. Originally indigenous to tropical Africa, horned cucumbers have been cultivated chiefly in New Zealand since 1981 and exported worldwide with increasing success. The peel, which is studded with numerous fleshy spines, encloses gelatinous flesh, which is pale in color to begin with, later becoming dark green. The many seeds, arranged in honeycomb-like compartments within a cavity, are also eaten. The taste—a mixture of banana and lime, with a hint of cucumber—can be enjoyed to best advantage when the fruit is eaten plain. **Fuzzy melon, hairy cucumber, (Chinese) wax gourd, winter gourd, ash gourd, ash pumpkin, white gourd, Chinese squash, Chinese preserving melon** (*Benincasa hispida*). The fuzzy melon plays a fairly significant role in the diet of the countries where it is traditionally grown—China, India, Japan, and Southeast Asia. The Americans and the Dutch cultivate this vegetable on a small scale; otherwise, it is imported in the West. Fuzzy melons come in the most varied shapes, from spherical, via ovoid, to an elongated sphere with a slightly nipped "waist." The color, too, varies from dark green to light greenish yellow. The fruit can be eaten both young and when mature. **Chayote, christophine, cho-cho, chow-chow, choyote, sou-sou, choko, vegetable pear,** (*Sechium edule*). This starchy fruit is indigenous to the mountains of Mexico, Central America, and Brazil. The Aztecs, who prized it as a vegetable, named it *chayotl*. Nowadays, it is grown

This wax gourd clearly displays the whitish bloom from which it gets its name. The waxy layer covers only fully grown fruit and is responsible for its particularly good keeping qualities—hence one of its other names, winter melon. The wax gourd is popular as a cooked vegetable in all the countries where it is cultivated.

Fuzzy melon is the name given to wax gourds which have been harvested young—an allusion to the hairy down which covers them.

Green and white chayotes: These pear-shaped, deeply ribbed fruits, which are sometimes also covered with soft prickles, grow to about 2¾–8 inches in length, reaching a weight of up to 2¼ pounds. Their flesh is firm and slightly sweet. Unlike all the other members of the gourd family, they have a single (edible) pit, which is nutty tasting.

Preparing chayote:

First wash the chayote thoroughly under cold running water. If necessary, scrub it briefly under hot running water.

Peel the chayote thinly with a swivel vegetable peeler, preferably under running water, as the juices that will leak out are sticky.

Once the fruit has been peeled, the furrows can be cut out with a sharp, pointed vegetable knife.

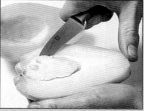

Halve the chayote lengthwise, cut around the large central pit, remove, and discard.

Like cucumbers, wax gourds are usually trained on trellises or other supports. The young, dark green specimens, known as fuzzy melons, are still firm-fleshed and have a more pronounced flavor than fully ripened wax gourds.

on a commercial scale in the United States, particularly in California, Central and South America, India, North Africa, and other countries. The slightly sweetish flesh of the fruit is ivory-colored to dark green and exudes a sticky juice. It may be prepared like potatoes, cucumbers, or zucchini, and it is also suitable for eating raw. It features in a number of Caribbean and Creole recipes. In the South American countries where it is cultivated, the starchy rhizomes are also eaten, prepared like potatoes. **Angled loofah/luffa, ridged loofah, ridged gourd, silk gourd, angled gourd, Chinese okra** (*Luffa acutangula*). Originally from Northwest India, the angled loofah has spread outward over the whole of Southeast Asia and the Caribbean. In spite of its low nutritional value, it is a popular vegetable in the countries where it is cultivated, particularly India. It is a vigorous climbing plant which is trained around supports. Although the fruits can grow up to 3 feet long, they are harvested young. The fruit is characterized by 10 raised ridges which run its length and which should still be soft. They harden in the mature fruits and the seeds develop unpleasant qualities, making the fully ripe fruits bitter and inedible. The angled loofah is good used raw, like a cucumber, and is also excellent braised or stir-fried. It can be cooked in the same way as zucchini. **Smooth loofah/luffa, sponge gourd, dish-cloth/dish-rag gourd, vegetable sponge** (*Luffa cylindrica*). The smooth loofah is the best-known of the ten or so different species of loofah. Scientists have developed varieties for producing sponge-like materials, as well as non-bitter varieties for use as a vegetable. Cultivation for extraction of the sponge-like vascular bundle from the mature fruits is commercially more important. Nowadays, this serves almost exclusively as the raw material for natural, exfoliant washing gloves and back-rubs, but before World War II, for example, 60 percent of the loofahs imported into the United States were used in filters for steamship and diesel engines. **Korila, wild cucumber** (*Cyclanthera pedata*). The korila is thought to have come originally from Mexico, but the Caribbean is another possible home. Today, it is still cultivated in both areas, as well as in Peru and parts of Southeast Asia. The 2–3-inch long, thick spindle-shaped berry fruits, which taper to a point, can be eaten either raw or cooked. **(Salad) cucumber**. Although the majority of the species belonging to the genus *Cucumis* come from Africa, the home of this familiar salad vegetable is North India, where it has been cultivated for over 3,000 years. The cucumber only reached Europe in the Middle Ages, and was first cultivated in greenhouses in

Preparing angled loofahs:
Clean under cold running water, then pat dry.

Peel the ridges off thinly using a swivel vegetable peeler. The remaining peel can be eaten.

Slice the loofah and sauté in butter or use as wished.

"Pepino hueco" ("hollow cucumber") is the name given to the korila by the Indios because of its meager flesh content.

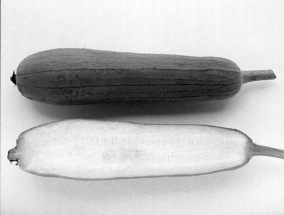

The smooth loofah differs from the angled or ridged loofah in that the ridges which run its length are only hinted at. The flesh of the young, 10-inch long fruit is white and cottony in texture. Special varieties which are free from bitter substances have been bred for vegetable cultivation. Smooth "vegetable sponge" loofahs and angled loofahs can be eaten peeled and raw or cooked.

The English cucumber is straight and elegantly proportioned. This popular salad vegetable is often sold shrink-wrapped in plastic to reduce transpiration and ensure that it stays fresh and crunchy for longer.

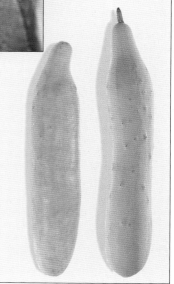

In terms of biology, cucumbers are an exception. Normally, female and male flowers exist on the same plant, but there are also predominantly female and all-female varieties. Growers increasingly favor the all-female cucumber plants, which form seedless fruit when they have not been pollinated. The herbaceous cucumber plant is grown creeping on the ground, or increasingly frequently trained on supports.

The Kirby cucumber is a mini variety that weighs just 3½–10 ounces and measures up to 6 inches in length. Although a popular pickling variety in the United States, it has only recently come onto the European market. It is gaining in importance because of its distinctive flavor.

Yellow and white cucumbers are popular for their decorative appearance, but come on the market infrequently. They are very good mixed with green cucumbers in salads.

The Japanese kuri cucumber resembles our outdoor ridge cucumbers only in appearance. It grows to a length of only about 10 inches and has a dark green, warty peel. It is also eaten like a normal cucumber, but for Western tastes, it has an unaccustomed fishy flavor. The peel is considered to be especially flavorful.

As its name implies, the **braising cucumber,** an outdoor (ridge) variety, is particularly well suited to cooking. Its firm, less watery flesh does not break down during cooking as fast as the greenhouse cucumber. It can, of course, also be eaten raw, but it frequently contains unpalatable bitter substances, especially at the base of the stalk.

A display of pickling cucumbers on sale at the *Viktualienmarkt* in Munich in late summer.

nineteenth-century England. Nowadays, cucumbers are grown almost everywhere, and are the fourth most cultivated vegetable in the world after tomatoes, brassicas, and onions. China is the largest producer, followed by Russia, Japan, Turkey, the United States, Romania and Holland. Other important producers are Greece, Spain, Italy, France, Belgium, and Germany. They are chiefly grown outdoors in warmer climatic zones, but because they are highly sensitive to frost cucumber plants are cultivated almost exclusively in hothouses in cooler regions. The cucumber is a fruiting vegetable bearing fruits in all sorts of different shapes and sizes. They start out green, becoming white, yellowish, orange-yellow, or brownish-yellow as they ripen, and may reach weights of up to 3½ pounds. Cucumbers grow to lengths of about 16 inches, with a maximum diameter of about 4 inches. The skin of the young fruit is covered with prickly warts which disappear as ripening progresses. Varieties of the cucumber worth mentioning are the especially aromatic **mini-cucumber,** the firm-fleshed **braising cucumber,** the Japanese **kuri cucumber**, quite unusual in the West, and **yellow** and **white cucumbers,** which are also uncommon. Ideal cut into rounds, sliced on a mandolin, or grated for salads, all these varieties are also good stuffed with a meat filling and broiled briefly, stir-fried with tomatoes, or in soup. Salad cucumbers are unsuitable for dishes with a very long cooking time. **Pickling cucumber, cornichon, gherkin** (*Cucumis sativus*). This variety of cucumber, best known in dill pickles, is cultivated almost exclusively outdoors and harvested when 2–8 inches long. The peak season for pickling cucumbers and cornichons is from mid-August to mid-September, when the first fruits have reached a length of about 3½ inches. A basic distinction is drawn between fruit types with nearly smooth skins and those with warty or prickly ones. Pickling cucumbers or gherkins are usually named solely according to their size or the way in which they are pickled or prepared. Cornichons are little cucumbers (about 2¼ inches long) which are not fully developed. They are generally pickled in vinegar. Larger cucumbers (2¼–4¾ inches long) are also pickled—usually unpeeled—in vinegar. The characteristic taste of larger pickled cucumbers comes from lactic fermentation. Commercial gherkins are usually sterilized slices, cubes, or strips of cucumber pickled with vinegar and spices. All cucumbers are very sensitive to the cold and should not be stored in the refrigerator. The ethylene gas given off by tomatoes and fruit also turns them yellow, so it is better to store them separately.

Pickling cucumbers are named according to their size and the manner in which they are pickled or spiced: **cornichons** (below), **larger pickling cucumbers** (below right and right), and **commercial gherkins** (above and above right). The latter are prepared in many varied ways by the pickling industry. When buying cucumbers for pickling at home, you should look for a smooth, unblemished peel, as otherwise the fruit will rot, spoiling the pickles.

Pumpkin
THE ORANGE GIANT, IN BIG DEMAND THE WORLD OVER

Pumpkins are thought to have existed over 10,000 years ago in Central and South America. The fact that five species of cultivated pumpkins or gourds are grown around the globe today, throughout the tropics and subtropics, as well as in the warmer regions of the temperate latitudes, is testimony to its value. In many countries, the pumpkin is among the most important vegetable species cultivated.

Young pumpkin leaves are a superb source of vitamin C and beta carotene. In Italy, and above all in Asia and Africa, they are valued as a cooked vegetable.

Preparing giant pumpkin:

Cutting larger pumpkins into sections or segments first makes them easier to handle. This is best done with a large, heavy knife.

Use the edge of a tablespoon to scrape out both the seeds and the fibrous core from the center of the pumpkin. Toasted pumpkin seeds make a delicious nibble.

Lastly, cut off the pumpkin shell in strips using a sharp kitchen knife. Dice or chop the flesh according to your recipe.

Aromatic pumpkin-seed oil is extracted from the seeds of the pumpkin.

(Giant) pumpkin, winter squash (*Cucurbita maxima*). Indigenous to South America, pumpkins grow vigorously in the tropics and are widely cultivated across the world—in the United States, Australia, China, Japan, Egypt, Argentina, Mexico, Spain, Romania, Turkey, France, Greece, and Italy, among many other places. The individual fruits of the frost-sensitive, creeping giant pumpkin plant are mostly spherical to cylindrical in shape. The name "giant pumpkin" graphically describes the enormous size of this winter squash, which can tip the scales at 65 pounds and more. The tough, thick, inedible shell encloses soft, juicy flesh, the color of which ranges from white to yellow to reddish orange. Besides its high water content—almost 95 percent—its chief constituents are carbohydrate, protein, calcium, iron, vitamin C, and a range of B vitamins. A dark green, highly aromatic oil is pressed from the very nutritious seeds, which is superb for dressing all kinds of salads. The dried seeds, sometimes toasted, are a popular snack. The delicate pumpkin blossoms, either stuffed or dipped in batter and fried, are prized as a delicacy. Small pumpkins are usually sold whole; large ones, on the other hand, are cut and sold by weight. Look for a smooth, clean shell with no spots, as well as the presence of a stalk or "neck" about 4 inches long. The flesh can be used in any number of different ways. It is ideal as a sweet-sour pickle, made into chutney or a compote, or as a purée with poultry or pork. It also good in a casserole or stew, cooked with cream and stock and made into a cream soup, or oven-baked. The traditional Thanksgiving pumpkin pie is, of course, now world famous. Pumpkin is not suitable for eating raw. **Musky gourd, musky pumpkin, (golden) cushaw pumpkin** (*Cucurbita moschata*). Archeological evidence shows that the musky gourd or cushaw pumpkin, of which no wild form is known, was grown as early as 1,000 to 3,000 B.C. in New Mexico and Peru. Because it can withstand high temperatures, it is the most widely cultivated pumpkin in the tropics of both hemispheres. The fruits, which do not develop tough shells, are extraordinarily varied in shape. The flesh is dark yellow in color, owing to its high carotene content. It is slightly gelatinous in consistency, and gives off a pleasant scent—hence the name "musky pumpkin." It is popular both as food for humans and as animal fodder. It is particularly worth emphasizing its superb keeping qualities—it can be stored for weeks, even months. Among the numerous varieties of this species is the butternut squash, highly prized for its buttery-soft flesh. It may be cooked in the same ways as the giant pumpkin.

The hard-shelled winter squash known as acorn squash, with its light orange-colored, sweet flesh, may be enjoyed stuffed and baked whole. It is also popular mashed with plenty of butter and pepper.

Cultivated gourds can be classified into five species of the genus *Cucurbita (C.):* the (giant) pumpkin or winter squash *(C. maxima,* 1), many varieties of which are now cultivated, mainly in the United States. The fig-leaf pumpkin *(C. ficifolia)* has little importance as a vegetable; it is chiefly used as a stock upon which cucumbers and melons can be grafted. The forms of the Ayote *(C. mixta),* which is widespread in Central and South America, are particularly diverse. The musky pumpkin or cushaw *(C. moschata, 2, 3, 4, 7, 8),* an important food in Central America, China, and India, comes in a great variety of shapes, colors, and sizes, and bears extremely aromatic fruit. Lastly, the summer squash *(C. pepo, 5, 6, 9, 10)* is, worldwide, the most widely distributed of all the species. Despite the fact that they are cultivated throughout the year, these species of gourd are roughly divided into summer and winter squashes, with the former generally assigned to the species *C. pepo,* which can be recognized by their small size, pale-colored flesh, and soft seeds. Because of their thin skins, young summer squashes, such as zucchini, can be boiled or sautéed without peeling. Winter squashes generally belong to the species *C. maxima* or *C. moschata* and are harvested only when fully ripe. Squashes of the species *C. maxima* have a hard shell and are not edible whole. Squashes of the species *C. moschata,* on the other hand, have a firm shell which can be eaten.

The **butternut squash** gets its name from the buttery consistency of its cooked flesh and its nutty taste. It belongs to the group of musky gourds or cushaws (top). This **"giant" pumpkin** with its rough green shell is a slightly small specimen (center). This **spaghetti squash** is still immature and white (above). Mature specimens are golden yellow.

This bell-shaped, strongly ridged specimen is a good example of the variety of shapes of cushaw.

Summer squash, (vegetable) marrow (*Cucurbita pepo*). Summer squash, probably descended from the **Texas squash** (*Cucurbita pepo* ssp. *texana*), which grows wild in Mexico and Texas, is the most widely grown squash in the world today. It is to be found both in the tropics and subtropics, as well as in temperate latitudes. It is cultivated from the sixtieth latitude in Scandinavia and Russia up to the mountain valleys of Asia lying at an altitude of 8,000 feet. As it grows quickly and is cold-tolerant, it is cultivated in preference to the more cold-sensitive giant pumpkin in subtropical mountainous countries and in temperate zones. Just 50 years after Columbus' discovery of the New World, summer squash was known throughout Europe; several varieties were mentioned in a famous German herbal as early as 1543. Today, there are countless varieties worldwide, all recognizable as descendants of the summer squash by certain common features: their fibrous flesh holds its shape when cooked, and the fruit stalk or "neck" is always strongly developed and deeply ridged. Among the most important squashes in this group are zucchini, pattypan, custard or scallop squash, vegetable spaghetti or spaghetti squash, and rondini. **Pattypan squash, yellow custard squash, scallop squash** (*Cucurbita pepo* ssp. *pepo* convar. *patissonina*). This species, probably developed from a cross between a cucumber and a squash, was already cultivated by Native Americans in pre-Columbian times, and is still a widely grown, highly-esteemed vegetable in the United States. The fruits of this annual creeper are characteristically a flattened sphere with scalloped edges in shape and the size of a side plate. Their color ranges from white via ivory and yellow to light green. There are only a few varieties, all of which are sold under the generic name "squash." Pattypan squash should be washed, but not peeled before cooking. It is excellent simply served with butter, but can also be braised with onions and tomatoes, or hollowed out, filled with ground meat, and served au gratin. **Spaghetti squash, vegetable spaghetti** (*Cucurbita pepo*). This species, which comes from Japan, is named after the peculiar tendency of its flesh to form spaghetti-like strands when ripe. Once cooked, the individual strands separate and become even more conspicuous. As it is cooked whole, the recommended cooking time varies between 20–50 minutes, depending on size. First pierce the end so that the heat can reach the inside. To serve, cut the squash in half, remove the seeds, and scoop the strands of flesh onto a plate with a fork. The slightly lemon-tasting flesh can be eaten like true spaghetti, with tomato sauce and grated Parmesan cheese, pesto, or garlic butter.

These slightly flattened, speckled cushaws come from Thailand.

Spaghetti squash or vegetable spaghetti (top) turns yellow as it ripens, and develops fibrous, spaghetti-like flesh. The popular very delicate **pattypan squash** is available in yellow and light green (above and right).

"Butterball," a Japanese hybrid variety of the giant pumpkin, measures only about 10 inches in diameter. Its green shell often turns orange when the fruit ripens. The flesh lends itself well to puréeing after cooking. Reminiscent of chestnut purée in color and flavor, it complements pan-fried and broiled meats superbly and goes well with chicken and turkey.

Giant pumpkin does justice to its name. It can tip the scales at hundreds of pounds. Since an average household could scarcely cope with a vegetable this size, large pumpkins are usually cut up and sold by weight. Smaller pumpkins are available whole and larger ones are commonly on sale—for non-culinary purposes—around Halloween.

Rondini (top) and **round zucchini** (above), although similar in appearance, actually belong to different varieties of *Cucurbita pepo*. For the consumer, the most important difference is that rondini, unlike zucchini, are not suitable for eating raw.

Throughout the Mediterranean region, zucchini are grown in an enormous range of colors and sizes. Italy leads all the other countries in the number of varieties cultivated.

"Goldrush" is the very apt name of this bright yellow zucchini variety. It was developed in the United States.

This light green zucchini variety from Turkey is extremely tasty, and is preferred in the Mediterranean and the Near East.

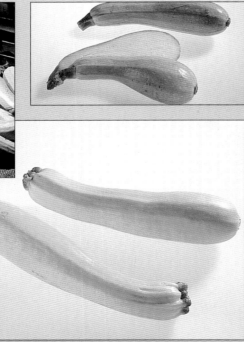

Zucchini (*Cucurbita pepo* ssp. *pepo* convar. *giromontiina*). Zucchini are the fruits of a fast-growing, non-creeping, and highly frost-sensitive plant. The name "zucchini" derives from the Italian *zucca*, and means "little squashes." Zucchini are, in fact, descended from the giant pumpkin. They are cultivated, among other places, in the United States, Mediterranean countries, Holland, Britain, and France. Zucchini are chiefly grown outdoors. They can grow up to 16 inches long and up to 4½ pounds in weight, but are generally harvested when quite small. The skin is usually light to dark green with light gray spots or yellow stripes. They resembles their relative, the cucumber, in appearance. There are numerous varieties, including white, cream colored, and yellow zucchini. Round zucchini is a special variety; "baby zucchini" are simply harvested very young, rather than being a separate variety. In summer, zucchini are sometimes sold with their flowers still attached; the blossoms are a special delicacy stuffed or deep-fried. All zucchini varieties and types have white to light green flesh, which is reminiscent of cucumber, but substantially firmer because of its lower water content. Yellow varieties have slightly firmer flesh than green ones. The flavor could be described as slightly nutty when raw and rather neutral when cooked. The numerous soft, pale seeds are eaten. In addition to carbohydrate and protein, the most important constituents of zucchini are the minerals phosphorus and iron, as well as provitamin A and vitamin C. They are usually harvested at half their full size, when they are about 6–8 inches long, or smaller. Zucchini are available all year round. When buying, look for straight, firm fruit with a glossy blemish-free skin. They can keep for up to three weeks in the vegetable compartment of a refrigerator (do not store below 50°F). Zucchini are sensitive to the ethylene given off by fruit and tomatoes, so they are best stored separately. They require only topping and tailing and are delicious braised, fried, deep-fried, roasted, steamed, in ratatouille, and stuffed with ground meat, cheese, and rice and broiled. They are also good as a gratin, in quiches, and raw as a salad vegetable. **Rondini** (*Cucurbita pepo*). Rondini are probably originally from the subtropics of Asia and Africa; they are relative newcomers to Northern countries, without much commercial importance yet. Although they are closely related to zucchini, they are distinct from the round varieties of zucchini, which they greatly resemble. Rondini plants are climbers, while zucchini plants are bushy. When ripe, rondini turn orange-red; zucchini remain green to yellowish. Rondini are harvested when unripe and green.

Very young "baby": zucchini may be sold in the summer with their flowers attached. They create a lovely splash of color in salads.

The especially large female zucchini flowers (top) with finger-long fruit, are best suited to stuffing. **The smaller male flowers,** on the other hand (above) are mostly pan-fried or deep-fried. The bushy **zucchini plant** (right) is extremely prolific and yields any amount of fruits over the course of the summer.

Zucchini
SMALL IS BEAUTIFUL

"Be fruitful and multiply"—this could be the motto of the zucchini plant. Undemanding with regard to growing conditions, it blooms and flourishes prolifically. It is hardly surprising, therefore, that zucchini, which have been cultivated in the Mediterranean since time immemorial, have in recent years enjoyed a steady rise in popularity with vegetable growers in many other countries. At the same time, demand has risen, since this low-calorie vegetable is second to none in terms of versatility. Sliced, or cut into matchsticks, it goes well with virtually all other ingredients—meat, fish, eggs, vegetables, herbs, and almost all spices and seasonings combine superbly with this very mild-flavored summer squash. Young zucchini are the most delicate.

Dark green zucchini varieties, which are more or less dappled with silver-gray—like "Elite," shown here— are the best known and most widely grown.

Water chestnuts
A FEATURE OF CHINESE CUISINE

In addition to a slight external resemblance to the sweet chestnut, the Chinese water chestnut also tastes similarly mild and has a crunchy texture. However, the two namesakes are botanical worlds away from each other: the water chestnut belongs to the sedge family and is cultivated in still water. The pseudobulbs mature slowly and are harvested painstakingly by hand. They are popular in East Asia. In the province of Canton in China, chopped water chestnuts are used as a filling for dim sum—little steamed dumplings enjoyed as a snack. In European cuisine, water chestnuts are known as a piquant hors d'oeuvre, wrapped in ham and broiled. If the dark brown- or black-shelled tubers are not available fresh, you can always fall back on canned produce from China or Japan.

Preparing water chestnuts:

Thoroughly wash the water chestnuts, then peel like an apple, using a sharp knife.

Sort through the tubers, discarding any that are becoming yellow and limp. Slice off the tough stalks from the remainder.

The peeled water chestnuts are now ready to be used, whole, sliced, or chopped, according to your recipe.

At Chinese markets water chestnuts are sold unpeeled and with soil still clinging to them. This keeps the white flesh under the skin fresh for a long time without refrigeration.

Tiger nuts are also known as earth almonds owing to their similarly nutty taste. The acorn-sized, chestnut-brown to blackish brown rhizomes are covered with a wrinkled skin.

Cyperaceae (**Sedge family**). This family chiefly contains useful, but inedible plants, such as rushes, sedges, and cotton grasses. However, the pseudobulbs of the tiger nut and water chestnut are used as vegetables. **Tiger nut, chufa, earth almond** (*Cyperus esculentus*). The Arabs brought the Cyprus grass plant from Africa to Southern Europe. This perennial, which, like a potato plant, sends out underground runners, is shunned as a weed in the majority of warm countries because of its creeping, rapidly expanding roots. It is cultivated only in North Africa and in Spain, where its high nutritional value and nutty taste are esteemed. Even there, cultivation is on a small scale. **Water chestnut, waternut** (*Eleocharis dulcis*). This marsh plant is native to West Africa, Madagascar, India, the Pacific Islands, and all of East Asia. In China, in particular, it is of great culinary importance: the dark-brown or black tubers located on the roots are prized for their sweetish, firm white flesh in both savory and sweet dishes.

Dioscoreaceae. This family was named after its most important genus, *Dioscorea* (yam), which, with 600 or so species, is widespread in the tropics. **Yam** (*Dioscorea* spp.). The yam was originally cultivated in Africa, Asia, and America. Ninety-five percent of the world's acreage given over to its cultivation is in Africa, where its high starch content makes it an important food. It is a labor-intensive, expensive crop to grow, so it is increasingly being superseded by cassava and sweet potatoes. Most of the 150 or so species of yam are right- or left-twining climbers with tubers differing greatly in color, shape, and size (4½–11 pounds). Among the most important species of yam are the **white yam** (*D. alata*) with tubers weighing up to 130 pounds, and the **Japanese yam** (*D. japonica*), as well as the **Asian yam** (*D. esculenta*) and the **cush-cush yam** (*D. trifida*).

Euphorbiaceae (**Spurge family**). Many ornamental plants belong to this family, but the most important tuber-producing plant is the **cassava, manioc** or **manihot** (*Manihot esculenta*). Thanks to its trouble-free cultivation, world production of cassava is constantly growing: the biggest producer is Thailand, followed by Brazil, and a number of African countries. The tuberous roots of this herbaceous perennial are the fourth most important source of food energy in the tropics after sugar cane, rice, and corn; as a foodstuff, it is in sixth place worldwide. This is primarily because of its high starch content, but the cassava is also very high in vitamin C, protein, and minerals. The raw tubers contain poisonous hydrogen cyanide, which disappears when they are cooked.

The white or water yam, also called the large yam, is the most widely grown species. The tubers, which often grow to an enormous size, usually have white to yellowish flesh.

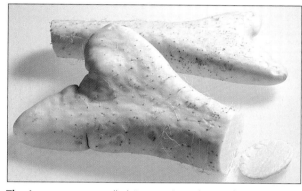

The Japanese yam, called "yamatoimo" ("mountain potato") in Japan, is distinguished from other species by its shape and snow-white color. It is usually used grated.

The Chinese or Asian yam has especially small, aromatic tubers that are cooked like potatoes. The shape is reminiscent of sweet potatoes.

The cush-cush yam originated in Northern South America and is now grown chiefly in the Caribbean. These spindle-shaped tubers come from Costa Rica.

Cassava roots grow up to about 3 feet long. Their nutritious flesh is always white, surrounded by a brown cork-like covering.

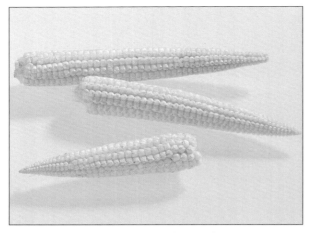

Baby corn is not a separate variety, but simply immature corn cobs, harvested when just under 4 inches long. These bite-size delicacies have long been a popular fresh vegetable in Asia, but now gourmets all over the world are appreciating these tiny, delicate off-white cobs.

Only the best quality is accepted when the contract farmers, here in Thailand, present their new baby corn crop for inspection.

Corn
BOTH GIANT AND MINIATURE COBS—A HIGHLY PRIZED VEGETABLE

The sweet young relatives of the age-old animal fodder corn are valued across the world. Hardly surprising, when one considers that the golden yellow cobs not only taste as sweet as sugar, but are richer in nutrients than most other vegetables, being on a nutritional par with peas. The main nutrients contained in corn are carbohydrate, protein, fat, calcium, potassium, iron, provitamin A, vitamins B_1, B_2, B_3, and B_6, as well as a great deal of vitamin C. This is not only true of the fully grown specimens, but also for the wonderfully delicate baby corn cobs.

Fresh corn is undoubtedly a delicacy, which unfortunately loses flavor quickly when stored too long or incorrectly. At temperatures of around 41°F, the cobs—except the new supersweet varieties—will lose about half their sugar content within a few hours. To be on the safe side, buy only freshly picked or well-chilled cobs and use them as quickly as possible.

A baby corn plantation in Thailand. Corn is an annual grass whose pith-filled stalk can reach a height of up to 8¼ feet. The irrigation canals ensure that the soil is sufficiently moist, which is especially important for optimal cob development.

Corn cobs are ripe when the silk at the tip of the cob turns brown. The kernels are plump and smooth, light to dark yellow in color, and contain a milky white juice. Older cobs, or those harvested too late, become sticky, the grains shrink, and quickly lose their sweetness as the sugar is converted to starch.

Labiatae. This family contains about 200 genera with around 3,000 species. The majority are classified as herbs or shrubs; many are cultivated as ornamentals, and quite a few as culinary herbs, tea and medicinal plants. The third largest genus is *Stachys*, with about 300 species. **Chinese artichoke, Japanese artichoke, crosnes, spirals** (*Stachys affinis*). In Japan and China, the rootstocks of the shrub are cultivated on a relatively large scale; France is the only Western country which grows them on any sizeable scale. Their mild flavor is reminiscent of scorzonera and artichokes. Since the rhizomes thicken primarily between, rather than on, the actual nodes, rootstocks are produced whose center sections are more swollen than their base and tip. The "nipping in" of the tubers results in their typically caterpillar-like appearance. Chinese artichokes may be prepared like Teltow turnips or asparagus.

Chinese artichokes or crosnes, each no longer than a finger, are the cream-colored, delicate, juicy tubers at the end of the underground stems of a plant native to China.

Gramineae **(Grasses).** With 600 genera and around 10,000 species, the grass family is one of the most extensive in existence, comprising such important plants as all cereals, rice, millet, corn, and sugar cane. **Corn, sweetcorn, sugar maize** *(Zea mays* convar. *saccharata).* In contrast to Indian corn, which originated in Mexico and has been known for millennia as a fodder plant, sweet corn has only been around since the mid-nineteenth century. It differs from Indian corn in its earlier ripening, smaller cobs, and tender, sweet kernels. Today the main producing country is the United States, where corn occupies a good 17 percent of the total vegetable-growing acreage. It is exported on a large scale. In Europe, it is cultivated in the temperate zones, chiefly in England, France, Spain, and Holland. The corn plant, an annual, grows up to 8 feet tall. The male flowers form a tassel at the tip of the stalk; the female flowers or silks are found in several cobs growing in the axils of the stalk sheathed in husks. The protruding, thread-like styles are fertilized by wind-borne pollen, which causes the kernels to develop at the cob axils. Around 300 varieties of corn, almost exclusively American, are known. The most widely distributed types are the particularly sweet hybrids, such as "Early Extra Sweet," "Tasty Sweet," and "Florida Stay Sweet." Some varieties are well suited to the cultivation of baby corn, the cobs measuring no more than 4 inches with nearly white kernels. Corn is ideal cooked whole in boiling water or barbecued. Baby corn can be stir-fried. The kernels may be boiled or creamed as a side dish, or served as a vegetable mixed with peas or bell peppers. It is also good in salads, puréed with cream as a soup, added to batter for corn fritters, or raw as a nibble.

Preparing Chinese artichokes: Scrub the small tubers well under cold running water, then trim. Blanch them, unpeeled, in boiling water and use in salads, or boil them and serve in a cream sauce.

To prepare corn, wash the cob, cut off both ends and scrape the kernels off with a sharp knife. They can then be boiled, sautéed, or otherwise prepared as a vegetable. The cobs can also be boiled whole, or spread with butter, wrapped in aluminum foil, and cooked on the barbecue.

Bamboo shoots (*Phyllostachys pubescens*). As a number of bamboo species take many years, even decades, to reach the flowering stage of maturity, many of them have only been described according to vegetative features, with the result that their botanical classification remains uncertain. The woody tree trunks of this plant have been used in tropical Asia since time immemorial in the making of furniture, kitchen utensils, and chopsticks, as well as for building entire houses, while the shoots are used as a vegetable. *Phyllostachys pubescens* is only one of over 200 species, but is best suited to cultivation on plantations for producing edible shoots. Originally from Southern China, it is now cultivated chiefly in Taiwan and Japan. There, the shoots, which are otherwise low in nutrients, are prized as a natural remedy for nervous complaints, and as a vegetable because of their delicate flavor and crunchy texture. The European climate is not ideal for growing bamboo shoots, but successful trials have been started in Northern Italy, where the Val Fontanabuona near Genoa, with its mild winters and hot, humid summers, offers excellent conditions. Six years after a small plantation was established there, the first shoots were harvested. Bamboo shoots are the young shoots of evergreen tropical grasses belonging to any of several genera. The pale shoots, which grow from the lower-leaf axils of young plants, are cut, like asparagus, while still tender, sweet, and non-woody. The best shoots are those harvested early ("winter bamboo"), which are cut as soon as the tips show above the surface of the soil. If allowed to grow well above the surface, they lose their delicate flavor. The shoots are 8–12 inches long, taper to a point, and weigh about 7 ounces–1 pound. Fresh bamboo shoots are encased in pale, tapering, oval lower leaves. Before use, they should be washed, trimmed, peeled, and sliced or chopped, according to the recipe. They are excellent in stir-fries and Asian rice dishes. They are also good blanched briefly and served in Asian-style salads with strips of roast chicken or shrimp and cellophane noodles. They are unsuitable for eating raw or for dishes which require long cooking. Fresh bamboo shoots are not widely available in the West. China, Taiwan, other Asian countries, and the United States export a wide variety of canned shoots. The young shoots are available sliced or chopped in cans or in vacuum-sealed glass jars. They may be used straight from the can or jar and only require draining and rinsing. They are ideal in rice and noodle dishes and in Asian soups and salads, providing a crunchy texture. They are also good with a spicy dip as an hors d'oeuvre or as an edible garnish for cold platters.

Fresh bamboo shoots are one of the most popular vegetables in the cuisine of Asia, although even there they are not cheap.

Bamboo shoots have more than one season. In contrast to the 1-foot long **spring shoots** (above), their smaller relatives reach a length of only 4–6 inches, which makes them ideal for cooking whole. **Winter bamboo shoots** (below) are much sought after in Asia because of their extreme tenderness. Fresh bamboo shoots are exported, but the vegetable is most commonly available in the West in cans.

Bamboo shoots
ONE OF THE MOST IMPORTANT PLANTS OF ASIA

With around 45 genera and over 200 species, the bamboo grasses (*Bambusoideae*) form a subfamily within the family of grasses (*Gramineae*). Referred to as "arborescent grass" because some species grow up to 98 feet tall, bamboo is the most important useful plant for the inhabitants of tropical and subtropical Asia, serving as the material for building bridges and houses and for making furniture, kitchen utensils, and musical instruments, as well as the raw material for the manufacture of paper. Last but not least, the young shoots of certain species of bamboo are a popular vegetable throughout Asia. It is chiefly the species of the genera *Bambusa, Dendrocalamus,* and *Phyllostachys* which are important as a vegetable.

Fresh bamboo shoots come onto Asian markets from plantations or natural bamboo orchards. Although they represent a rare delicacy in the West, they are a widely available, sophisticated, and popular vegetable in China, Taiwan, and Japan. Bamboo shoots are also used as an ingredient in many dishes in Korea, Thailand, Indonesia, and the Philippines.

BAMBOO SHOOTS: PREPARATION AND PECULIARITIES

Since raw bamboo shoots contain a poisonous hydrogen cyanide glycoside which is destroyed only by heating, they must always be cooked. They are prepared by cutting off the tips with a sharp knife and making a lengthwise incision in the shoots. This makes it easy to remove the tough outer leaves. The inedible base of the shoot is then cut off, the vegetable is washed, cut up according to preference, and cooked. Depending on the size of the chunks, strips, or cubes, 5–10 minutes cooking time is sufficient—they should still have a crunchy "bite."

Bamboo shoots cooked whole (below) are especially decorative. They should be cooked for about 40 minutes in boiling salted water. Chiles added to the cooking water counteract the bitter substances from the bamboo shoots.

The ripe bamboo shoots are harvested early in the morning. There is much to do before they can be packed for shipping, several to each wooden crate. The grass mulch layer is removed by hand, the shoots are exposed with an ax, and then cut from the soil like asparagus. Lastly, the remains of the roots around the cut surface, as well as the lower basal leaves must be cut or torn off.

Avocado trees growing in the wild reach heights of up to 65 feet. Cultivated trees, on the other hand, seldom grow more than 25 feet tall. It takes four to seven years for the tree to produce its first fruits. The avocados, which grow on long stalks, do not ripen and become soft on the tree and are always harvested when they are still hard.

Lauraceae (**Laurel family**). Ranking among the members of this family, which is chiefly indigenous to the tropics, are the camphor, laurel, and cinnamon trees, in addition to the avocado tree, its only fruit-bearing species. **Avocado, avocado pear, alligator pear** (*Persea americana*). The fruit of the large evergreen avocado tree almost defies classification: although botanically a fruit, it is usually prepared like a vegetable. It originated in tropical and subtropical Central America, where it was named *ahuacatl* ("butter of the forest") by the Aztecs. The fruit, which contains up to 30 percent fat, was one of their most important foods. First mentioned around 300 B.C., the avocado reached European shores in the sixteenth century with the Spanish Conquistador Cortés. Today, in addition to its native Mexico, the main producers are the United States, Brazil, the West Indies, Peru, Kenya, Australia, South Africa, Indonesia, Israel, and Spain. Around 400 varieties of avocado are cultivated worldwide. Some, the so-called mini or cocktail avocados grow to the size of plums, others reach weights of up to 4½ pounds. Among the most important varieties are "Bacon," "Edranol," "Ettinger," "Fuerte," "Hass," "Nabal," "Pinkerton," "Reed," "Ryan," and "Wurtz." Fruits weighing 5–14 ounces are cultivated and exported. Depending on the variety, they are about 4–5 inches long and are generally pear-shaped, but they may also be round or elongated. The skin varies in color according to variety, ranging from light and dark green, to purple to black, and may be thick or thin, and rough or smooth. The delicate green to yellowish, creamy flesh surrounds a large, brown, inedible pit. In addition to nutritious polyunsaturated fatty acids, the avocado contains plenty of the B group vitamins, vitamin E, and minerals, such as iron, calcium, and potassium. Avocados are nearly always sold underripe, so they should be allowed to ripen for one to three days at room temperature. To speed up the ripening process, they can be wrapped in newspaper and stored with an apple or banana. When they feel soft, but not squashy, and the skin yields to slight pressure, the fruit is completely ripe. It is only then that the fine avocado flavor develops fully; before that they just taste insipid or bitter. Fully ripe avocados can be prevented from overripening for a few days by storing them in the vegetable compartment of the refrigerator. However, they will spoil at temperatures below 43°F. They are perfect eaten fresh, stuffed with shrimp, crab meat, smoked salmon, or tuna. They may be served in slices with ham, or with a vinaigrette dressing as a starter or salad. They are also good mixed with piquant

Preparing avocados:

Cut the avocado in half by cutting around the pit with a sharp knife.

Using both hands, twist the two halves in opposite directions, so that one half comes away from the pit. Do this carefully to avoid squashing the fruit.

If the pit does not come away easily, carefully ease it out with a pointed kitchen knife.

To stop the flesh from turning brown, drizzle or brush it with lemon or lime juice immediately.

If the avocado halves are to be sliced or diced for a salad or mashed, rather than filled, they may be peeled with a swivel vegetable peeler.

If the avocado is very soft, it is advisable not to peel it, but to lift the flesh out with a spoon.

Nabal is an almost spherical, smooth-skinned fruit from Israel. It has the lowest fat content.

Fuerte is both the most frequently cultivated and most popular variety—it is said to be particularly aromatic.

Ettinger, pear-shaped and with an excellent flavor, is exported by Israel from September to December.

Hass is small variety with pale green flesh and a wrinkled, dark skin. Its nutty flavor is highly prized.

Edranol is one of the Guatemalan varieties. It is also extensively grown in South Africa.

Ryan, is a rough-skinned avocado widely grown in South Africa.

Bacon is the avocado variety that is most widely grown in Spain.

Mini avocados are small, elongated fruits which contain no pit, as they grow without fertilization.

Wurtz is a slender pear-shaped variety grown in Australia and Israel. The fruit has light yellow flesh and contains a large, slightly tapering pit.

Avocado
BUTTER OF THE FOREST

Revered by the Aztecs and Mayans as a miracle fruit, the avocado has lost nothing of its delicious taste and nutritional value. In fact, improvements to the avocado over millennia have led to a constant increase in quality, as well as to an incredible number of varieties—around 400 worldwide. Although botanically a fruit, avocados are usually prepared and served like a vegetable, both in their native Central and South America and everywhere else in the world.

Benik, is a variety from Israel. It is one of the types whose skin turns dark when ripe—a sign of spoilage in many other varieties.

Pinkerton is a less common variety from Israel. It can be recognized by its slender shape and rough skin.

Reed, a late variety of avocado, comes from Guatemala. It is very high-yielding and for this reason has been cultivated for some time in Israel. The thick-skinned, roundish oval fruit has dark yellow, highly aromatic flesh and weighs about 11 ounces.

seasonings and mashed as a sandwich spread, in the classic guacamole, cooked briefly and blended with cream to make soup, in mixed green salads, or in fruit salads. They are not suitable in dishes with relatively long cooking times.

Leguminosae (Fabaceae) **(legumes).** With some 700 genera and around 18,000 species, legumes are the third largest order of flowering plants. They are found in the temperate latitudes and humid tropics, as well as in dry regions, savannas, and mountain ranges. All bear legumes, which are extremely varied in appearance—round, flat, or winged, long or short, thick or thin, straight or curved, papery or leathery, woody or fleshy. They range from the size of a pinhead to over 3 feet long. Generally speaking, their pods burst open lengthwise at one or both ends when ripe, releasing the seeds, which are the actual fruits, many of which are known as pulses. The importance of many legumes lies in their high protein content, which is two to three times that of grains. In many Third World countries, where animal protein is available only to a limited extent, and in countries where vegetarian diets predominate for religious reasons, they constitute a major source of protein. A few species, such as peanuts, soybeans, and Goa beans, are also rich in fat. **Soybean** (*Glycine max*). The soybean has been cultivated in China for centuries, but it did not reach Europe and America until the end of the eighteenth century. It is now one of the world's most important plants in economic terms, as well as being the most important source of plant protein and oil in the world. North America is the biggest producer and exporter of soybeans. Other important growing areas are in China, India, Indonesia, the Philippines, Africa, Central and South America, and Russia. On a worldwide scale, the soybean is also the most important legume. The soy, an annual, grows 8–39 inches tall. The hairy, yellow, gray, or black shells contain two to five round or flat seeds $\frac{1}{5}$–$\frac{1}{2}$ inch in diameter. Generally ivory colored, there are also varieties with green, red, or blackish brown seeds. The crop is harvested before the pods burst open. Ripened seeds keep practically indefinitely if stored in a cool, dry place. Green ripe legumes keep for several days in the refrigerator. **Stink-bean** (*Parkia speciosa*). At least five species of this genus, are cultivated in Asia and Africa. The trees, which grow up to 66 feet tall, are useful as shade-providers. The pods are used as animal fodder and the seeds as a vegetable and condiment. The best-known species is *Parkia filicoidea*, called the African locust bean, which is cultivated chiefly in Nigeria for its edible fruits and seeds.

Soybeans and soy products
A VERY VERSATILE LEGUME

The soybean is, in the truest sense of the word, a wholefood: anyone who was so inclined could live almost exclusively on these beans and the products derived from them. The little seeds of the soybean provide all the nutrients we need to survive, containing up to 48 percent high-quality protein, around 11 percent carbohydrate, and about 18 percent valuable oil. This is why soybeans are not only an important food fresh or dry as a vegetable, but also play a central role as the raw material for a range of other foodstuffs. First and foremost, the oil of the bean is obtained by pressing or extraction. It contains nutritious, essential linoleic acid. In addition to its use as a salad or edible oil, it is made into cooking, frying, and spreading fats. A by-product of the oil-refining process is lecithin, much in demand as an emulsifier in the food industry. What remains is the so-called pressed cake from which soy flour, soy milk, bean curd, miso, and soy yogurt have been made in Asia for thousands of years. Of more recent origin are pasta and industrial meat substitutes made from soy. More traditional, however, and also long popular in the West are the especially vitamin-rich soybean sprouts and spicy soy sauce. Bean curd (foreground above), available from health food and wholefood stores, Asian markets, and many supermarkets, plain, marinated or smoked, is a particularly versatile foodstuff. Its high protein content, coupled with its bland taste and consequent ability to absorb other flavors, make it suitable for use in both sweet and savory preparations. Puréed and blended with cream, bean curd is a superb base for creams and desserts. Marinated with garlic and herbs in oil, it makes a tasty hors d'oeuvre, while diced and stir-fried with a variety of vegetables, it makes a light but satisfying vegetarian main meal. Bean curd also harmonizes superbly with pork or fish. Seasoned with salt, pepper, and spices and puréed, it makes a protein-rich sandwich spread.

The pods of the stink-bean, cultivated in East Asia, grow up to 17 inches long. The seeds are cooked with fish and meat dishes, or are toasted and liberally salted, when they taste like nuts.

Known only as a legume on the European market, fresh soybeans still in the pod play a considerably more important role in the United States and East Asia. The unripe seeds are stripped from the green ripe pods and cooked like fresh green beans or peas as a vegetable.

Sugar snap peas are annual, non-self-supporting, bare plants, whose tendrils need a trellis on which to grow.

The sugar snap pea (top) is distinguished by its high sugar content and the fact that it does not have an inedible parchment layer inside the pod. This means that the fleshy, delicate pod containing the unripe seeds can be eaten whole.
Wrinkled peas (above) are the favored fresh market peas. The tough pod is discarded after the seeds are shelled. Wrinkled peas are also well suited to freezing, retaining their nutritional value, shape, and most of their taste when frozen.

Asparagus peas grow from bright red flowers. The 2-inch long, almost oblong, light green pods are given a winged appearance (hence the alternative name winged peas) by their side frills. Briefly sautéed whole, the young pods are somewhat reminiscent of asparagus. The dried, roasted seeds were once used as a coffee substitute.

Dried peas may be any sort of peas, but are mostly round peas, which ripen fully on the plant. There are white, yellow, green, gray, and marbled types, in the pod and shelled, as well as whole or split. In every case, their nutritional value is higher than that of fresh peas. Since the outer seed pod is tough and indigestible, dried peas are usually shelled. Shelling makes their surface blunt, for which reason they are rounded and polished afterward. During this process some of the seeds split into two. These are then sold more cheaply as shelled split peas.

Capucin peas (above left) and **gray peas** (above right) are specialty dried peas and look more like some varieties of beans than round peas. In Holland they are considered delicacies. There are several varieties, including one known as *Blauwschokkers* ("blue shocker") because of its blue pods.

Goa bean, winged bean, four-angled bean (*Psophocarpus tetragonolobus*). This perennial bush has been cultivated for centuries throughout Asia, West and East Africa, and the Caribbean. In addition to the seeds, the pods, young leaves, flowers, and shoots are eaten as a cooked vegetable. In some countries the root tubers, which are very rich in protein, are also prized. Goa beans are seldom exported. **Asparagus pea, winged pea** (*Tetragonolobus purpureus*). Indigenous to Southern Europe, the asparagus pea is now cultivated in Western Europe almost exclusively as a connoisseur's vegetable in garden plots. They are available in very small quantities from June to October. **Pea, garden pea, green pea** (*Pisum sativum* ssp. *sativum*). The pea is the oldest useful plant among the Leguminosae, as well as one of the oldest cultivated vegetables. There is evidence that it was cultivated as long ago as 5,700 B.C. It is descended from the wild form *Pisum elatius*, which is indigenous to the Eastern Mediterranean and to the Middle East. Nowadays the pea is cultivated in almost all the countries of the world and is the fourth most important vegetable. The largest growing areas are the United States, Europe, and India. It is cultivated almost exclusively outdoors. Only about 5 percent of the pea crop reaches the fresh produce market; the vast proportion of the remainder finds its way into the food processing industry for canning, drying and freezing in particular. The actual peas are the seeds in the pods. There are only two varieties of plant in terms of growth habit: bush peas, which are low growing, and climbing peas, which may be up to 6½ feet tall. Commercially, peas are classified as wrinkled, round or smooth, and edible-pod peas. Petits pois are a dwarf variety, not peas harvested when immature. **Wrinkled pea, wrinkle-seeded pea** (*Pisum sativum* ssp. *sativum* convar. *medullare*). This type of pea is particularly sweet and tender and has large, wrinkled seeds. As they do not become soft when cooked, they are sold only as fresh vegetables. **Round pea, round-seeded pea** (*Pisum sativum* ssp. *sativum* convar. *sativum*). This pea can be recognized by its mostly smooth, round seed. The tough, green pods are harvested while the seeds are still small and tender, or as dried peas when the seeds are completely ripe, dry, and yellow or green. Because of their high starch content, round or dried peas taste slightly mealy and less sweet than wrinkled or sugar snap peas. **Sugar snap pea, snow pea, mangetout, sugar pea, edible-pod(ded) pea** (*Pisum sativum* ssp. *sativum* convar. *axiphium*). These are harvested when immature and eaten whole. They have a particularly high sugar content.

The Goa bean, both the pod and tuber, constitutes a first-class source of protein (37 percent) for many East Asians. It owes another of its names, winged bean, to the wavy wings running the length of its 2½–16-inch long pods.

An immense variety of **garden beans** is widely available, fresh, frozen, and canned.

The climbing bean is an annual twining creeper which requires a trellis or canes to support growth. Especially important for the fresh market because of its high quality, it must be harvested by hand.

Green bean, French bean, garden bean (*Phaseolus vulgaris* ssp. *vulgaris*). These are classified either as climbing or bush varieties. **Climbing green bean, climbing French bean** (*Phaseolus vulgaris* ssp. *vulgaris* var. *vulgaris*). The numerous types of climbing beans are distinguished according to the color and shape of their pods. Important varieties are the yellow wax bean and the purple-pod snap bean. **Thin bean, dwarf French bean, bush bean,** (*Phaseolus vulgaris* ssp. *vulgaris* var. *nanus*). The thin bean is a mutant variety which arose by chance from creeping forms. Varieties are distinguished according to the color, length, and cross-section of the pods. Among the most important types are the tender princess bean, the wax bean, the snap bean, and the sugar bean. **String bean, (scarlet) runner bean** (*Phaseolus coccineus*). Rough pods, up to 1 foot in length, develop from the scarlet or white flowers. The tender young pods are eaten, but it is the colorful, mostly red-and-black-flecked seeds which are of greater importance. **Lima bean, butter bean** (*Phaseolus lunatus* var. *lunatus*). The seeds of the lima bean, which is indigenous to tropical America, are large and white to cream in color. Although white varieties are usually free from bitter substances, dark varieties may contain a hydrocyanic acid glycoside called linamarine. This means that the beans must be soaked twice (with a change of water) and cooked for about 1½ hours. **Fava bean, broad bean** (*Vicia faba* ssp. *faba* var. *faba*). These have been cultivated for almost as long as the pea and were an important source of protein for centuries. Botanically, the fava bean belongs to the vetches. It is not the pods, but the large green, brownish, or even red seeds that are eaten. These should always be cooked, since they may contain toxic substances. **Rice bean, small red bean** (*Vigna umbellata*). The rice bean is grown throughout tropical Asia and Africa. It is a typical intercropping plant in rice cultivation, which, owing to its rapid growth, ripens between one rice harvest and the next sowing. **Yard-long bean, asparagus bean, Chinese long bean, snake bean** (*Vigna unguiculata* ssp. *sesquipedalis*). This bean, which is native to Southern Asia, has a sweeter, earthier flavor than Western garden beans, but is prepared in the same way. **Black-eyed pea, black-eyed bean, cowpea** (*Vigna unguiculata* ssp. *unguiculata*). The black-eyed pea originated in Western or Central Africa, where it is still an important food plant. It is used fresh or dried, and is canned on a large scale in the United States. **Moth bean, mat bean** (*Vigna aconitifolius*). The fully ripe pods contain four to nine seeds, each measuring only about ¼ inch in length and ⅛ inch in width.

Bush beans, available in many shapes and sizes, are the type most often used in commercial canning and freezing, not least of all because they can be harvested by machine.

These purple-pod snap beans live up to their name. The pod color of this bush or climbing bean specialty, however, disappears immediately upon heating.

Kenya beans are varieties with almost knitting-needle-thin, tender, seedless pods which are imported from Africa. They are highly prized and expensive.

Wax beans are yellow-podded bush or climbing beans. The brightness of their color varies. Those which are almost white are usually canned or pickled.

Fresh beans
LITERALLY AN INTERNATIONAL VEGETABLE

Numerous, often contradictory, stories exist regarding the origins and evolution of the various species of beans. This is partly because bean seeds—tropical ones in particular—are often hard to tell apart. In addition, the term "bean" is used in tropical countries to refer to a number of genera, such as *Phaseolus, Vigna, Vicia, Cajanus, Dolichos*, or *Lablab*. Elsewhere, "bean" is generally taken to mean the genus *Phaseolus*. Beans are an important staple food in many countries and number among the most important of all vegetable plants.

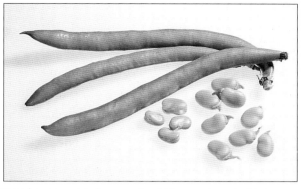

Fava beans contain large seeds which are extremely rich in carbohydrate, protein, and minerals. Varieties are distinguished according to the color of their flowers.

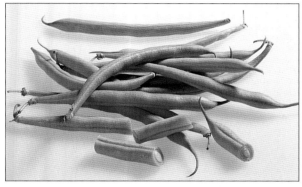

Bobby beans are garden beans of plump cross-section with a fairly large number of seeds.

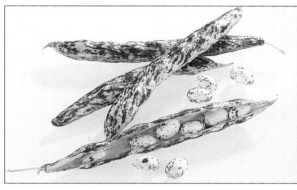

Reddish-brown speckled borlotti beans are prized in Italy, either fresh or dried for salads and soups.

All kinds of beans should be cooked for a minimum of 10 minutes, since phasin, the toxic protein that they contain, is broken down during cooking.

Princess beans are short-podded green bush beans that are picked young. Because they are stringless and contain only small, thin seeds, they are ideal for canning.

The rice bean takes its name from its use and its small seeds, which are only ¼–⅓ inch long. As a dried bean, it is eaten with, or instead of, rice.

Climbing beans with broad, flat pods are marketed as "coco beans" or "wide beans." Their main advantage is that they are quick and easy to trim.

Yard-long beans are so named because of their length (35–36 inches). The shoelace-like, mostly gray to grayish green pods contain 10–30 edible seeds.

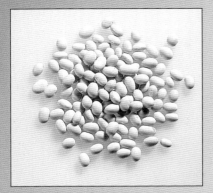

The navy bean, is mealy-textured when cooked. This variety is very popular in soups and stews.

Cannellini beans are medium-size, soft-cooking, mealy beans that are especially popular in Italy.

Puy lentils (right) have a brownish green, firm hull and are especially popular because of their strong flavor. **Green lentils** (far right), which hold their large, firm shape very well when cooked, are also popular.

The lima or butter bean turns soft and mealy when cooked, but does not disintegrate, making it suitable for salads.

The pinto bean is a mealy bean, but remains firm when cooked. Its name means "dappled."

Legumes: beans and lentils
IMPORTANT STAPLES ON THREE CONTINENTS

Well over 150 million tons of legumes are cultivated worldwide each year, the majority of which are grown in home gardens and on small commercial farms. Next to soybeans (*Glycine max*) and peanuts (*Arachis hypogaea*), from which oil is commercially extracted, beans are in the forefront internationally. These legumes are the most important sources of protein for the poor rural populations of Africa, Asia, and South America. In addition, for around 600 million vegetarian Indians, *dhal*, as legumes are called in Hindi, are absolutely essential. Next to peas, it is mainly the many varieties of lentils and beans that supply the inhabitants of this huge country with desperately needed protein. Eaten together with rice or bread, the hot, spicy bean and lentil curries provide an ideal combination of nutrients, comprising high-quality protein, a good deal of carbohydrate in the form of starch, and plenty of dietary fiber. The Indian, as well as the South American, way of preparing legumes with a variety of seasonings and spices is not only exemplary from a culinary standpoint, but also helps the body to cope with the seeds of the leguminosae, which are fairly indigestible. Spices stimulate the flow of digestive juices, alleviating the unpleasant consequences of the indigestible carbohydrate stachyose that is contained in beans and lentils. Otherwise this could lead to flatulence if, as in India, South America, and parts of Africa, large quantities of these legumes are regularly consumed. Both Indian and Western cooks are aware of a second way of reducing this undesirable side-effect of eating beans and lentils: they are used hulled. Although the starchy seeds disintegrate very quickly when cooked after the tough, fiber-rich hull has been removed, and usually have a less distinctive flavor, they are considerably easier for the body to digest.

The black bean with its white inside becomes soft when cooked and has a pleasantly spicy, sweetish flavor.

The black-eyed pea is so called because of a black spot which resembles an eye. It absorbs seasonings and flavors well.

The small borlotti bean from Italy softens during cooking. Its taste is typically bitter-sweet.

The large borlotti bean is used in many Italian dishes and is an indispensable ingredient in minestrone.

Hulled red lentils disintegrate quickly, but have a fine flavor.

Unhulled red lentils have a stronger flavor than hulled ones.

Hulled green lentils are ideal for soups, as they disintegrate easily when cooked.

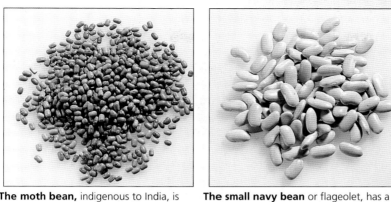

The moth bean, indigenous to India, is the most drought-resistant species of bean and the basis of many dishes there.

The small navy bean or flageolet, has a delicate flavor and is popular in France in dishes with lamb or in salads.

The brown bean is quite superb in soups and stews because it has a very hearty flavor.

The red kidney bean is mealy when cooked and sweetish in taste. It is one of the main ingredients of chile con carne.

The scarlet string bean has been cultivated for millennia in the subtropical mountain ranges of Central America.

The lima bean with its high nutritional value constitutes a (sometimes difficult to digest) "power food."

Unhulled black gram or *urid dhal* is most often available dried. Young, green pods are used as a cooked vegetable.

Shelled black gram or *urid dhal* often splits into two halves. Milled into flour, it can then be used for making bread.

The adzuki bean becomes very tender when it is cooked. It has a slightly sweetish taste.

The soybean, with its high protein, carbohydrate, and oil content, is a very valuable source of nutrients.

The black soybean differs in appearance, rather than in flavor, from the white or yellow soybean.

The green mung bean is often germinated—at home and commercially— for bean sprouts.

Jicama or yam bean
owes its name to its
bean-like hull and yam-
like tubers, which
measure up to 1 foot in
diameter and weigh up
to 22 pounds. The
slightly sweet vegetable,
which is very watery
when fresh, may be
eaten raw; older, drier
tubers are usually
ground into flour.

The kudzu was
originally cultivated both
for its starchy tubers,
which reach weights of
up to 13½ pounds, and
as a fiber plant. At one
time a staple food, it has
been superseded by the
sweet potato. Its flesh,
which is white and
sweet, is also tough, and
becomes edible only
after at least 2 hours'
cooking time.

Preparing garbanzo beans:

Dried garbanzos should be
soaked in cold water for at
least 5 hours and preferably
overnight, so that they will
soften when cooked later.

After soaking, rinse the beans
thoroughly under cold
running water.

"Kabuli-type" garbanzos
are an important staple in
many countries because
of their protein
content and high
nutritional value.

Black gram, urd, urid dhal, mung bean (*Vigna mungo*). This is classified into two varieties: early-ripening, with large black seeds, and later-ripening, with smaller, olive green seeds. **Adzuki bean, aduki bean, Chinese red bean** (*Vigna angularis*). This bean is cultivated on a large scale in Japan and China. The pods are 2½–6¾ inches long, ¼ inch wide, and cylindrical. They contain five to 12 relatively delicate, dark red seeds. **Mung bean, green gram, golden gram** (*Vigna radiata* var. *radiata*). This bean, which is probably more widely distributed than any other, is available in two varieties, producing yellow and green seeds, respectively. The green seeds are better known in the West. **Lentil** (*Lens culinaris*). The lentil, which has been grown in Egypt for between 8,000 and 10,000 years, is one of the oldest cultivated plants. **Jicama, yam bean, potato bean** (*Pachyrhizus erosus*). Originally from Central and South America, this plant is now cultivated in Asia. Ripe pods and seeds are thought to be poisonous, but the young pods may be cooked and eaten. It is primarily the tuber that is eaten, usually raw. **Kudzu** (*Pueraria lobata*). This East Asian plant is cultivated for its tubers, which are used mainly to produce starch. **Garbanzo beans, chick-peas, gram** (*Cicer arietinum*). There are two types. The small, dark, heavily wrinkled seeds come from India, while the larger, plump beige seeds are from the Mediterranean. They may be ground into flour. **Hyacinth bean, Egyptian bean, lablab** (*Lablab purpureus* ssp. *purpureus*). Although originally from Africa, the hyacinth bean is now cultivated almost exclusively in India and Southeast Asia. The wide, flat pods are 2–6 inches long and about ¾ inch wide. They contain between three and six round or oval seeds, which are white, red, brown, black, or speckled. **Guar, cluster bean** (*Cyamopsis tetragonoloba*). Guar gum, made from the seeds, serves as the basis for adhesives, cosmetics, and thickening agents. **Water mimosa** (*Neptunia oleracea*). The root shoots are cultivated in still water, like rice, chiefly in tropical Asia. **Tamarind** (*Tamarindus indica*). The ripe pods of this plant supply a highly valued sweet-sour fruit pulp. The unripe pods are eaten as a vegetable. **Katurai, cork wood tree** (*Sesbania grandiflora*). From Southeast Asia to Australia, this fast-growing tree is valued for the shade and wind protection it supplies. The seeds are among the most protein-rich of the Leguminosae. **Cha-om** (*Acacia pennata* var. *insuavis*). The young shoot tips of this acacia tree are eaten as a vegetable in central Thailand. **Wild tamarind** (*Leucaena leucocephala*). Native to Central America, this tree or bush serves as a shade tree, fertilizer, and source of animal fodder in the tropics.

The pods of the hyancinth bean or lablab are prepared as a cooked vegetable and the young leaves are eaten much like spinach. The ripe seeds contain a bitter substance which is destroyed only after a relatively long cooking time. They can also be sprouted.

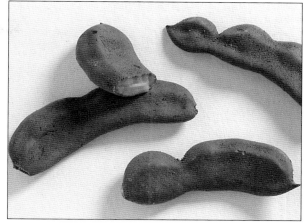

The unripe pods, the pleasantly sharp-tasting young leaves and the flowers of the tamarind tree are used to season curries, soups, and stews. The ripe pods contain a sweet-sour fruit pulp, which forms the basis of sweet drinks and foods. In India and Mexico the dried pods are a well-known seasoning.

In Southeast Asia, only the young leaves, flowers, pods, and seeds of the **wild tamarind** are prized as cooking vegetables. The gum from the seeds is used in the food and pharmaceuticals' industries.

The guar bean, an upright, bushy plant, probably originated in Africa. It has been cultivated since time immemorial in India and Pakistan, and has been grown in the United States since the 1950s. The pods, which are 2–4½ inches long and stand upright when ripe, contain 5–12 pea-sized seeds. Pods and seeds must be cooked thoroughly before eating.

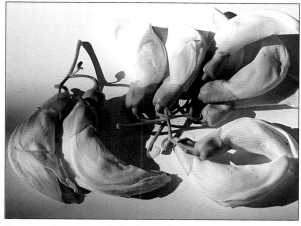

The huge blossoms of the katurai tree can grow up to 4 inches long and are considered a particular delicacy in Asia. After the bitter heart is removed, they are boiled or sautéed very briefly. The protein-rich leaves and pods are prepared like cooked vegetables.

The water mimosa is particularly rich in minerals and vitamin C. The leaves are sold in Asian markets, together with their root shoots. The young leaves, shoot tips, and the young pods are cooked as vegetables. The roots are used as a natural remedy in Asian medicine.

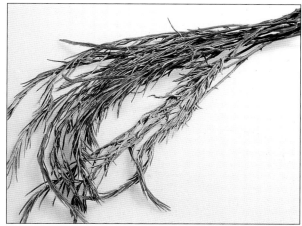

Cha-om is an acacia tree, the cuttings of which are planted for vegetable cultivation in Thailand. The young shoot tips or shoots of this annual plant are harvested and used as a vegetable. It is valued for its mildly spicy taste and very high mineral, protein, carbohydrate, and vitamin C content.

Leeks, depending on the variety, can grow up to 2½ feet long, but these are more highly prized by home gardeners than by cooks. **Stalk thickness** differs according to variety and season. Winter leeks can reach a diameter of up to 2 inches, but early leeks are marketed with a minimum diameter of ½ inch.

Leeks and scallions
A WELCOME ADDITION TO OUR DIET YEAR-ROUND

Members of the *Allium* genus, including the leek, have a particularly delicate taste in late spring and summer; their flavors are stronger in fall and winter. Scallions and Welsh onions are, in any case, available year round. Both leeks and scallions owe their typical aromatic taste to various volatile oils (chiefly allyl mustard oil). The high concentrations of potassium, calcium, phosphorus, sodium, iron, vitamins B_1, B_2, C (30 mg), and provitamin A in these vegetables make them healthy as well as delicious. In addition, their sulfur content acts as a natural antibiotic. Leeks and scallions can be prepared in numerous ways. They are suitable for eating raw, sautéed, or boiled as a vegetable side dish. They can also provide the basis of, or a substantial garnish for, soups. Cook them in stews and casseroles, as a filling for hearty pies and quiches, or serve au gratin with ham and cheese. The green part of the scallion, like snipped chives, is a superb seasoning for herbed cream or cottage cheese, sauces, and salads. It also makes a hearty sandwich topping.

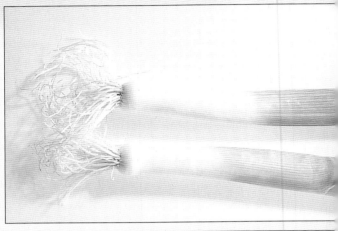

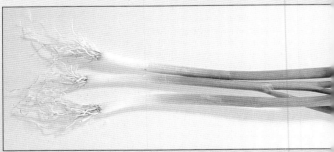

Despite their numerous similarities, leeks and scallions belong to different species. They can be identified by their leaf shape: the leek (top) has broad, flat leaves, while the scallion has

Liliaceae (**Lily family**). This family comprises some 220 genera with around 3,500 species, including such well-known ornamental plants as tulips, lilies, and hyacinths. Only very few genera are cultivated as vegetables, the most important of which is *Allium*, which includes leeks, garlic, and onions. Others are *Lilium*, *Muscari*, and *Asparagus*. **Leek** (*Allium porrum* var. *porrum*). The leek is thought to have developed from the field or summer garlic of the Eastern Mediterranean and Middle East. It was grown in ancient times in Egypt and also eaten by the Greeks and Romans. In the Middle Ages and for a long period afterward it fell out of fashion, although it probably remained a useful part of poor people's diets. Today, it is cultivated throughout the Western world and is especially valued as "king of the soup onions." A robust vegetable, it flourishes chiefly outdoors, and only early crops are grown in greenhouses or plastic tunnels. Leeks are classified as summer, fall, and winter types, which vary in the length and firmness of stem, as well as differing slightly in strength of taste. A biennial, the leek plant develops in the first year from the bulb-like thickening of a leaf rosette. The stalk base and sheaths form the white to greenish white stem, which grows up to 16 inches long—the actual vegetable—with broad green leaves toward the top. The stem is blanched by placing the plant in trenches up to 8 inches deep, then progressively filling them with soil as the leek grows. Look for a strong, straight, snow-white stem with no bulb-like thickening, surmounted by dark-green leaves. Leeks do not store well, so it is best to buy them only when you need them. They can be cooked in a variety of ways, but should not be allowed to brown if they are sautéed or stir-fried, as this makes them tough and gives them an unpleasant taste. There are also many types of wild leeks. Probably the best known is Canadian ramp, which resembles the scallion in appearance, but has a stronger flavor. **Welsh onion, spring onion** (*Allium fistulosum*). Like the leek, the Welsh onion is unknown in its original wild form. It is thought to have originated in Central and Western China, where it is still of importance as a herb and vegetable plant. It is closely related to the Japanese bunching onion, known as *chang fa*. The term spring onion means no more than an onion whose green part is eaten and which is available all year round. Although much more delicate, the Welsh onion is strongly reminiscent of the leek in appearance and taste and is similar to the scallion. It is distinguished from the bulb onion by its round, hollow leaves and only slight bulb formation.

narrow, tubular leaves (center and bottom). The scallion does not form a spherical bulb, but is prized for its delicate, aromatic green portion.

Since sand or soil often lurks between the leaves of the leek, cut the stalk lengthwise to just above the end before washing.

Rinse the leek stalk very thoroughly under cold running water, while fanning out the leaves with your fingers. This is the most reliable way to get rid of sand and soil.

Chinese chives, Chinese leeks, flowering chives, garlic chives, gau choy fa, kuchai (*Allium tuberosum*). Although a relative newcomer to the West, Chinese chives have been a popular cultivated plant in Southeast Asia and India for centuries. In contrast to garlic, this perennial plant develops a strong root, rather than a bulb. The grass-like leaves grow to a height of up to 20 inches. They have a mild garlic taste, and may be used like chives. They may be cooked with or without the flowers. Chinese chives with unopened flower buds are young and therefore more tender. **Chives** (*Allium schoenoprasum*). The wild plant, thought to have originated in Central Asia, is grown as a culinary herb in almost every country in the world. The hollow leaves, which are 6 inches–2 feet long, owe their onion-like taste to their high content of allium and mustard oil. Chives also contain a great deal of vitamin C. The outdoor crop is harvested from May to October, and from November to April, chives come from the greenhouse. Varieties are classified as fine, medium-fine, and coarse-leafed. Fine-leafed chives are often sold during the winter planted in pots with their root bales attached. **Ramson(s), bear's garlic** (*Allium ursinum*). Once cultivated in Northern and Central Europe as a medicinal plant, herb, and vegetable, ramson is now naturalized throughout Europe, as well as in Asia. Its leaves resemble those of the lily-of-the-valley, but have a strong garlic aroma and taste owing to their allicin content. **Garlic, common garlic** (*Allium sativum* var. *sativum*). One of the oldest cultivated plants, garlic is thought to have originated in Southwest Asia. Even in ancient times, it was a popular medicinal plant and seasoning herb. Today, it is one of the 20 most important vegetable species in the world, with an annual production of around 3 million metric tons. It is cultivated worldwide, principally in hot, dry places. The world's largest production area is around Gilroy—"Garlic City"—in the Santa Clara Valley in California, where a huge garlic festival is held every year. Other major growing areas are in Spain, Egypt, France, and Italy. The garlic bulb is formed at the base of the perennial plant and is surrounded by several dry, white, red, or purple layers of skin. It is composed of up to 12 bulblets, called cloves, which in turn, are surrounded by papery layers of skin. The high nutritional and culinary value of the cloves, as well as their characteristic taste, come from the sulfurous volatile oil allicin. It also contains carbohydrate, protein, fat, calcium, phosphorus, iron, magnesium, several B vitamins, and vitamin C. It has been proved to lower blood cholesterol levels and has antibiotic properties.

Chinese chives are valued in Asia for stir-fries or as an accompaniment to fish. The flower stalks with their unopened white buds have a honey-like flavor, and are considered a delicacy. They are available fresh and in jars, from Chinese foodstores.

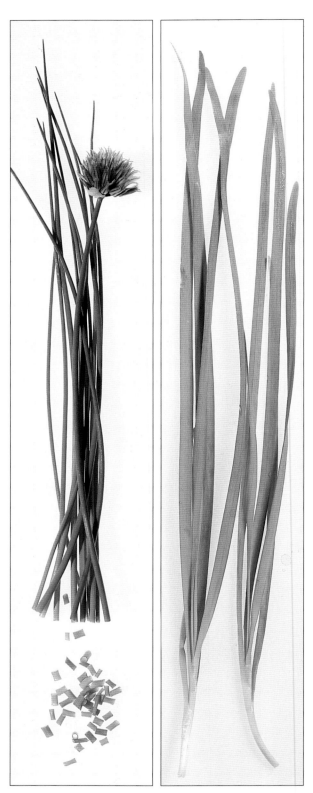

Chives are best enjoyed fresh, as almost all their flavor is lost when they are dried. The spicy-hot tubular leaves of the chive plant are popular worldwide as an ingredient in egg dishes, salads, soups, sauces, and cottage cheese dishes, and to flavor herb butter. The flowers are edible and may be used in salads or as an attractive and unusual garnish.

Nira is a Japanese variety of the Chinese chive, which is used as an aromatic substitute for chives, garlic, and shallots. Blanched Chinese chives, which are milder in taste than their dark green cousins, are also sold there. Nira is also a popular seasoning for spring roll fillings.

Head garlic is a Thai specialty: the garlic is planted so close together that it remains small and does not form the typical bulb with numerous cloves. In Thailand, the little bulblets are popular used raw, in hot pickles, or with sautéed shrimp. It is not well known in the West.

Garlic & Co.
VEGETABLE AND SEASONING IN ONE

This member of the family *Liliaceae* is both famous and infamous for exuding an odor because it contains large concentrations of the volatile oil allicin. This highly sulfurous oil is responsible not only for seasoning all sorts of foods, but also for the healthy effect of garlic. It acts as a natural antibiotic against many different inflammatory ailments, and can help to reduce high cholesterol levels and high blood pressure, if consumed in large quantities. It is precisely this beneficent oil, however, which makes some wrinkle their sensitive noses in distaste at the seasoning-cum-vegetable, otherwise so well-loved worldwide. There is a solution for garlic-haters: Chinese or garlic chives, which combine the good qualities of garlic with a substantially milder aroma and flavor. It is, so to speak, the culinary compromise between garlic and chives, whereas ramson or bear's garlic, which grows only in the wild, has both a very strong taste and a powerful smell. Whichever member of the genus you choose, they are superb both as a seasoning for foods from all around the globe and as a vegetable.

In Asian marketplaces, Chinese chives are a popular everyday vegetable, available both green with their white flowers attached, and blanched (especially tender).

Ramson or bear's garlic is closely related to cultivated garlic, sharing its pungent smell and taste. In Northern Europe, it grows wild in damp deciduous forests and in shady, moist locations, as well as in home gardens. The leaves are picked before the plant flowers in May and are chopped and added to salads, cheese dishes, soups, and sauces, as well as vegetable dishes.

Fresh garlic is available in white or reddish-purple bulbs (right). These especially mild heads of garlic can be recognized by their juicy green stalks. It can be kept for only about two weeks; however, it can be dried, or preserved in oil. It makes its appearance on the market at the beginning of the season in the producing countries and is mainly available in spring and summer.

Red onions are an Italian specialty. Their thin, red to purple skins and mild reddish flesh make them especially popular as a decorative salad onion.

Onions
LARGE OR SMALL, THEY PACK A PUNCH IN ALL SAVORY DISHES

Its fairly unprepossessing appearance notwithstanding, the onion has a venerable history. At least 5,000 years ago, it already ranked among the most important medicinal and culinary plants of Central Asia, present-day Pakistan, Northwest India, and the Mediterranean. Its importance was also appreciated by the ancient Egyptians, who used it as a sacrificial offering and fed it to the slaves who built the pyramids to give them strength. Today, this sharp-tasting vegetable is popular because of its unmistakable flavor, which it owes to the sulfurous volatile oils it contains in abundance. Smaller, darker onions generally contain more of these oils than large, pale specimens and so taste stronger. The large onion family has a member to match every taste and purpose: the basic brown-skinned onion, the red and white onions so popular in Italian cuisine, the mild Spanish onion, and the pale yellow Vidalia onion from Georgia, to name just some of the most important.

White onions are prized, especially in Italy and Spain, for their sweet flavor. They vary from mild to strong, depending on the variety.

The red Semian onion is a popularly variety in Italy. It has an unusually elongated, narrow shape and can grow to a length of 1 foot.

These large, flat-spherical white onions are a further example of the great diversity of form of the bulb onion.

Onion, bulb onion (*Allium cepa* var. *cepa*). Over 5,000 years ago, the onion was already one of the most important vegetable and medicinal plants of Central Asia, present-day Pakistan, Northwest India, and the Mediterranean. It is one of the oldest of all cultivated plants and is now grown in many different forms, chiefly in the warmer subtropics and the temperate zones of all continents. The world's major producers are the United States, China, Russia, India, Turkey, and Spain. Measuring up to about 4 inches in diameter, onions, which can be round, flat, or oval in shape, are encircled by several layers of dry skin. Their color may be yellow, brown, red, or white. The plant is a perennial, but is usually cultivated as an annual or biennial. As with garlic, the volatile oil allicin is responsible for the mild to pungently hot taste. It acts as an irritant to the mucous membranes, which is why peeling onions can make your eyes water. To avoid this, peel them under cold running water. Cooking causes allicin to evaporate, with the result that the cooked vegetable is much less pungent than raw onion. Allicin also acts as a natural antibiotic. The onion contains about 8 percent glucose and saccharose and up to 90 percent water, as well as protein, calcium, sulfur, fluoride, provitamin A, vitamins B_1, B_2, and B_6, and vitamins E and C. Onions are enormously diverse in form. The different colors and sizes also vary considerably in flavor. Red onions are popular for salads, antipasti, and for eating raw, because they are mild and sweet. They are especially attractive as their flesh is tinged with red. Spanish or yellow onions, which are actually a pale copper color, are large and mild, often weighing 7 ounces or more. Their sweet, spicy flesh is ideally suited for braising, for salads, and for stuffing. Bermuda onions are similar to Spanish onions, as they are large and mild. White onions flourish chiefly in relatively warm, dry climates and vary considerably in both size and shape. Small white onions are usually mild, but larger ones may be mild or pungently flavored. Vidalia onions are large, yellow, and sweet-tasting. They are delicious roasted or raw in salads. **Tree onion, Egyptian onion, top onion** (*Allium* x *proliferum*). This is a cross between the Welsh and the bulb onion. It is of virtually no commercial importance, but is very popular plant with amateur gardeners. It is unusual in that it does not produce flowers, and so cannot be propagated by seed. Instead, small bulbils are produced on the plant itself. These send out roots, which grow down to the ground and eventually produce new plants. The main advantage of the tree onion is that it is winter-hardy. The fresh green leaves and the tiny bulbils can be eaten.

Indispensable in everyday cooking
The brown-skinned onion with its fairly sharp taste is available large or small, spherical or elongated, all year round. However, it is at its best and thinnest-skinned in early summer. These onions, as with all other types, should be peeled and sliced or chopped just before use or they develop an off-taste.

Instead of flowers, the **tree onion** produces little bulbils on its cylindrical leaves. They have a strong taste that is vaguely reminiscent of garlic.

Onions tied together on a rope: a decorative way of storing them in the kitchen.

Small onions like these are known in Britain as pickling onions. In addition, they are superb in stews, meat sauces and casseroles. Peel, add them whole, and braise with other ingredients. They are also good cooked alongside a roast.

These round, brown-skinned shallots (here, "Bretonne Ronde" from Brittany, France) are deceptively similar to onions. Because of this, round shallots are less popular than other, more clearly distinguishable varieties. As far as flavor is concerned, though, they have just as much to offer.

Silverskin onions reach a diameter of only ½–1½ inches. Not only can they be pickled (as they are commercially), but they are also suited to braising and serving with pan-fried meats. Their mildly spicy taste makes them a great delicacy. Silverskins are the onions used to decorate cocktails.

"Bretonne Longue" (Long Breton) is an elongated French variety of shallot.

Extra small red onions are very popular in Thailand.

These flat-spherical bulb onions belong to early varieties that are widely grown on the Canary Islands. The mildness of young onions makes them especially suitable for eating raw and for preparing onion soups, quiches, and vegetable side dishes.

"Grise de Bagnolet" are gray shallots that are not so widely available as brown or red ones. They can be prepared in the same ways. Highly regarded by the French, they are used not only to lift salads and many other dishes out of the ordinary, but also to flavor white or red wine vinegar.

Silverskin onion, pearl onion (*Allium cepa* var. *cepa* and *fistulosum*). This particularly small onion or Welsh onion species is seldom sold fresh. It is mainly grown for the food industry, which uses these in mixed or other pickles. **Pearl onion** (*Allium porrum* var. *sectivum*). Although pearl and silverskin onions are almost similar enough to be mistaken for one another, they belong to different species. True pearl onions are closely related to leeks and are also used chiefly in pickles. **Shallot** (*Allium cepa* var. *ascalonicum*). The mildest and most delicately-flavored of all onion types is named after the Palestinian town of Askalon, although the original home of the shallot is thought to be tropical Asia. Other producing areas are West Africa, South America, the Caribbean, and Europe. Its subtle taste makes it indispensable in haute cuisine and it is very useful in all dishes where only a hint of onion flavor is required. It is an essential ingredient in many fine sauces because it disintegrates into the liquid. Onion is not a satisfactory substitute. There are a number of different varieties, but the variation is mainly in color, size and shape, rather than in flavor. **Tassel grape-hyacinth** (*Muscari comosum*). Twenty species belong to the genus *Muscari*, some of which grow wild. The plant grows up to a height of 2 feet and in early summer produces bluish-violet flowers that resemble a bunch of grapes. The upper flowers form a tuft, and in contrast to the lower flowers, are infertile. While the tassel grape-hyacinth is gathered and eaten as a vegetable in Mediterranean countries, it is classified as a protected species in some others. It is not generally available commercially. **Lily bulb** (*Lilium* spp.). Several species of the lily, known in the West only as ornamental plants, are cultivated in Southeast Asia, particularly in China and Japan, for their starchy bulbs, which are used as vegetables. One of the best-known is the tiger lily (*Lilium lancifolium*). Its fresh bulb consists of around 18 percent starch, as well as at least 2 percent protein. Drying these mildly sweet bulbs increases their starch content to over 60 percent, making them a particularly nourishing vegetable. Dried lily flowers, also known as golden needles, are used as a seasoning in soups and in Chinese vegetable dishes. They must be soaked in hot water for 30 minutes before use. **Hop sprouts** (*Humulus lupulus*, **Moraceae**). Although hops do not belong to the lily family, their sprouts are very like young asparagus in both appearance and taste, and are prepared in the same way. The above-ground parts of hops die off in the fall. The roots, which are frost-hardy, overwinter in the ground and produce new shoots in the spring. It is these shoots that supply the hop sprouts.

Wild bulbs of the tassel grape-hyacinth are a prized vegetable in the Mediterranean countries, particularly Italy, Spain, and Portugal. They grow wild in fields, vineyards, and olive groves, as well as being cultivated on a small scale.

Lily roots or lily bulbs are cultivated as a vegetable in Southeast Asia because of their nutritional value and spicy taste. The species used, such as the tiger lily, are known in the West only as ornamental plants. Their starch content is particularly notable: in dried bulbs it comes to over 60 percent.

Hop sprouts were highly regarded as a vegetable in the Middle Ages, and still play a modest role in France, Belgium, and Italy because of their fine taste.

The delicate hop sprouts must be painstakingly harvested by hand so that they do not break. They should be no more than 3 inches long and white to yellowish—never green—in color.

Once the asparagus tips have broken through the soil, they take on color or open quickly. It is best to cut them as soon as fine cracks appear on the surface of the soil.

Asparagus
SPRING'S MOST LUXURIOUS VEGETABLE

As far back as 2,000 years ago, asparagus was known as a natural remedy because of its blood cleansing and diuretic properties, and was cultivated as a medicinal plant in monastic gardens. Today, however, it is prized around the globe—in Europe, the Americas, Asia, and Africa—for its uncommonly fine taste and delicacy. International opinion is divided on which type of asparagus is the most desirable. In some countries they prefer the delicate spears to be white all over, while elsewhere they are more fond of aromatic green asparagus. This is truly a royal tradition, since in the seventeenth century, green asparagus was still absolute ruler of the tables of the European royal houses and monasteries. The custom of blanching asparagus by growing it underground only came into fashion toward the end of the nineteenth century. Since then, a host of recipes for preparing asparagus has been developed. It is also an important vegetable for the canning industry. In China, Taiwan, Spain, and Holland, in particular, a large part of the harvest is peeled and preserved in jars or canned.

Blanched asparagus grows in light, sandy soils in soil mounds that are built up in early spring. It is cut once or twice daily in the main growing season. The spears are dug free by hand and then cut with special knives. The surface of the mounded earth is then smoothed flat again with a trowel.

Asparagus (*Asparagus officinalis*). Thought to have originated in Eastern Europe and the Middle East, asparagus is now widely cultivated in all temperate and warm countries. Major European producing countries are Germany, France, Spain, Holland, Belgium, and Greece, and asparagus is grown in both North and South America and in Africa. It can be grown wherever a light, warm soil provides the ideal conditions for the time-consuming business of cultivation. Asparagus spears are shoots, which are covered with fine, scaly protective leaves and are formed each year from the perennial rootstock. It is always harvested by hand, preferably in the early morning, which makes the spears relatively expensive. In Europe, the harvest traditionally lasts from the beginning of May to St John's Day, 24 June; after that the shoots are left "to run to seed." The richly-branched asparagus foliage then builds up reserves which are stored in the rootstock and ensure a good harvest early the next summer. In warmer countries, however, the asparagus season is longer, stretching from March to the end of June. South Africa and South and Central American countries export asparagus to the Northern hemisphere during the rest of the year. The color of the asparagus reveals nothing about the variety, but everything about the method of cultivation. White or blanched asparagus is grown under mounded soil, protected from the sun's rays and is most popular in Northern Europe. Green asparagus grows in flat beds, completely exposed to sunlight and this method of cultivation is most typical in the United States and in Britain. Violet- or green-tipped asparagus spears come from mounded beds, but have been exposed briefly to the sun. Exceptions are the special pink to purple varieties cultivated in France and California. Asparagus is commercially classified as whole spears, broken spears (with or without tips), and asparagus tips. The more uniform the appearance of the spears, the higher the quality. The best asparagus has straight spears with firm, closed tips and cut ends which are light in color, fresh, and free from withering or discoloration. Improperly stored, inferior quality asparagus can be recognized by gray or yellow discoloration or spots and an unpleasant musty smell, as well as the lack of "crackle" when the spears rub together. Good quality fresh asparagus can be stored for several days wrapped in a damp towel in the refrigerator. Freezing is also a possibility, but because of their 95-percent water content, the spears will become limp when defrosted. Imported asparagus, while still good, lacks some of the flavor of home-grown because the spears start to lose flavor as soon as they are cut.

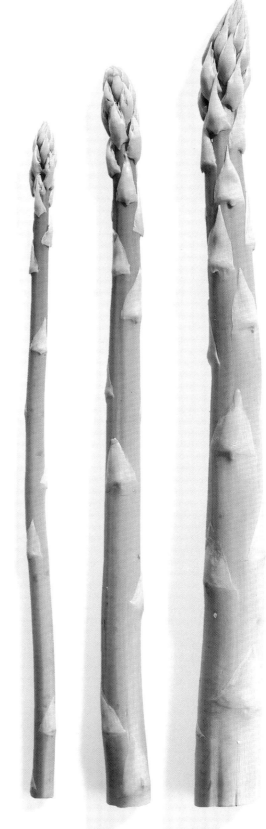

In contrast to blanched asparagus, violet-green asparagus grows in full sunlight—at amazing speeds in warm weather, during which time the spears can be harvested once a day by cutting or breaking them off just below the soil level.

"Genuine" green asparagus is completely green in color; not even the scaly leaves are tinged purple. Because of its high chlorophyll content, it has a strong taste and contains more vitamin C than white asparagus. Green asparagus is also sold in categories according to thickness, shape, and tip firmness.

Trimming white asparagus: Cut off the bottom end and peel the spears from top to bottom with a special peeler or a swivel-blade vegetable peeler. Begin under the tip and peel more thickly as you move downward.

TIP: Asparagus should be boiled or steamed until just tender. Cooking times vary from 10—15 minutes, according to the quantity and thickness of the spears.

Cooking asparagus:

Place the trimmed, peeled asparagus in cold water before cooking. This stops it from drying out.

Tie the asparagus into bundles weighing about 1 pound each, using thick, soft string or trussing thread. Wind it around the bundle two or three times to keep the asparagus secure.

Finally, knot the evenly wrapped thread firmly or tie in a bow, so that the bundle cannot fall apart while the spears are cooking.

If the asparagus spears are of different lengths, it is advisable, if only for the sake of appearance, to trim them at the bottom to the same length.

Using a skimmer, carefully lower the asparagus bundles, one by one, into boiling water, to which salt, sugar and one or two slices of lemon have already been added.

White and green asparagus, topped with fresh butter and perhaps served with ham or salmon, is not just a pleasure to look at. The taste contrast between the mild, delicate white spears and the hearty, aromatic green spears is also a delight for the palate. This is also an excellent idea for soups, salads, and cold platters.

Trimming green asparagus:

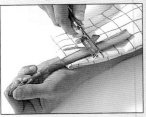

Green asparagus does not require peeling unless the skin is very thick and unappetizing.

Generally, it is sufficient to cut or break off the bottom end of the stalk and thinly peel the lower third of the spear.

Cooking asparagus upright: The tender tips are the most delicate part of the asparagus spear, and break off easily during cooking. Tall, narrow asparagus kettles like this one, made from stainless steel and fitted with a basket, protect the tender vegetable. After cooking, the asparagus can simply be lifted out of the water in the basket.

Purple asparagus is obtained from varieties containing the pigment anthocyanin. Sometimes the top third of the spears may also be colored. This purple asparagus tastes noticeably more bitter than the snow-white type. It is popular in France, Spain, and Greece.

Cooking asparagus flat is a gentle and practical method. You can buy a special flat asparagus kettle with a grid which can be lifted out. Such kettles are also suited to steaming whole fish or poaching large, tender pieces of meat.

Cooking asparagus peelings:

Washed asparagus peelings, when cooked for 10–15 minutes, produce an aromatic stock for making soup or in which to boil the spears.

After cooking the peelings, pour them into a fine strainer and press the excess liquid out with a ladle or the back of a wooden spoon.

This rare and accordingly expensive asparagus is marketed as **wild asparagus or baby green asparagus.** It is grown as a specialty vegetable in France, where it is particularly prized for its slightly tangy taste. It is only washed, never peeled.

The green, finger-length pods of okra develop from the yellow flowers of the bush. They are available fresh, canned, and frozen.

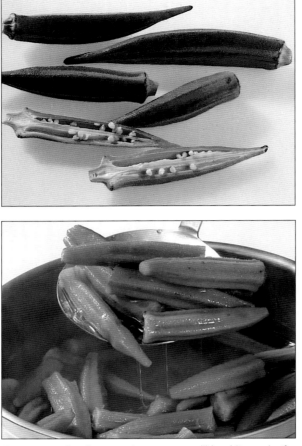

Young, angular okra contain numerous edible white seeds. If they are not blanched or acidulated, the pods exude a milky viscous fluid during cooking, which, although neutral in taste, is disliked by some people. On the other hand, it gives body to certain dishes, such as gumbos.

TIP: If okra is blanched for a few minutes in boiling water to which vinegar has been added, then rinsed under cold water, the mucilage exuded by the pods remains in the blanching water. The vegetable can then be prepared according to the recipe. Okra may be eaten raw in salads, but is usually cooked as a vegetable accompaniment to fish, meat, and poultry, or added to casseroles, curries, and stews.

Preparing okra:

Using a small, sharp bird's beak knife, trim the top of the pod to a pencil point without damaging the fruit.

This method of trimming the pod allows it to remain closed. Cutting straight through would let the liquid to run out.

After trimming, place the okra in water that has been acidulated with lemon juice until you are ready to proceed with your recipe. This prevents the pods from bursting while they are cooking.

Malvaceae **(Mallow family).** Members of this family include shrubs and annual to perennial herbs, such as the hollyhock, marshmallow, and hibiscus, to which the now separate genus *Abelmoschus* is closely related. **Okra, lady's fingers, gumbo, bhindi, bamia** (*Abelmoschus esculentus*). Native to Ethiopia, okra is one of the oldest vegetables, already in existence in the second millennium B.C. It is highly valued, particularly in Africa, but also in India, Thailand, tropical Asia, the whole of America, the Middle East, the Balkans, France, and the Mediterranean. The annual or perennial plant, which grows up to 8 feet tall, bears pod-like fruits or narrow, angular seed capsules about the width of a finger. The skin is yellowish green to dark green and covered with a fine down. The pods, which exude a milky juice when cooking, are harvested before they are ripe and fully grown. Okra is delicious boiled, fried, or stewed with other vegetables, and is also good in stews, braised dishes, and curries. It is featured in gumbo, the Louisiana stew of meat or seafood.

Moraceae **(Mulberry family).** The mulberry family contains around 60 genera and over 1,500 species of trees and shrubs, which are found mainly in the tropics. Only a few are used as fruit (fig, mulberry). Breadfruit and jackfruit are fruit and vegetable rolled into one. **Breadfruit** (*Artocarpus communis*). Native to Polynesia, the breadfruit tree is now naturalized throughout the tropics. In addition to water, protein, fat, various B vitamins, and a maximum of 50 mg vitamin C, its fruits, weighing up to 4½ pounds, also contain up to 28 percent starch. This makes the breadfruit a nutritious staple food, rich in carbohydrates. It can be prepared in a variety of ways. It is picked before it is ripe and is boiled, baked, or roasted. Alternatively, it may be dried and ground into flour. **Jackfruit, nangka** (*Artocarpus heterophyllus*). Native to India, the jackfruit is one of the largest fruits grown in tropical Asia. Fruit that has been allowed to ripen is used chiefly as a fruit, but when picked before it is ripe, it is used as a vegetable. The flesh, may be diced, dried, and used as a vegetable, in soups, or pickles. The seeds are boiled and roasted. The cooking water should be thrown away.

Moringaceae **(Moringa family).** This family consists of a single genus from which it takes its name, the trees of which grow chiefly in tropical Asia. **Horseradish tree** (*Moringa oleifera*). The cress-like leaves, flowers, and underripe fruits of this drought-resistant tree can be used as vegetables. The roots contain a mustard oil, so are used as a condiment. The rich oil from the seeds is also edible and is used for industrial purposes.

The jackfruit, fruit and vegetable rolled into one, is especially impressive on account of its size. Often weighing over 90 pounds, the fruits are up to 3 feet long and 20 inches wide. Next to pumpkins, they are the largest fruits in the world. Under the nubbly green shell, a large number of fruit segments nestle in a gelatinous skin. The taste is fruity and mild.

The breadfruit tree (top), with its dark green feathery leaves, grows to a height of 49–66 feet. It flourishes on just about every Caribbean island and after the plantain, the breadfruit (above), with its high nutritional content, is the most important staple of the West Indies. Its seedless fruits, which are harvested while still green and unripe, are versatile and nutritious. The flesh is fine-fibered and juicy, with a mild, subtle taste.

Preparing jackfruit:

Halve the fruit crosswise with a cleaver or heavy knife, so that the individual segments of flesh can be removed.

Carefully remove the fibrous covering from each segment, exposing the smooth, yellow flesh. Halve and pit it.

The long (6–47 inches), bean-like fruits of the horseradish tree are called **drumsticks**. From its root to its flowers, this tree serves some useful purpose.

Preparing banana flowers: First, remove the reddish leaves enclosing the flower. Cut off the stub of the stem with a knife. The banana flowers can then be cooked for about 15–20 minutes in boiling, salted water to which lemon slices have been added.

The fruits develop from the female banana flowers, but the male flowers, which remain on the end of the stalks, are a popular vegetable in Asia. Bananas start off growing downward, but then turn toward the light, that is, they bend their tips upward. That is why the banana has a curved shape.

Banana flowers, (above), mostly from Thailand, are rarely available in the West. These small, green vegetable bananas (below) are marketed as **Matok bananas**. They are always cooked, for example in curries. These **plantains** (bottom) are typical examples of the vegetable bananas which are now sold all over the world. They turn yellow when ripe. They are not suitable for eating raw.

Banana flowers and fruit
AFRICA'S ANSWER TO THE POTATO

Although the plantain contains very little in the way of protein, minerals, and vitamins, its high starch content makes it an important staple throughout Africa and the Caribbean, where it is prepared like our potato: fried, baked, roasted, or boiled.

Musaceae (**Banana family**). This small family with only six genera and approximately 220 species is native to the tropics and subtropics. Fifty to sixty species belong to the genus *Musa*, which in turn is subdivided into two categories: *Australimusa* is of virtually no commercial importance on a worldwide scale; *Eumusa* contains the popular banana and also the plantain or vegetable banana. **Plantain, vegetable banana, kayla** (*Musa* x *paradisiaca*). In their native Asia, bananas are among the oldest cultivated plants, but they have been known in the West only since 1885. The banana is more important on a worldwide scale, but the plantain plays an important role as a staple food, particularly in Third World countries, because it is extremely rich in starch. The biggest producer of plantains is Africa, with 75 percent of the world's production, followed by South America, North and Central America, and Asia. Plantains are quite different from bananas. They can grow up to twice the size and are often squarer in shape. They vary in size (up to 20 inches), shape, color (green, yellow, red to violet), and taste (dry, sweet, or sweet-sour). The flesh is coarser and more savory than that of sweet bananas. Plantains are harvested unripe and may be stored until they turn yellow (in the case of green fruits). With their mealy consistency, they resemble the potato and are also prepared quite similarly: peeled and boiled, fried, roasted, or mashed. They are completely inedible raw. Mild-tasting they go well with spicy braised dishes. Unless they are ripe, they can be difficult to peel. It is easiest to cut them into short lengths, slit the skin along the natural ride with a sharp knife, and ease it away from the flesh. **Banana flowers** (*Musa* x *paradisiaca*). These are the male flowers of the banana plant, which are only rarely available. They can be prepared like globe artichokes: the boiled, fleshy leaves may be dipped in a spicy sauce, or they may be boiled whole or roasted.

Nymphaeaceae (**Water lily family**). This family of aquatic or swamp plants with round, floating leaves and strong underwater rhizomes includes, in addition to the water lily (*Nymphaea*) and the yellow water lily (*Nuphar*), the Indian lotus flower. **Lotus root, sacred lotus** (*Nelumbo nucifera*). Originally from the Volga delta, Iran, and India (where to this day it is considered sacred), the lotus is now mainly distributed throughout Southeast Asia. The rhizomes form three or four sections, resembling sausage links in appearance. They have an attractive lacy appearance when cut. Lotus roots are grown in ponds or flooded fields, just like rice, and are harvested from the end of September into the spring. Lotus root is good stir-fried or steamed.

Lotus roots
EAST ASIA'S SYMBOLIC VEGETABLE

In East Asia, the Indian lotus flower is a symbol of rebirth, purity, and perfection. At the same time, it is as important as a food. Both its leaves and its flowers (right) are prepared as a fine vegetable, and the peeled seeds are munched as a snack or used to make flour. Even the husk leaves are used as the basis of a medicinal tea in China. Finally, there are virtually endless ways of preparing the lotus root. Not only is it made into a starchy flour, but, well-washed, peeled, and sliced, it is used in a variety of Asian specialties. Fresh lotus root is sometimes available in the West and well-stocked supermarkets will certainly be able to supply canned lotus root. Slices of lotus root are superb in exotic rice dishes or Indian curries. Fresh roots, particularly if cooked whole, require a relatively long cooking time, but should always retain a little "bite"—this is how they taste best.

The decorative lotus root may be boiled, baked, or braised. The Chinese traditionally serve it candied as a New Year's treat; the Japanese like it fried in oil and then cooked in water acidulated with lemon. The Indians use it in hot pickles.

Preparing lotus roots: Wash the root thoroughly, then cut off the ends and peel with a swivel vegetable peeler.

Fresh olives
A HIGHLY NUTRITIOUS FRUIT

Since Biblical times, if not before, the olive tree has been the quintessential symbol of peace and plenty, but the olive tree is thought to have existed in Palestine as far back as the Bronze Age. What is certain is that its fruit has been a real blessing for the peasants of the Mediterranean for thousands of years, yielding an extremely nutritious and flavorful oil. Unlike the small varieties of olives, however, the large, fleshy eating olives are not pressed for their oil. Green, purple, and black olives are available on the market, but cannot usually be bought "fresh" in the true sense of the word. This is because olives harvested unripe or only partially ripe taste bitter and this disappears only when they are preserved in alkaline or salt solutions. Black olives are harvested ripe, but are then fermented and oxidized to preserve their deep color.

Barba di frate is the Italian name for buck's horn plantain, which is not a widely used vegetable or salad plant. In Italy, however, the long, grass-like leaves growing from the plant's roots are valued as a salad ingredient. When boiled, it tastes similar to spinach.

Labiatae (**Labiates**). **Perilla, shiso, beefsteak plant** (*Perilla frutescens*). Native to the Himalayan region as far as China and Mynamar, the perilla has long been cultivated throughout Asia, as well as in Iran and Southern Europe. It has been valued as an oil-yielding plant, a seasoning herb, and a medicinal, aromatic, and ornamental plant. The entire plant may be used in a variety of ways. In China, Korea, and Japan, the young plants— flowers, leaves, and seeds—are a popular vegetable. The buds and seeds are used as a condiment.

Oleaceae (**Olive family**). Named after the olive tree, this family includes such ornamentals as lilac, forsythia, and jasmine. **Olive** (*Olea europaea* var. *europaea*). The olive tree spread from Palestine and Greece throughout the Mediterranean region. Today, it is cultivated worldwide in all suitable climatic zones. However, 97 percent of olive trees are still to be found around the Mediterranean, where they are of major importance for the production of olive oil. The fruits are harvested, particularly in Italy, Spain, Greece, and Turkey, and processed for export or preserved in jars.

Phytolaccaceae (**Pokeweed family**). **Pokeweed, pokeberry, skoke** (*Phytolacca americana*). This North American species was introduced to Europe in the eighteenth century. It is now cultivated in the Mediterranean and in India: the juice is used to color wines, liqueurs, and baked goods, and the young shoot tips and leaves are eaten as a vegetable.

Plantaginaceae (**Plantain family**). The most important genus of this family is the plantain (*Plantago*), a weed well known to gardeners in temperate climates. A few species are also used for medicinal purposes. **Buck's horn plantain, barba di frate** (*Plantago coronopus*). This species of plantain is cultivated in Italy as a salad plant and is very occasionally exported.

Polygonaceae (**Knotgrass family**). This family contains around 30 genera with 750 species, of which the most important are buckwheat, sorrel, and rhubarb. **Rhubarb** (*Rheum rhabarbarum* and *rhaponticum*). As long as 4,000 years ago, rhubarb was of great importance in China as a medicinal plant. It has been known as a vegetable only since the mid-eighteenth century. This perennial, with its tuberous, thickened, fleshy roots, is grown worldwide in all temperate zones. Although a vegetable, rhubarb is almost always prepared like fruit. **(Garden) sorrel** (*Rumex rugosus*). This perennial herb, which grows wild in damp areas in Europe, Asia, and America, is also cultivated on a small scale. It is very popular in France, where it is traditionally combined with eggs and cream. It goes well with fish, and young leaves are good in salads.

Pokeweed juice is used in Mediterranean countries and India to color foods, and the shoot tips of the young plant provide an asparagus-like vegetable. It is also grown as an ornamental.

Shiso leaves (top) may be green or reddish-purple. Purple leaves are used in Japan as a food coloring for pickled fruits and vegetables; the green variety serves as a condiment or garnish. **Shiso sprouts** (above) in both colors are beginning to become available. They can be used like other sprouted vegetables.

Early rhubarb (above left) has light red flesh, a green stalk-end, and a mild flavor. Tangier tasting is the **maincrop rhubarb** (above right), which has dark red flesh. Red-fleshed varieties contain less oxalic acid than green-fleshed ones. The fruit can be made to taste less acidic by adding sugar.

Sorrel, which grows chiefly in the wild, is closely related to rhubarb, and similarly contains large amounts of oxalic acid. Young leaves taste best, the older ones being unpleasantly hot. The cultivated form is aromatic and astringent. It tastes good in mixed salads or prepared like spinach.

Harvesting hearts of palm on Martinique: After a coconut palm is felled, the large leaves are chopped off and the coconuts removed. Next, the pith or heart, which lies over the base of the leaves, is chopped out and freed from its fibrous husk.

Hearts of palm: a luxury vegetable
THIS DELICACY IS OBTAINED AT THE COST OF THE TREE'S LIFE

To harvest this vegetable, you must literally go straight to the heart of the matter: it is the pith or heart lying over the base of the large leaves that you are after. To obtain 2 pounds of hearts of palm, you need one to two palm trees between 10 and 15 years old. Very often, the heart is nothing more than an accidental by-product of palms being felled or uprooted in storms, but healthy coconut and assai palms must often give up their lives for this sought-after delicacy, since the removal of the heart spells their death. This is the main reason for the high cost. The delicate white heart is characterized by a crunchy consistency and an intensely nutty flavor. It is particularly popular eaten raw as a salad ingredient. Canned hearts of palm are widely available from most supermarkets.

The heart of a coconut palm about 32 feet tall weighs 4½–6½ pounds. It is surrounded by a series of inedible fibrous husks which must be removed completely to expose the pith. Heart of palm is extremely delicate and is crunchy in texture, and can be separated by hand into its individual leaves.

Hearts of palm, with their intense, nutty flavor, taste best raw. When cooked together with the unopened young leaves surrounding them, they are referred to as "palm cabbage." When they are pickled and fermented, they are known as "palm cheese."

Oxalidaceae (**Oxalis or Wood sorrel family**). **Lucky clover, good-luck plant** (*Oxalis tetraphylla*). This herb is native to Mexico, but has been cultivated as far away as Europe as an ornamental plant and vegetable since the beginning of the eighteenth century. Both the turnip-shaped roots and the tangy little leaves may be eaten. **Oca** (*Oxalis tuberosa*). This herbaceous perennial is of great importance as a food in Latin America, but is hardly known elsewhere. It produces underground root tubers which resemble the potato in nutritional value and flavor.

Palmae (**Palm family**). There are about 225 genera with some 2,600 species, but only a few are used as vegetables. The most important are hearts of palm, obtained from some 20 different species of palm. **Hearts of palm** *Euterpe edulis* and *oleracea*). These are obtained from the Assai palm, the only species cultivated on plantations in Brazil, Argentina, and Paraguay for this purpose; otherwise the hearts are a by-product of palm felling.

Piperaceae (**Pepper family**). This family, consisting of 10 genera and over 1,000 species, is mainly native to the tropics. Its representative genus *Piper* contains around 650 species, the most important of which is pepper (*Piper nigrum*). **(Indian) long pepper** (*Piper longum*). Indian long pepper grows wild in the foothills of the Himalayas and is cultivated chiefly in India and Sri Lanka. In ancient times it was preferred to pepper because of its milder taste, but has been commercially supplanted by the latter all over the world.

Polypodiaceae (**Polypod or Brake root family**). **Fiddlehead fern, ostrich fern, bracken, brake** (*Pteridium aquilinum*). Fiddlehead ferns grow wild, reaching a height of up to 6½ feet. Distributed from the temperate latitudes to the tropics, it is particularly popular in Asia. The young shoots of this and other ferns are eaten as vegetables.

Portulacaceae (**Portulaca or Purslane family**). The 30 genera and 300 species of this family are chiefly indigenous to the tropics and subtropics. **Purslane, common/kitchen-garden purslane, portulaca** (*Portulaca oleracea* ssp. *sativa*). This plant mostly grows wild and is cultivated (on a small scale) only in France, Belgium, and Holland and for specialized markets in the United States. The nutty, tangy leaves are available only infrequently, from March to October. They can be prepared like spinach or used raw as a condiment. **Winter purslane, miner's lettuce, claytonia, spring beauty** (*Montia perfoliata*). Originally from North America, winter purslane is now cultivated under glass in England, France, and Germany. The tender leaves, are rich in vitamins and minerals.

Cha-plu is what the Indian long pepper is called in Thailand, where the hot, spicy leaves of the plant are used in vegetable soups and stir-fries, or as wrappers for shrimp or diced ginger. In India and Sri Lanka, on the other hand, the long pepper, whose fruit is substantially milder than that of the black pepper, is cultivated chiefly as a herb and a medicinal plant.

Purslane is a fast-growing herbaceous annual with thick, fleshy oval leaves. Esteemed in ancient Egypt and cultivated in Europe as far back as the Middle Ages, it fell victim to neglect over the course of the centuries. Now it is known as a delicate vegetable to connoisseurs only. Like sorrel, it has a high oxalic acid content and should not be eaten in large quantities.

Oca is the thickened root shoot of *Oxalis tuberosa*. The color of the scalloped tubers ranges from yellow and orange to purple.

Winter purslane is usually harvested while the leaves are still young and small. These contain between 30 and 60 mg of vitamin C per 4 ounces—around 30 times as much as the stems, which are also edible. It lends itself to being prepared like spinach, but its taste is also shown off to advantage in a salad, on its own or mixed with other salad greens.

The tender little leaves of the lucky clover are a superb seasoning for salads and fine soups. Unfortunately, they only come on the market very infrequently. If necessary, wood sorrel can be substituted. The turnip-shaped roots of the lucky clover can be prepared like Teltow turnips (glazed with bacon), but are never available commercially.

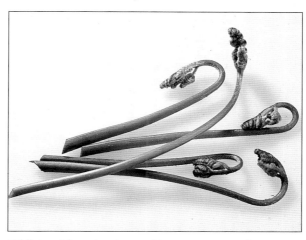

When **winter purslane** is allowed to grow for a little longer than usual, the leaves develop a characteristic bowl or plate shape. In order to retain their high vitamin C content and delicate texture, the leaves should be cooked only briefly.

Fiddlehead fern shoots resemble green asparagus in appearance and taste. Their young, tightly furled fronds are an especial delicacy, highly valued in the United States, Japan, China, and Korea as a spring vegetable.

Bell peppers
IN ALL COLORS

The rise of the bell pepper in the cuisines of many different countries has been meteoric. For example, it was virtually unknown in Northern Europe until the end of World War II, but it is now one of the most popular vegetables. The Dutch have rendered outstanding service to the bell pepper, cultivating it on a large scale. They are also responsible for today's ever-increasing variety of shapes and colors. Dutch greenhouses not only provide green, yellow, and red bell peppers, but in the last few years have also produced black, purple, lilac, brown, and orange varieties. The particularly aromatic Hungarian wax bell pepper, however, comes from the classic land of paprika and bell peppers. It is particularly important in the food industry and is used, among other things, for pickling.

Orange, purple, and black bell peppers are among the most recent strains produced by the Dutch. When raw, they are an attractive addition to salads and cold platters. When cooked, however, they quickly lose their decorative color. Their flavor and nutritional value is much the same as those of other bell peppers.

The fruits of the bell pepper plant crowd together on the bushes, which grow up to 3 feet in height (top). As they need a great deal of warmth, in Northern latitudes they flourish only under glass or plastic tunnels, with the harvest possible about six to ten weeks after planting (above). Bell peppers are always harvested by hand.

Solanaceae **(Nightshade family).** Approximately 85 genera, with around 2,000 species, belong to the nightshade family. The upright or climbing herbs, bushes, or small trees are distributed worldwide, but most of the species occur in the tropics. The family is named after the genus *Solanum* (nightshades), which contains a great many species: from among the fruits, the lulo and pepino, and from among the vegetables, the eggplant and potato. Other important cultivated plants from different genera of the nightshade family are tobacco, tomatoes, and bell peppers. **Bell pepper, sweet pepper, capsicum** *(Capsicum annuum* var. *annuum)*. The Spanish Conquistadors took this plant from the tropics of Central and South America back to Europe in the sixteenth century, and from there it spread to Asia. It is not related to the spice pepper, but may have been misleadingly named because the native South Americans flavored their food with ground bell pepper. Originally cultivated solely as an ornamental, the bell pepper came to be used as a vegetable plant relatively late in the day. Only at the beginning of the twentieth century did intensive breeding trials result in the development of the relatively mild, more or less capsaicin-free, large-fruited varieties that are known to us today. Until then, varieties consisted exclusively of burning-hot fruits, such as those used to make cayenne pepper. The capsicum plant, which requires plenty of light and warmth to flourish, is cultivated outdoors as a summer crop in numerous countries with a hot, sunny climate. Among the important producing countries are the United States, Italy, Spain, France, Greece, Israel, Hungary, Bulgaria, Romania, and the former Yugoslavia, as well as a great many African, Asian, and Central and South American countries. The fruits of this herbaceous annual, which grows to a height of 1–3 feet, are, strictly speaking, berries. They vary widely in shape, color, and size. Bell peppers grow to about 6 inches long and up to 9 ounces in weight,. They may be flattened, spherical, cylindrical to conical, more or less triangular, heart-shaped, trapezoidal, blunt, or tapering in shape. The color of the shiny skin varies from green and red to yellow, orange, white, purple, and even black. Green bell peppers are fruits harvested before they are ripe and have a sharper flavor. In theory, if they are further exposed to sunlight, they can still turn a reddish color, but they will never be as uniformly red as fruit harvested when fully ripe. With one exception, all other varieties have developed from intensive breeding trials, which have been successfully carried out since the 1980s, many of them by the Dutch. The

Red bell peppers are left to ripen fully on the plant, which not only makes for a pleasantly milder taste, but also greatly increases their vitamin C content.

Slicing bell peppers into rings:

If you wish to stuff a bell pepper whole or slice it into thin rings, first cut around the base of the stem with a sharp knife.

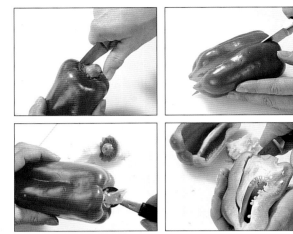

Using a melon baller, pull out the seeds and the white core.

Wash the bell pepper briefly under cold running water and cut the flesh into rings with a sharp knife.

Coring bell peppers:

Halve the bell pepper crosswise or lengthwise and cut out the stem, seeds, and core with a sharp kitchen knife. Wash briefly and dice or slice according to your preference.

Charleston or Carliston (below) is a thin-fleshed, delicate bell pepper from Turkey, which accounts for one fourth of the country's total production. **Tomato bell peppers** (bottom), which owe their name to their similarity to beefsteak tomatoes, have the highest vitamin C content of all fresh vegetables. Yellow varieties also exist. They are especially valued by the food-processing industry because of their intense flavor.

These elongated, pointed peppers from Turkey are sweet bell peppers. Be careful when tasting, though—they are almost indistinguishable in appearance from fiery hot chiles.

Hungarian bell pepper, developed in Hungary about 100 years ago, is the exception. It has a pleasantly sweet, hot flavor. Judged by appearance alone, it might be mistaken for a cross between a bell pepper and a ribbed tomato. The chambers and seeds of the fruit are separated by thin, whitish membranes in which the majority of the alkaloid capsaicin, responsible for the hot taste of the pepper, is to be found. Further important constituents are vitamins P and C. Vitamin P was named by a Hungarian scientist after the pepper, which contains the vitamin in very large quantities. Bell peppers are reckoned to be the absolute leader among vegetables and fruits for vitamin C. Depending on ripeness, they can contain from 150 mg (green bell peppers) to 300 mg (red bell peppers) per 100 grams (3½ ounces). Hungarian wax peppers can even contain up to 400 mg of vitamin C per 100 grams (3½ ounces). Their many valuable constituents means that bell peppers also have a therapeutic value. They act as an appetite stimulant, assist digestion, and act as a diuretic, as well as having a disinfectant effect on the mucous membranes. When buying bell peppers, make sure that they are firm, smooth, shiny, and unblemished—wrinkles or spots indicate that they have been stored too long, with a consequent loss of vitamins and flavor. They can be stored for 1–2 weeks in the refrigerator vegetable compartment (although not at temperatures under about 44°F°), although there will be some loss of flavor, texture, and vitamins. To prepare bell peppers, cut them in half lengthwise, remove the stem, seeds, dividing membranes, and bitter ribs, wash thoroughly, and cut the flesh into strips or dice, according to your recipe. For more sophisticated recipes, as well as for dishes that are being prepared for those with sensitive digestive systems, it is advisable to remove the skin, which is hard to digest. This is most easily done by placing halved or sliced bell peppers, skin side up, under a preheated broiler or in a preheated oven at 400°F until the skin begins to blacken and blister. Using tongs, transfer them to a plastic bag and seal the top with a loose knot. Leave for a few minutes until they are cool enough to handle. Remove them from the bag and peel— the skin will come off quite easily. There are countless recipes for bell peppers and a great number of suitable methods of preparation. They are ideal raw in salad, mixed with other vegetables in a stew, roasted, or braised with tomatoes and onions. They are also good in other braised dishes, such as goulash, in pasta sauces, mixed with scrambled eggs, or halved, stuffed with ground meat or tuna, and broiled.

This light yellow, tender, pointed type of bell pepper was once grown mainly in Hungary, but is now cultivated in many other countries. If left to ripen fully on the plant, it will turn red.

Peeling bell peppers:

Whether green, yellow, or red, bell peppers taste better peeled. Bake the whole peppers in an oven at 425°F, roast over an open flame, or broil until their skins blister and develop brown patches.

Signs of freshness in a bell pepper are smooth, firm skin and a crisp, green stalk. At one time bell peppers were often broken off the plant, but they are now usually cut in order to avoid damaging them.

Allow to cool briefly, or rinse under cold water if necessary. Pull off the skin from top to bottom with a kitchen knife.

Cut the bell peppers in half lengthwise, taking care not to squash the soft flesh.

Remove the stalk, including the base, from the bell pepper halves, and cut out and discard the core and seeds, leaving just the flesh.

The prepared bell pepper halves may now be halved again, quartered, or cut into strips or cubes of any desired size, according to the recipe.

This yellow rokoto pepper (top) is a very hot chile from Peru, where green and red versions are also cultivated. At first glance it is indistinguishable from a bell pepper, so it pays to be careful with unknown peppers. **Green bell peppers** (center) come in many different shapes—produce grown outdoors, in particular, can be very oddly shaped. **These thin-fleshed, tender dolma bell peppers** (above) are grown in Turkey. They are among the smallest varieties of the block-type, squarish bell peppers, and with their highly digestible skins are especially suitable for adding raw to salads.

The light green or striped forms of the eggplant variety serpentium, cultivated in India and Thailand, may grow up to 3 feet long. Sometimes they also grow into a snake-like spiral.

These glowing purple eggplants with the white band under the calyx are typically **Italian** (top). **In Asia, eggplants** are an integral part of any vegetable display. They play an important role in the marketplace, as here in Singapore during the Mooncake festival (above).

These long, light purple fruits are found in every Asian market. This color is typical for this variety, but a normally dark purple Western variety sporting this shade would already be overripe.

Eggplants
A MULTI-FACETED DELIGHT IN A VARIETY OF COLORS, SHAPES, AND SIZES

Until comparatively recently, the eggplant was considered to be somewhat exotic in many Western countries, but it has been known for thousands of years in its native India and in China. The original eggplant, descended from the wild forms of the plant which are still numerous there to this day, was like a hen's egg in shape and color, which satisfactorily explains its name. The Arabs brought the eggplant to Europe in the thirteenth century, where it became naturalized, mainly in the South because it requires lots of sun and warmth. In Italy, eggplants were already being cultivated in about 1550; other Southern countries followed suit. Today, throughout the Mediterranean, the eggplant is as much a byword of everyday cooking as the tomato, onion, or garlic. Nor is it by any means just the purple eggplant which graces the markets and tables of Southern Europe and Asia, but a seemingly infinite variety of shapes and

Despite its misleading English name "pea eggplant", *Solanum torvum* is actually not an eggplant. Its bitter-tasting fruits grow to only ¼–½ inch in size.

colors: long, slender, light green or striped specimens, in addition to round or long, plump violet eggplants. Small, egg-shaped eggplants are available in white, yellow, reddish-orange, or green and white stripes. The range of recipes from all four corners of the world is correspondingly large. In addition to such famous dishes as the French *ratatouille*, the Greek *moussaka*, or the Turkish *imam bayeldi*, there are countless other ways of preparing this vegetable. Perhaps the nicest thing about the eggplant is its adaptability: its white, very mild flesh goes well with just about any other ingredient. It harmonizes particularly well with strong seasonings, such as garlic, cinnamon, allspice, or aromatic herbs. Broiled or baked, eggplants taste superb with a tomato or yogurt sauce; they can be filled, not only with ground beef and lamb, but also with rice and pine nuts, cheese mixtures, mushrooms, or even fish. Eggplant is also a winner in braised dishes. It is only unsuitable for eating raw, firstly, because it tastes mushy and insipid, and secondly because it contains the toxin solanine, which can cause gastrointestinal problems. Salting the spongy flesh before cooking, removes excess water and bitter substances.

Elongated dark purple eggplants with green calyces and shining skin (below) are popular everywhere. On average, they weigh about 9–11 ounces. Southern European countries prize **dark purple, long and slender eggplants** (center). On the other hand, **Japanese eggplants, *Konasu*** (bottom), with their very differently shaped calyx, are hardly ever to be found in Europe, although they are grown in the United States. Growing only to about 4 inches in length, they taste considerably milder and sweeter than Western varieties.

Small, snow-white eggplants have been grown in Asia for thousands of years. They are now cultivated in the West, along with large, long white varieties. In contrast to purple, green, yellow, and red eggplants, their skin contains no pigment at all, so the white flesh can shine through.

Eggplants in the greenhouse: one to two fruits develop at each inflorescence of the 3-foot tall, bushy plants.

Like the tomato, the eggplant is self-fertilizing, producing 1–2-inch light purple or, infrequently, white flowers.

Preparing eggplants:

Specimens with unblemished skin need not be peeled—just wash them thoroughly and remove the calyx.

If the eggplants are to be stuffed, halve them lengthwise. Otherwise, dice or slice the flesh after halving.

It is best to brush the white flesh liberally with lemon juice to stop it turning brown on contact with the air.

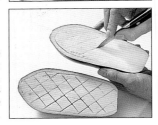

In order to make it easy to remove the somewhat tough flesh from each eggplant half, carefully cut a criss-cross pattern (without damaging the skin), then lift out the pieces.

Eggplant, aubergine, brinjal, madapple (*Solanum melongena*). Originally from India, eggplants are now distributed throughout almost every tropical, subtropical, and temperate climatic zone. They can be cultivated outdoors in warmer regions only, as they need temperatures of 72–86°F. This perennial member of the nightshade family, which is grown commercially only as an annual, bears fruits up to 1 foot in length, 2–5 inches in diameter, and up to 1¼ pounds in weight. While oval, dark purple eggplants dominate the market, shapes and colors vary considerably. There are egg- and teardrop-shaped, elongated, club-shaped, cucumber-shaped, and even snake-like eggplants, with purple to almost black, but also greenish yellow, reddish orange, white and green striped, or white skin. Regardless of the skin color, the flesh of the fruit is always white, and contains numerous edible seeds, which should also be milky white. Seeds which have turned brown indicate a lack of freshness or overripeness. Eggplants contain 92 percent water and only a few nutrients (calcium, iron, vitamins B and C). Unripe fruits may also contain relatively large amounts of the toxin solanine, most of which disappears after a fairly long cooking time. Eggplant is available year round. When buying, look for firm fruits with glossy skins that feel heavy in the hand. Storing eggplants for a long time after purchase does them no good: if refrigerated, their skin quickly becomes blemished and the flesh turns slightly brown. Since they are sensitive to ethylene given off by ripe fruits and vegetables, they should be stored separately. Newer varieties of eggplants are much less bitter than older ones and rarely need salting before cooking to get rid of the bitter substances. However, if the eggplants are to be fried, it is still worth salting them in order to draw out some of the moisture. Otherwise they will absorb enormous quantities of oil. Even so, they will still absorb quite a lot. Cut the eggplant into slices or segments and sprinkle them generously with salt. Place in a colander and set aside to drain for at least 30 minutes. Rinse thoroughly with cold water and pat dry with paper towels. **Potato, Irish potato, common white potato** (*Solanum tuberosum*). The potato's origins lie in the Andean countries of South America, where it was cultivated as far back as 2,000 years ago. Introduced into Europe toward the end of the sixteenth century, the "gold of the Incas" only really became popular some 200 years later. For a long time it was scorned by the fashionable as lacking flavor and being fit only for the poor, and some church ministers preached against eating this "ungodly" vegetable because it was not mentioned anywhere in the Bible. The

The potato
NUTRITIOUS FOOD STAPLE WITH A LONG TRADITION

Ever since it was discovered that this plant from the nightshade family—originally used in Europe only as an ornamental—could be cultivated as a vegetable, the potato has gone from strength to strength. The cuisines of many Western countries have long been unimaginable without this tuber from the Andes. It could rightly be said that you can make anything from a potato, since this staple food is rich in starch, minerals, vitamins, and protein. It is suitable for salads, soups, the most varied side dishes, casseroles, gratins, stews, and even for distilling spirits. Incidentally, the potato's reputation for being fattening is undeserved: with around 75 calories per 14 ounces, it is actually a boon for the calorie-conscious— unless, of course, it is heaped with butter or fried in oil.

Predominantly waxy potato varieties are ideal for boiling in their skins. They taste best with salt and butter. However, they are also suitable for side dishes, such as boiled or roast potatoes. Crème fraîche or sour cream and caviar turn them into a high-class delicacy.

Jersey Royals are often the first new potato of the season. They have firm, yellow flesh and a distinctive flavor. They are best boiled or steamed and served with butter.

Christa is a first early, yellow-fleshed variety. Predominantly waxy, it is distinguished by an especially hearty taste and an attractive tuber shape.

Maris Piper is a good all-round potato with white flesh and a fine flavor. Use for baking, frying, mashing, and roasting, and in salads.

Désirée, is a mid-season, predominantly waxy Dutch variety with rounded oval tubers. It is good for making French fries, mashing, and roasting.

Maris Bard is a slightly waxy potato with firm flesh. This is a good variety for boiling and steaming, and is particularly excellent in salads.

Pentland Dell is a mealy oval-shaped variety that tends to fall apart when boiled. It is slightly lacking in flavor, but is good roasted or baked.

Sieglinde, is a waxy variety, that keeps its shape and color when it is cooked. Because of this and its fine taste, it is very popular.

Maja, a midseason variety, has rounded oval tubers with predominantly waxy, yellow flesh. Its skin becomes slightly rough and cracked in a dry atmosphere.

Maris Peer is a waxy variety with very good flavor. It is best boiled or steamed and is good in salads.

Carlingford is available as a new and maincrop potato. It has firm white flesh, but tends to be mealy on the outside.

Grenailles ("shot") is the name given by the French to the smallest grade of potatoes (1–1¼ inches).

Cara is large, maincrop variety. It is a good all-round potato that is particularly tasty baked or boiled.

Linda, is a mid-season German variety. It is waxy, making it ideal for boiling unpeeled and roasting.

Truffle potatoes are superior quality, rare potatoes from France with a fine nutty flavor.

Yukon Gold has yellow flesh and pale skin. It is a good all-round variety and is perfect for mashing.

Romano, with its red skin and creamy flesh, is similar to Desirée and is also a good all-rounder.

La Ratte is a mid-season, waxy variety from France. It is pointed and tastes of chestnut. It is excellent in salads.

Aula, a mid-to-late maincrop fall variety with bright-yellow, floury flesh. Its taste is mild to strong.

Wilja is a waxy potato with pale yellow flesh. It has a slightly sweet flavor and is a good all-round variety.

Nicola, a midseason, waxy variety, is a popular salad potato with a fine taste and pleasant texture.

Pink Fir Apple is a maincrop variety with many characteristics of new potatoes. It has pinkish yellow flesh.

Chugauas are relatively small potatoes from Colombia, named after their place of origin.

Paramuna is a Colombian variety. Its name, too, is a designation of origin rather than variety.

Tuquerrea is a floury variety from Southern Colombia. It is frequently used for mashed and roast potatoes.

Pastusa, a potato with dark yellow flesh, was named after Pasto, which is its region of origin.

Tocarena, a good all-round floury potato, was also named after its region of origin.

Capiro is characterized by particularly juicy, waxy flesh. It has a slightly reddish skin.

Ica Huila is a new strain which is especially suitable for making French fries and potato chips.

Sabanera is one of the most popular varieties in Colombia. Suitable for roasting, steaming, and baking.

Potatoes

LATIN AMERICAN SPECIALTIES: A GOURMET'S DREAM

For a potato-growing country to import ordinary potatoes from abroad would, at first sight, seem to smack of sheer snobbery. Those who have tasted the different varieties in the Andean countries of South America, however, will see things differently. In point of fact, varieties—new strains, in some cases— exist there which promise a culinary experience and which could spur an imaginative cook onto new creations. The small varieties in particular, such as "Purace" and "Chugauas," can be eaten with their skins. They are best simply boiled or steamed, or cooked on the barbecue. Naturally, they must be washed very carefully beforehand. It is worth trying these specialty potatoes in order to bring a splash of culinary color and an interesting change to the potato landscape.

Storing potatoes:

Whether you wish to store a relatively large or only a small quantity of potatoes, you should heed the following points:
- Only store completely undamaged potatoes without any bruises.
- Protect from both daylight and artificial lighting, which could cause them to develop green spots, rendering them inedible.
- Store where air can circulate, preferably on wooden slats.
- Protect from frost. When stored at temperatures below freezing, they develop a sweet taste. The ideal storage temperature range is 37–43°F.

Purace, a new Colombian variety, which, as its name indicates, is particularly suitable for mashing (purées).

Criolla is cultivated at an altitude of 6,500 feet and is always roasted or boiled in its skin.

potato was not introduced to North America until 1719, when it was brought to New Hampshire by Irish settlers. Today, it is one of the seven most important food staples in the world. It is an excellent source of carbohydrate and also contains iron, potassium, and vitamins B and C. Most of these minerals and vitamins are contained in or just under the skin, so it always better to eat potatoes cooked in their skins. New potatoes should be washed under cold running water, but maincrop potatoes will need to be scrubbed. If you are going to peel them, remove only the very top surface. Alternatively, boil the potatoes in the skins and peel them afterwards. Potatoes consist of the thickened parts of the annual plant's underground shoots. Each plant produces 10—25 sprouting tubers. Propagation is not carried out by sowing the seeds of the white or purple flowers, but by planting the overwintered tubers (seed potatoes). Generally speaking, the flesh of the round, oval, or kidney-shaped potato is white or a shade of yellow, while the color of the skin can vary, according to variety, from whitish, light yellow or ocher yellow, to light red and purple. A basic distinction is drawn between first early, second early, midseason and early maincrop to late maincrop varieties. The first early potatoes are available in January, and should be consumed as soon as possible after harvesting. Maincrop varieties, on the other hand, may be stored for weeks and even months. A cool, frost-free cellar is ideal for this, but as potatoes are now in sufficient supply all year round, it is hardly worth it. If you buy potatoes in a plastic bag, remove them when you get home, otherwise the humidity will rot them. Do not store where they will be exposed to light. The cooking qualities of different sorts of potatoes are important: waxy varieties keep their firm consistency when cooked, so they are very good for salads, roast potato dishes, casseroles, and gratins, as well as boiling in their skins. Mainly waxy applies to varieties with a medium-firm to slightly mealy consistency; these are ideal as an accompaniment for dishes with a lot of sauce, and for boiled, baked, and roast potatoes. Mealy potatoes are ideal for soups, mashed potatoes, dumplings, potato pancakes, *rösti*, hash browns, and croquettes because of their high starch content. A particular specialty, the "truffle potato," comes from France. These small, purple-skinned tubers, known there as *truffes de Chine*, have pleasantly sweet flesh with a slightly nutty flavor. Red- and purple-colored flesh does not indicate a lack of quality, but is characteristic of the variety. Other specialty varieties, such as the small, elongated fingerlings, have also become popular.

Adretta, Likaria, Liu, and Arkula (from top to bottom) are varieties characterized by a really fine taste.

Tomatoes
RIPENED UNDER THE SOUTHERN SUN

November and December on the Canary Islands see the tomato harvest in full swing. The "apple of Paradise" is by far the most important export of the Canaries: Around 200,000 tons of tomatoes per season are exported from Tenerife, Lanzarote, and Fuerteventura into chilly Northern Europe. The vast majority of this produce is then shipped to Holland, from where it is dispatched onward to neighboring countries, such as Germany. Small quantities are also imported by Great Britain, Scandinavia, and the Spanish mainland.

OUTDOOR GROWING ON THE CANARY ISLANDS: IS ALL WELL IN PARADISE?

Thanks to a constant average temperature of around 72°F, tomatoes can be cultivated outdoors on Tenerife and the neighboring islands. The tomato plants are trained onto strings and supported by canes (opposite far left). Large plantations contain numerous rows of tomato plants (opposite left). Irrigation is crucial for the success of the crop, since problems, such as bursting, could arise with fruit grown without a steady water supply. The tomatoes, which are harvested by hand, are sorted automatically in packing houses according to color and size, and packed in crates (opposite below). When they are dispatched, palletized, on refrigerator ships to their destination ports, they are, however, still green, since in spite of the short transportation time of about 5 days, they would hardly survive the journey undamaged if fully ripe. Unfortunately, there is a trade-off in taste involved, since despite all the Southern sun they have received, tomatoes harvested while still green cannot be as aromatic as fully ripened specimens. Damage from the cold can also impair flavor. Mature green tomatoes are more sensitive to the cold than ripe fruits, and must not be stored below 55°F. Damage due to cold may manifest itself in pallid color (light red to yellowish), fruit turning prematurely soft and waxy, and quicker spoilage.

GREENHOUSE TOMATOES: AS BAD AS THEIR REPUTATION?

Over the decades, the Dutch in particular have continually perfected the cultivation of tomatoes under glass. Under uniformly warm conditions, the plants are trained on strings, like those grown outdoors. Optimum nutrients are supplied by planting not in soil, but in peat substrate, mineral wool, or water channels with nutrient solution. The harvesting wagon (right center and bottom) which runs along the heating pipes is used for picking. In the larger greenhouses, the crop is conveyed for sorting according to size and color via water channels (far right), with the advantage that damage in transit, such as squashing, can be prevented almost completely. Tomatoes cultivated as carefully as this need not be strikingly inferior to outdoor-grown tomatoes. Continual improvements of the cultivated varieties of tomato by means of selective cross-breeding, constant monitoring of optimal nutrient provision, and biological pest control ensure that tomatoes grown in greenhouses can aspire to the quality of fruit raised outdoors—a proviso of quality for cultivation under glass also being that the fruit is harvested as late and as ripe as possible.

Outdoor tomatoes: post-harvest ripening. In order to obtain maximum flavor from tomatoes picked and transported before they are fully ripe, it is best to let them ripen for a few days more after purchase. This works well if they are stored at room temperature with ripe fruit.

In addition to the Belgians, the Dutch have for many years been leaders in the cultivation of tomatoes under glass. Dotted about the country are numerous huge greenhouses (top), in which harvesting can take place throughout the entire year under steady climatic conditions. Using a harvesting wagon to pick the crop ensures low costs, as well as undamaged tomatoes (center and above); the pickers travel down the long rows of tomato plants which are suspended in nutrient solution, pick the fruit that is very nearly ripe by hand, and send it on its way in the wagon to the sorting and packing stations.

Transporting the tomatoes in water channels (top) to the station where they are sorted according to color and size saves time and labor, as well as being particularly easy on the fruit. At the end of the channel, the tomatoes are picked up by conveyor belts (above).

Old varieties native to the area of origin, such as these Colombian cultivated tomatoes, produce highly ribbed, often misshapen fruits weighing up to 2 pounds. Generally speaking, they are extremely high-yielding and disease-resistant.

Elongated bush tomatoes grown outdoors, belong to the Roma and Napoli types. They are chiefly canned, bottled, and used to make tomato juice and tomato paste.

Round tomatoes (top) with two to three chambers and many yellowish seeds in a gelatinous liquid are widely cultivated and dominate the European market. **Beefsteak tomatoes** (center) are large-fruited, round to semicircular, and slightly to strongly ribbed. They have over four chambers, more flesh, and fewer seeds, and are particularly firm-slicing. They are very popular in the United States. **Plum tomatoes** (above) are grown outdoors in warm climates. Their large proportion of flesh and intense flavor make them ideal for sauces, soups, salads, and many Mediterranean dishes.

Tomato (*Lycopersicon esculentum*). After the potato, the tomato is probably the most important useful plant from the nightshade family. There are even historical similarities with the potato. Peru and Ecuador are thought to be the original home of the tomato, with the first cultivated forms probably having originated in Mexico. From there the Spanish Conquistadors took the plants and fruit, known in Latin America as *tomatl*, to Europe. Like the potato, the tomato—yellow in those days—was regarded with suspicion. Spain was the first country to regard them as anything other than ornamental, followed by Italy. Then they spread throughout the world, although it was another 200 years before Europeans made the supposedly poisonous ornamental into a vegetable plant. The first red tomatoes did not arrive in Europe until the eighteenth century, brought to Italy by Jesuit priests. Nowadays, the world's biggest tomato producers are the United States, Russia, China, and Egypt. The tomato plant is a herbaceous perennial, but it is cultivated as an annual. It grows to a height of about 5 feet. The stems and leaves are covered with fine hairs. The yellow flowers and the yellow, pink, orange, red, or purple fruits hang in clusters on the branching stems. There are many varieties, which differ chiefly in shape, size, and weight. Most in demand in Europe are round tomatoes, which weigh up to 3½ ounces each, while Americans have a preference for the larger beefsteak varieties that can measure as much as 4 inches in diameter. Plum tomatoes, which are less watery than round tomatoes, are crucial to Italian cuisine. Color intensity is promoted by light and hindered by extremes of temperature. Taste is determined mainly by the ratio of sugar to fruit acids. During ripening, the sugar content increases, while the acidity decreases. Eating unripe, green tomatoes should be discouraged, since they contain the alkaloid solanine, which can cause headaches and other complaints. **Cherry tomato** (*Lycopersicon esculentum* var. *cerasiforme*). In addition to the well-known round cherry tomato that is only about ¹/₂ inch in diameter, there are three further variants: *L. esculentum* var. *pyriforme*, is the same size as a cherry tomato, but pear-shaped; var. *pruniforme*, is also the same size, but plum-shaped; var. *ribesiforme*, is the smallest of all the tomatoes. **Tomatillo, jamberry, Mexican husk tomato** (*Physalis philadelphica*). The area from southern Texas to Guatemala is home both to the wild forms of the tomatillo and the present-day cultivated forms. These tomato-like relatives of the ground cherry, Cape gooseberry, or physalis (*Physalis peruviana*) grow to no more than 2 inches in diameter.

Here in Naples (right) and elsewhere, sun-ripened, highly aromatic tomatoes are hung out to dry. These intensely flavorful dried tomatoes, available preserved in oil, are delicious as an antipasto. **A glut of tomatoes** fills southern markets (below) during the long season.

Yellow, round tomatoes, here the variety "Golden Queen" (top), are thick-skinned with a particularly sweet taste. Market resistance probably stems from the mistaken belief that they are unripe red tomatoes. **Yellow, plum-shaped cherry tomatoes** (above), unlike the increasingly commonly found red, round cherry tomatoes, are still unusual.

The cherry tomato is enjoying great popularity and considerable expansion in the areas where it is cultivated. This has to do with its appealing taste, a result of higher sugar content, and more acidity.

The *tomatillo*, also known as the green tomato, is popular in Mexico for chile dishes, stews, soups, and sauces. It is widely available in the United States, but it is rather less frequently seen in Europe. The berries, which are eaten cooked, ripen protected by a papery calyx.

The nasturtium, with its funnel-shaped orange to red flowers and flat leaves, is not only an ornamental for gardens; it also adds a decorative note to salads, soups, and delicate egg dishes, enriching them with its piquant taste.

The floury, sweet flesh of turnip-rooted chervil can be roasted or boiled like potatoes, or even prepared like Teltow turnips (glazed with bacon). In spite of its pleasant taste and high mineral content, turnip-rooted chervil is infrequently cultivated. Rare supplies come almost exclusively from vegetable plots in late summer and fall.

It is only the highly toothed leaves of the **fitweed** that may be used as a vegetable. The herbaceous shrub is cultivated all year-round. In Thailand, for example, it is prized in hot-and-sour soups, or prepared with ground meat, toasted rice flour, lime juice, and various seasonings.

Parsnips are the traditional American Christmas vegetable, served in a sweet glaze. These aromatic roots are also popular in the other main growing countries—England, France, Scandinavia, Hungary, and Holland. They are harvested from October onward.

Umbellifers
VEGETABLES, HERBS, AND MEDICINAL PLANTS

The species mainly used as vegetables originated in Asia and the Mediterranean. They are annual, biennial, or perennial herbs or shrubs, characterized by a high content of vitamins, minerals, and flavoring substances, as well as volatile oils in their seeds, leaves, and roots. For this reason almost all plants in this family are not only vegetables, but also seasoning plants, and in some cases, medicinal herbs as well. Anise, dill, chervil, cilantro, caraway, lovage, common burnet, cumin, and angelica: these and others are familiar to us as kitchen herbs and spice plants.

The Peruvian parsnip is a plant up to 3 feet long with celery-like leaves and roots 6–8 inches long and 1½–3 inches thick. It is eaten while still young and tender. Its high starch content (20–25 percent) makes it very important as food for invalids and children, as well as for the obtaining of starch.

Tropaeolaceae **(Nasturtium family).** The genus *Tropaeolum* gives its name to this family of New World climbing plants, whose 35 or so species are all native to South America. **(Common) nasturtium** (*Tropaeolum majus*). The nasturtium, best known as an ornamental, as well as its tuber-forming sister *T. tuberosum*, can also be used as vegetables. In addition to minerals, the flat, shield- to kidney-shaped leaves of this herbaceous perennial contain vitamin C, as well as a natural antibiotic. Their slightly hot taste is caused by a mustard oil glycoside and they are a pleasant addition to salads, not unlike watercress. The large orange-yellow to scarlet red flowers are also edible and the buds may be pickled and used like capers.

Umbelliferae (Apiaceae) **(Umbellifers).** The umbellifer family contains about 300 genera with around 3,000 species. Some 75 of these are cultivated plants. **Fitweed** (*Eryngium foetidum*). The seaside thistle is a close relative of this noble thistle, which is native to Central and South America. It serves as a vegetable, seasoning herb, and drug, and is cultivated in Cuba, Liberia, Brazil, Cambodia, and Thailand. **Peruvian parsnip, Peruvian carrot** (*Arracacia xanthorrhiza*). This plant, cultivated by the Andean Indians, is similar to celery root. Cultivated by the Incas for its agreeable tasting roots, it is now grown in the highlands of Peru, Bolivia, Colombia, Ecuador, and Venezuela. **Turnip-rooted chervil, tuberous chervil** (*Chaerophyllum bulbosum* ssp. *bulbosum*). Turnip-rooted chervil is native to the area from Northern and Central Europe to Asia Minor. The herb is considered a particular delicacy. The part of the plant used as a vegetable is the taproot, which may be straight, oval, spindle-shaped, tuberous or almost spherical. From ¾ inch to 4 inches long, it reaches weights of up to 7 ounces. **Parsnip** (*Pastinaca sativa* ssp. *sativa*). One of the oldest gathered plants of the original inhabitants of Eurasia, the parsnip was an important food staple until it was superseded by the potato and the carrot in the mid-eighteenth century. Although regarded as something of an old-fashioned vegetable, they are still valued as a winter vegetable for soups and stews and are delicious roasted with beef. Parsnips contain vitamins A, B, and C, as well as calcium, iron, and potassium. **Parsley root, Hamburg parsley** (*Petroselinum crispum* convar. *radicosum*). These strong, aromatic roots closely resemble those of the parsnip. They are used mainly as a seasoning for soups; their leaves can be used like normal parsley. **Parsley** (*Petroselinum crispum* convar. *crispum*). A distinction is drawn between flat leaf or Italian and curly parsley. Both owe their vivid taste to the volatile oil

Parsley root, or Hamburg parsley, native to the Southeastern Mediterranean, is now cultivated worldwide both outdoors and under glass. Its yellowish white to light brown flesh can be cooked as a vegetable or puréed into a creamy soup. Available from October and November, parsley root is a very typical winter vegetable.

Curly parsley (right) is especially suitable for garnishing salads, soups, and cold platters, while **flat leaf parsley** (below) is the better seasoning herb on account of its stronger flavor. The typical parsley taste goes well with practically all dishes.

Celery: root and branch
A VEGETABLE FOR ALL SEASONS

The first thing many people think of when celery is mentioned is losing weight because the act of chewing it is said to use up more calories than the celery supplies. Be that as it may, doctors and dieticians are more interested in the fact that, with their high concentrations of volatile oils, vitamins, and minerals, celery stalks, celery root, and cutting celery are all very health-giving. With the trend for eating salads and raw foods, stalk celery is becoming more and more popular. The intensely flavored celery root, on the other hand, has been left out in the cold. Mostly, it is used only as a soup vegetable and in stews, despite the fact that its quality has increased considerably in the last few years. The tubers now remain white-fleshed when cooked, whereas in the past a chemical reaction of the volatile oils with the cooking water often caused black discoloration to appear.

Celery: The dark green, unblanched stalks (top) almost always taste just as delicate as the pale, yellowish heads of **blanched celery** (above) or the so-called self-blanching varieties, which come mainly from Britain and the United States. Depending on origin, the plants weigh from 1¼–2½ pounds. The most important signs of quality for all varieties are unblemished, crisp fresh stalks with no discoloration or dried-up patches.

Cutting celery outwardly resembles flat leaf parsley. However, its leaves, which are used as a seasoning in soups and are excellent for drying, have an intense celery taste.

Celery root is a hearty Eastern European vegetable with a time-honored place in good home cooking. Recently, however, consumption has fallen—perhaps because many people now prefer the juicy, mild stalk celery with its shorter cooking time.

apiol. In addition to its high iron and protein content, parsley is also remarkable for its vitamin C content (166 mg per 100 grams/3½ ounces). **Celery** (*Apium graveolens* var. *graveolens*). The wild form, from which present-day celery and celery root developed, is native to the Mediterranean. Three varieties are now sold as a vegetable: stalk celery, celery root, and cutting celery. **Celery** (*Apium graveolens* var. *dulce*). Stalk celery forms only poorly defined tubers, as growth takes place mainly above ground. With older varieties of celery, it was necessary to blanch the stalks by mounding soil or by covering the plants; with newer, self-blanching varieties, this is no longer necessary. Celery tastes just as good raw as it does boiled, braised, or stir-fried. **Celery root, celeriac** (*Apium graveolens* var. *rapaceum*). This is grown widely throughout continental Europe from the Mediterranean to Scandinavia, but it is less popular in Britain and the United States. In addition to France and Germany, the main producers are Holland and Belgium. Celery root is a softball-size tuber with tough yellowish-white or grayish-brown skin. The flesh is whitish, and spongy to firm. Fifty percent of the European harvest goes to the food processing industry for pickling. **Cutting celery, soup celery** (*Apium graveolens* var. *secalinum*). Cutting celery is very similar to wild celery. Like stalk celery, it does not develop any tubers, but is cultivated for its aromatic leaves. It is raised in greenhouses or outdoors, where it can be harvested by machine. **Carrot** (*Daucus carota* ssp. *sativus*). Wild forms are frequently found in Southern Europe and Asia, suggesting an extensive original distribution over two continents. Originally purple in color, carrots as we recognize them were first exported from Holland in the seventeenth century. Now one of the most important of vegetables, the carrot is cultivated worldwide. Root color ranges from white to yellowish and reddish orange; there are also purple-skinned Asian varieties. An important characteristic for judging the quality is the ratio between the juicy, nutrient-rich outer fleshy part and the woody core or heart. A high proportion of fleshy outer part and a small, tender core, similar in color, is considered ideal. The brighter the color, the higher the content of carotene, the precursor of vitamin A. The sugar content, averaging about 6 percent, is higher for early varieties sold in bunches than for the larger carrots sold loose in the fall and winter. Both types should always be stored without further washing, since once washed they do not keep well, even if refrigerated. Carrots become bitter when exposed to ethylene.

It is mostly early varieties, harvested young in the spring and summer, which are sold with their tops on in bunches. **Long carrots** (top) are lifted somewhat later than the very sweet, round **Paris carrots** (above), which are cultivated chiefly for the canning industry.

Washed carrots are sold without their green tops from July onward, either loose or pre-packed. Cylindrical, smooth varieties are often chosen for this purpose.

Carrot harvest in Sicily: Here, in the vicinity of Siracusa, the main carrot-growing region in Italy, bright orange-red, firm-fleshed carrots are cultivated for the fresh market. In the winter months they are exported to other European countries.

Florence fennel comes in different shapes, depending on variety: elongate, narrow bulbs (top) or rounded, almost spherical ones (above). They are identical in taste. Important quality criteria are that the feathery leaves should appear fresh and shiny green, and that places where the stalks are cut should not be dried up.

Wild fennel, with its elongated bulb—roots and abundant green tops still attached—is displayed at a market in Palermo.

Preparing fennel: Wash the bulbs. Cut off the base of the root and any dry outside leaves. Starting from where the cut was made, pull the fine strings up and off. Next, halve or quarter the bulb according to your recipe and cut out the hard core in a wedge shape so as not to detach the leaves.

Fennel (*Foeniculum vulgare*) is native to the Near East and the Mediterranean, where it grows wild in dry, stony places. In addition to pepper fennel (ssp. *piperitum*), which is also cultivated as a vegetable in Italy, sweet fennel (var. *dulce*), and bitter fennel (var. *vulgare*), it is primarily bulb or Florence fennel which is of interest. **Florence fennel, bulb fennel, fennel** (*Foeniculum vulgare* ssp. *vulgare* var. *azoricum*). The main growing areas are Southern Italy, the South of France, Spain, Greece, and North Africa. To prevent bolting caused by long summer days, fennel is now cultivated as a winter plant in the Mediterranean, with the main harvest season running from October to May. The ribbed leaves are thick and fleshy at their base and form a white to greenish white bulb-shaped tuber.

Urticaceae. **Nettle** (*Urtica*). The nettle can be found in the temperate zones of every continent. **The greater nettle** (*Urtica dioica*) grows up to 5 feet in height, while the **lesser nettle** (*Urtica urens*) grows to only about 1 foot tall. Both varieties have stinging hairs which leave an itchy rash on the skin when they are touched. They are thought to be powerful medicinal herbs, and are surprisingly rich in vitamins and minerals, as well as nitrates.

Valerianaceae. **Mâche, corn salad, lamb's lettuce** (*Valeriana locusta*). This undemanding herb, widely distributed in Europe and Asia and only cultivated since the beginning of the twentieth century, is eaten raw as a salad green.

Vitaceae. **Grape leaves, vine leaves** (*Vitis vinifera*). The leaves of the grape plant are harvested when young. They are found in every market in Greece and Turkey, where they are stuffed and made into packets. Fresh leaves are difficult to find in countries where grapes are not grown, but preserved leaves are widely available.

Zingiberaceae **(Ginger family).** This family contains 47 genera and 1,400 species of tropical herbaceous perennials with starchy, fleshy rhizomes. The plants are often rich in volatile oils and prized for their seasoning qualities. **Ginger** (*Zingiber officinale*). Fruity, hot-tasting ginger is now cultivated in many tropical regions. Fresh and dried rhizomes are exported by Hawaii, India, Taiwan, and Nigeria. **Japanese ginger, mioga ginger** (*Zingiber mioga*). Native to Japan and China, it is now cultivated there and in Hawaii. The rhizomes are considered inferior to those of the ginger plant, but the flower clusters and buds are regarded as delicacies. **Galangal, galingale, Thai ginger** (*Alpinia galanga*). There are two varieties: greater galangal or *laos* and lesser galangal or *kenchur*, with a more intense flavor. It is grown mainly in Malaysia and Java for its highly spicy and pleasant smell.

Grape leaves are an everyday food in the Middle East and several Mediterranean countries, such as Greece and Turkey. They are used primarily as wrappers for meat and rice fillings. If fresh grape leaves are not available, you can use preserved ones.

Mâche, or corn salad is a frost-hardy herb. It places no great demands on soil or climate, rather just on one's patience in sorting through and trimming the leaf rosettes. These may differ widely in size and leaf shape, according to variety and time of harvest. The main season for this healthy salad green is the winter and early spring; throughout the rest of the year it is hardly available.

Japanese ginger buds (below) are considered a delicacy in their native land, and are a popular seasoning for soup. The young leaves and shoots of the plant are also used as a seasoning. Stalks, leaves, and young roots of the **galangal** plant (bottom)—here, bundled together for sale—are mild, and are cooked in vegetable dishes. Older galangal roots have a spicy, bitter, gingery taste and are used as a seasoning, chiefly in curry pastes.

The lesser nettle is not just harvested as a wild herb; in Western Switzerland, it is cultivated as a vegetable. As the leaves soon wither, 4-inch high plants are sold in pots, so that the consumer can keep on harvesting the tender leaves for salads and soups, as required.

Ginger harvest in Sri Lanka: The reed-like ginger plant is dug up one year after planting and the tuberous, branching, root-like rhizomes, measuring up to 20 inches in length, are sold fresh or dried.

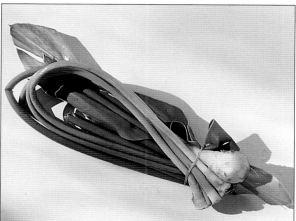

To obtain nori, fresh seaweed is chopped, pressed between bamboo mats, and dried either in drying rooms or in the sun. Good-quality nori is mild-tasting and black in color with a purple sheen. It should be packed airtight. **Arame,** a brown alga or kelp, is one of the most nutritious of all plants.

The best varieties of kombu grow in the cool precoastal waters of the northernmost Japanese island of Hokkaido. Their broad *thalli* (leaves) grow up to 33 feet long and are sweet-tasting.

Hijiki, a highly-branched black seaweed, is so tough that after its first drying it must be cooked for up to 4 hours under pressure, and then allowed to dry again. It has a uniquely astringent, but at the same time somewhat nutty, flavor.

Kombu must be thoroughly soaked in cold water before preparation to allow the thick dried leaves to swell sufficiently. It can then be boiled, sautéed, or deep-fried.

Edible seaweeds belong to entirely different families.. They are actually algae (from the Latin *alga*, "sea grass"),

Around 30 different red and green seaweeds, mostly species of *Porphyra*, are sold under the name of **nori.** The most important of these are *Porphyra umbilicalis, P. tenera, P. yezoensis,* and *P. haitanensis.* Nori is important from a culinary and an economic standpoint in Japan, where 300,000 metric tons fresh weight is harvested each year. It is cultivated on raft-like screens. The widely distributed species *P. umbilicalis* is native not only to Japan, but also to the coasts of the Atlantic, the North Sea, the Baltic Sea, and the Pacific coasts of North and South America, the coasts of East Asia, and the beaches of Hawaii. In Ireland it is called sloke, in Wales it is known as laver, and is eaten there as a fresh vegetable. **Susabi nori** (*Porphyra yezoensis*) flourishes best on coasts with a cold current and now predominates in all regions of Japan.

Kelp, kombu, konbu, laminaria (*Laminaria japonica*). The best-known species of kelp, which has broad, shiny leaves, flourishes in cool waters off the coasts of Japan, Korea, and Siberia, as well as in Brittany in Northwest France. It has been cultivated in Japan for 300 years, and elsewhere on a large scale for about 40. A rich stock (*dashi*) can be prepared from kelp because of its concentration of the flavor-enhancer glutamic acid.

Wakame (*Undaria pinnatifida*). Next to nori, wakame is one of the most important species of seaweed on the Japanese menu. It is eaten both dried and fresh. The nutritional value is high, as the leaves consist of 13 percent protein and substantial amounts of calcium.

Hijiki, hiziki (*Hizikia fusiformis*) is among the most mineral-rich of plants, containing 14 times as much calcium as cow's milk.

Arame (*Eisenia bicyclis*) is also known as sea oak because of the shape of its leaves. It grows wild on solid rock a few yards under the water's surface on many Pacific coasts.

Dulse, dilisk (*Palmaria palmata*) flourishes in the cold coastal waters of both the Atlantic and the Pacific. Today this species is successfully cultivated along the coast of Brittany, France.

Haricot vert de mer, sea spaghetti (*Himanthalia elongata*) are long, dark seaweeds, rich in trace elements and vitamins, which are successfully cultivated in Brittany, France. They are increasingly exported fresh for the restaurant trade.

Sea lettuce, sea laver, lettuce laver, laitue de mer (*Ulva lactuca*). This mild, green seaweed is exported fresh from Brittany, France. When dried, it is reminiscent of spinach in smell and appearance.

Sea vegetables

FRESH AND DRIED ALGAE: A RICH ADDITION TO THE ARRAY OF VEGETABLES AVAILABLE

Of all the exotic plants, species which grow exclusively in the sea seem to be the strangest. In fact, however, the Japanese discovered the plant riches of the seas as far back as 10,000 years ago, and incorporated them in their cooking. Dried wakame found in clay burial pots bears witness to this. Even in Northwestern Europe, the use of seaweed as a food is not altogether uncommon: some species have been on the menu for over 1,000 years. The red seaweed **dulse** (bottom right) was prized by the Celts and Vikings, and has been harvested on beaches at low tide, air-dried, and boiled in soups from Ireland to Iceland into the twentieth century. For some time now, algae have been cultivated in Brittany and Normandy, France, and exported fresh to other countries. Thus, **_haricot vert de mer_** (top), **nori** (second), **_laitue de mer_** (sea lettuce or green laver) (third), and dulse have been successfully raised in France, and, owing to their high quality, exported to Japan in some quantity.

Haricot vert de mer, also known as sea spaghetti, is a long, vitamin-rich seaweed. Before preparation, the furry layer must be removed by hand under cold running water.

Wakame, a brown alga or kelp, grows in water 20–33 feet deep. Usually harvested from boats by means of long hooks, it is sold fresh or sun-dried. Since this seaweed is salted for transport, before eating, it must first be rinsed thoroughly under running water, then placed in boiling water, boiled for 30 seconds, and rinsed in ice water, before spreading out the leaves and removing the hard midrib.

Practical Guidelines

THE BEST WAY TO PRESERVE FRESHNESS AND QUALITY IS
BY HANDLING INGREDIENTS SCRUPULOUSLY.

This chapter is about how vegetables are prepared before cooking. It
provides detailed guidance on the ideal ways of preparing them and
essential basic recipes to ease your entry into the demanding world of
vegetable cuisine. The six following chapters explain various cooking
methods, with step-by-step illustrations. These include the basic
techniques, such as boiling, sautéing, braising, and frying, as well as
recipes for classic and international vegetable dishes. The entire
spectrum is covered—soups and sauces, Italian risottos, French gratins
and quiches, and Asian wok-cooked specialties. Useful background
information makes interesting reading for creative cooks, serving as
inspiration for trying out and varying the recipes.

Washing and peeling
PREPARING LEAVES, STALKS, TUBERS, AND ROOTS

This gets rid of any residual pesticide, along with the dirt and peel. When calculating how much to buy, remember that the amount of waste depends chiefly on the quality of the raw materials. Wherever possible, rinse vegetables before rather than after peeling, so that soluble vitamins and minerals are not simply washed down the drain.

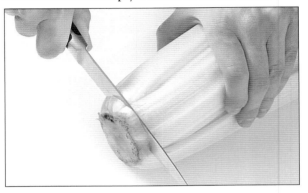

Drying lettuce: Put the washed leaves in a wire basket, hold it by the handle, and shake vigorously over the sink so that the water is spun out. Outdoors, you can dry the lettuce by swinging your arm. If you do not have a basket, you can wrap the lettuce in a clean dish cloth.

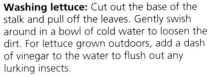

Washing lettuce: Cut out the base of the stalk and pull off the leaves. Gently swish around in a bowl of cold water to loosen the dirt. For lettuce grown outdoors, add a dash of vinegar to the water to flush out any lurking insects.

This big electric *salad* spinner is used in the catering trade and can dry huge quantities of lettuce in 10–15 seconds. Smaller hand-operated spinners are suitable for all lettuce leaves, leafy vegetables, and herbs. Centrifugal force gently and thoroughly removes all the water clinging to the leaves.

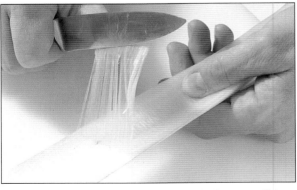

Preparing Swiss chard: Use a large, sharp knife to cut off the base of the root, if necessary. Place individual leaves flat on the counter and cut out the white stalk, together with the rib. Cut into the upper tip of the stalk so that you can take hold of the delicate inner skin and pull it off toward the base of the root. With some newer varieties of chard, and with young or thin-ribbed chard, this skin need not be removed.

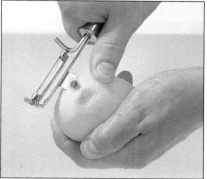

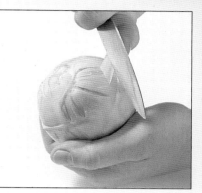

Washing celery root: Clean the skin with a stiff brush under cold running water. If there is a lot of ingrained soil, place the unpeeled tubers briefly in water to loosen the dirt. Peel smaller tubers whole with a sharp vegetable knife. Very large tubers are easier to deal with if quartered or cut into thick slices first.

Trimming kohlrabi: First cut off the leafstalks. If desired, reserve the tender leaves for seasoning and garnishing. The skin of young kohlrabis pulls off easily—always start at the base of the leaf. Fully grown tubers are best peeled.

Peeling potatoes: Either wash the potatoes first and then peel, or peel them under cold running water. This is best done with a swivel-blade vegetable peeler. Any eyes may be removed with the pointed end of the peeler. Place the peeled potatoes in a bowl of water until they are needed to prevent them from turning brown.

Radishes, zucchini, and other vegetables to be cooked unpeeled should be scrubbed thoroughly under cold running water. This removes dirt and pollution.

Slicing or "sculpting"
SIMPLE SLICING IS NOT ALWAYS ENOUGH FOR DECORATION

Depending on the shape of the vegetable, rounds, slices, cubes, or strips are formed almost automatically during cutting. Just how coarsely or finely the vegetable should be sliced depends on how it will be used. The smaller the pieces, the shorter the cooking time. It is important not to leave cut vegetables standing around for long, since light- and heat-sensitive vitamins will be lost. If you have to leave prepared vegetables, cover them with plastic wrap and put them in the refrigerator. For visual impact, roots, tubers, and fruiting vegetables are usually cut into uniform shapes. Leftover, oddly shaped pieces can be used in fillings, soups, and purées. You can cut waved surfaces with a crinkle-cut knife, and spheres with a melon baller. For most other shapes all you need is a sharp, slightly curved kitchen knife, known as a bird's beak paring knife.

Slicing carrots: First cut lengthwise into thin slices, then into long strips, and lastly into dice. Any of these three shapes may be used, according to the recipe and the desired effect. The thinner the initial slices, the finer the dice.

Dicing onions: Cut the onion in half. Place one half, cut side down, on a chopping board, hold it firmly with your fingertips, and make a number of cuts very close together. Slice the onion once or twice crosswise in such a way that it still holds together. Finally, cut the onion half into slices, which will create dice.

Mirepoix: This classic vegetable mixture from France usually consists of carrots, celery, and onions or leeks, the proportions of which are varied according to taste. Sometimes parsley root is added, as well as a piece of bay leaf and a sprig of thyme or parsley. The mirepoix mixture is sautéed in butter over a low heat until lightly colored, then used to flavor sauces, stews, and casseroles. The size of the dice depends on how you intend to use the mirepoix: coarsely diced for dishes with a long braising time, finely diced for quick sauces and soups.

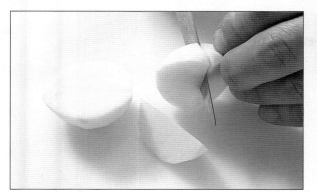

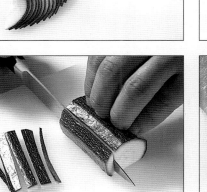

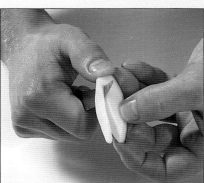

Slicing round vegetables, such as turnips, short carrots, or beets. Cut into quarters, eighths, or matchsticks, according to size. It is important to cut pieces of equal size so that they will all finish cooking at the same time. A rolling cut can be used for carrots and other elongated root vegetables. This Asian cooking technique produces uniform chunks with a large surface area, useful for stir-frying in a wok. Slice the vegetable diagonally, giving it a quarter turn after each cut before making the next. Hold the vegetable properly when cutting it. The tips of the fingers holding the vegetable should be resting vertically on it and be bent slightly inward, so that the knife glides along the second joint and the fingertips are hidden. At the same time, this also lets you determine the thickness of the slice.

Balls can be cut out with melon ballers, which are available in different sizes. When using a bird's beak paring knife, make sure that the blade is thin so that the vegetable does not break apart.

Shaping elongated vegetables: The simplest way to do this is to slice them into rounds with a crinkle-cut knife. For fan shapes, halve the vegetable lengthwise and make a series of cuts close together, taking care not to cut all the way through. For batons, leave a piece of peel on one side.

Classically shaped: The vegetable is cut into an olive shape. The size can vary greatly, so just cut large pieces roughly to the proper shape, then round off toward the ends. The French method recommends seven cuts.

Trimming red cabbage: Remove the ragged outer leaves and cut the head into quarters using a large, sharp knife.

Slicing cucumber: Rounds can be cut to the desired thickness on a plastic or metal mandoline with an adjustable blade.

Slicing Savoy cabbage: Press down firmly on the tip of the knife, then raise and lower the blade in a seesaw motion. A large, sharp kitchen knife is best for this.

Place each quarter round-side down and make a wedge-shaped cut to remove the stalk and a portion of the thick leaf ribs.

Cutting radishes: A series of vertical blades on the mandoline creates these neat and uniform batons.

Chopping and shredding
KNIFE AND MANDOLINE

A food processor saves time and effort when chopping, grating, and shredding—particularly when large quantities are being prepared—but it cannot cut as perfectly and uniformly as practiced hands and a sharp knife. The blades are seldom as sharp as a good knife, so the structure of the vegetable is often damaged, and vitamins and minerals are lost. A mandoline offers a compromise, especially for grating and shredding.

Place the cabbage quarters on their cut surfaces and cut off thin slices, which will then naturally fall into strips.

Shredding carrots: Elongated vegetables can be quickly shredded into thin strips using a mandoline.

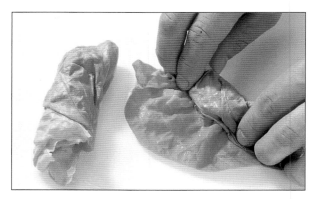

Chiffonade is a technique for shredding leafy vegetables, such as lettuce, spinach, and sorrel. Wash and dry the leaves, then roll up loosely. Slice into paper-thin shreds using a sharp knife. Use for garnishing cold meat platters, soups, and sauces.

Salting eggplant: Depending on the variety, the spongy flesh of the eggplant contains greater or lesser quantities of bitter substances. To achieve a firmer texture and milder taste, slice the eggplant into rounds and sprinkle with salt. After about 30 minutes, rinse and pat off the juices with paper towels, squeezing the eggplant rounds slightly as you do so. Doing this removes air in addition to the bitter liquid from the flesh of the eggplant, which will then not absorb so much fat during frying.

Soaking legumes: Dried beans and peas cook more quickly and are more digestible when they have been soaked for 8–12 hours first. Any beans which float to the surface should be discarded, as they could contain harmful substances. Discard the soaking water. Legumes are ready to cook once they have doubled or tripled in size.

Dried legumes are usually soaked, as this reduces their cooking time.

Sprouts
CRUNCHY SPROUTS AND SHOOTS—A NUTRITIOUS ADDITION TO MANY DISHES

Traditional Asian medicine attributes therapeutic properties to the different types of sprouts. It is certainly true that when seeds germinate, their vitamin content increases dramatically within a short time span. In addition, volatile oils and fiber ensure good flavor and nutrition. Sprouting seeds and beans is simple: just sort through and rinse untreated grain, herb, or vegetable seeds and soak them for several hours. The seeds will germinate within 2—5 days under the influence of light, moisture, and heat. A constant temperature of about 68°F and watering regularly, but sparingly, are essential for growth. Lack of moisture causes the sprouts to dry up; conversely, if they are sitting in water they suffocate and go moldy.

Sprouting in a preserving jar:

Cover garbanzos or other beans in lukewarm water and soak for several hours. Secure a piece of cheesecloth over the jar with an elastic band.

Pour out the water and rinse the beans several times. Fill with fresh water and let stand for 10 minutes. Pour off the water and drain thoroughly.

Rinse the beans several times a day. Let them stand briefly in water, then drain thoroughly.

Sprouting techniques: Nowadays, a large variety of ready-to-eat sprouts are available. In Europe, radish sprouts (left), for example, are sold like cress in papier mâché pots. Equipment for sprouting seeds and beans at home can make the procedure easier and more hygienic. There are various designs of sprouter, but their function is always the same: to provide the seeds with a uniform amount of moisture while avoiding a buildup of water. With stackable translucent plastic bowls, shown above with sprouted mung beans, grooves and tiny siphons distribute the water evenly over all the levels, and excess liquid collects in a container. An advantage of the see-through container is that the seeds sprout in the light and so collect less nitrate. Mucilage-secreting seeds, such as cress and mustard, are best sown on a flat plate and moistened three to four times daily with an atomizer. The mucilage quickly renders sprouting devices unusable. Seeds and beans can be sprouted simply and successfully in a large glass jar—see the garbanzos above.

Black radish: Rinse once a day. Sufficiently sprouted after 4 days at most. The seeds have an antibacterial effect and prevent mold.

Adzuki beans and small red soybeans: Rinse twice a day. Ready after 5 days. Blanch them before eating.

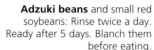

Garbanzos: Sprouted after 3–5 days. Blanch for a few minutes or cook briefly with other ingredients before eating.

Alfalfa: Sprout in a preserving jar for 4 days without prior soaking. The tiny sprouts can clog up the water channels of a sprouter.

Cress: Rinse 2–3 times a day, spread out flat. Preserving jars and sprouting devices are unsuitable because of the mucilage formed.

Lentils: Soak for up to 10 hours and rinse twice a day. Ready after 4 days. Use unhulled lentils only.

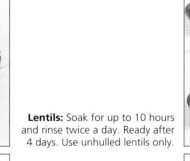

Mung beans: Easy to sprout; ready after 3–5 days with twice-daily rinsing. Must be blanched before eating.

Dried peas: Soak for 12 hours and sprout for 5 days. Rinse twice a day. Hulled peas may also be sprouted.

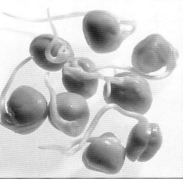

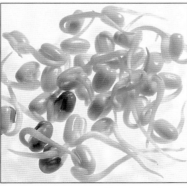

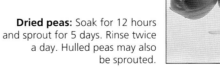

Pumpkin seeds: The sprouts are ready after 3–4 days. Rinse once a day. These work particularly well in a preserving jar.

Mustard: Sprout the seeds in flat bowls or on plates, rinsing once a day. Ready to eat after 4 days.

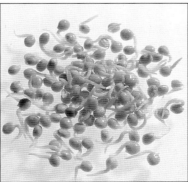

Basic stocks are easy to prepare in large quantities and then freeze. It is usually advisable to freeze the stock in small portion-sized containers. Thoroughly defatted meat stocks keep for about 6 months when frozen. Vegetable stock can be stored for up to a year, although it will lose some of its flavor over time.

TOMATO ESSENCE

Tomatoes provide color and flavor to this superior mixture of vegetable bouillon and meat stock, provided they are aromatic outdoor fruits. Canned peeled tomatoes also make a useful contribution. Finely ground beef clarifies the essence, and the liquid proteins exuded give the essence a concentrated flavor that cannot be achieved with vegetables alone.

Makes 5–6½ cups
7 ounces carrots, 4 ounces celery root
14 ounces boneless shin of beef, 1 cup thinly sliced leeks
½ caramelized onion (see page 155), finely chopped
½ clove garlic, finely chopped
2 sprigs thyme, 1 sprig rosemary
1 sprig basil, 1 bay leaf
1 clove, 5 allspice berries
10–12 white peppercorns
10 crushed ice cubes, 8 egg whites
1 tablespoon balsamic vinegar
1¾ pounds beefsteak tomatoes, finely chopped
2¼ pounds canned peeled tomatoes
1 cup white wine, salt

The method is shown in the step-by-step illustrations and described below.

VEGETABLE STOCK

Not as strong or as rich as meat stock, but vegetable stock is light, aromatic, and low in fat. Leftovers from trimming and shaping almost any sort of vegetable can be used, although too much cabbage will give a pungent taste. Celery root, too, should be used with caution. Asparagus and mushroom trimmings, on the other hand, lift the flavor. Carrots and diced tomatoes give the vegetable stock an attractive golden color.

Makes 6–8 cups
2 onions
2 tablespoons butter
4 ounces broccoli stalks
9 ounces leeks, 11 ounces carrots
7 ounces celery root, 15 ounces zucchini
1 cup white wine, 13 cups water
½ caramelized onion (see page 155)
1 sprig each thyme and rosemary
1 bay leaf, ½ clove garlic, finely chopped
1 clove

The method is shown in the step-by-step illustrations and described below.

TIP: Do not add salt to basic stocks, since they could become too salty when further reduced.

Tomato essence: Peel the carrots and celery root. Put the carrots and celery through the medium plate of a meat grinder, together with the beef. Stir in the leeks, onion, garlic, herbs and spices, ice cubes, egg whites, and vinegar. Add the fresh and canned tomatoes, the wine and a pinch of salt. Transfer to a large saucepan and bring to a boil, stirring constantly. When a scum forms and the meat rises to the surface, reduce the heat, and simmer for 15 minutes. Pour through a strainer lined with cheesecloth into a clean pan, bring to a boil again, and skim.

Vegetable stock: Peel and coarsely slice the onions. Melt the butter and sauté the onions until lightly colored. Wash all the remaining vegetables, dice, and add to the pan. Sauté briefly. Pour in the white wine and water. Add the caramelized onion, the herbs and seasonings. Bring to a boil over a medium heat, and simmer for about 30–40 minutes, skimming frequently. Pour the vegetable stock through a cheesecloth-lined strainer into a clean pan. Return to the heat, bring to a boil and cook until reduced to 6–8 cups.

Preparing chicken stock:

Rinse the boiling fowl inside and out with cold water and place in a large saucepan. Add the water and bring to a boil.

Simmer gently over a low heat for 40 minutes, occasionally skimming off the scum and fat that rise to the surface.

Tie the vegetables and herbs together in a bundle. Add to the stock, together with the caramelized onion.

Simmer for 1 further hour over a very low heat. Remove the boiling fowl with a slotted spoon or skimmer.

Carefully ladle the stock through a cheesecloth-lined strainer into a clean pan. Return to the heat and, if necessary, skim off the fat once more.

Bring to a boil and cook until reduced by about a half to two-thirds, depending on how it is to be used.

Caramelized onion: When roasted without any fat, the sugars and proteins contained in the onion caramelize and combine. This has the dual effect of lending more color and flavor to the stock.

Vegetable stocks are not the classics that meat and chicken stocks are, but creative cooks seriously concerned with healthy eating have developed superb vegetarian recipes.

Basic stocks and sauces
THE AROMATIC BASIS FOR ASPICS, SAUCES, SOUPS, AND BRAISES

In strictly vegetarian cuisine, stocks made from mixtures of vegetables and herbs are used. However, meat- or poultry-based stocks lend greater substance and a more rounded flavor to many vegetable dishes.

CHICKEN STOCK

Makes 6–8 cups
1 boiling fowl, about 4–6 pounds
14 cups water
1 carrot, 1 celery stalk
½ leek
½ clove garlic
1 sprig thyme, 1 bay leaf, 1 clove
½ caramelized onion (see right)

Substituting 2¼ pounds of veal or beef bones and a calf's foot for the boiling fowl will produce a rich meat stock. Whichever variant of the recipe you use, it is important to season carefully, preferably only after the dish is finished—otherwise the liquid becomes too strong-tasting when reduced. The method for making a light chicken stock is shown in detail in the step-by-step photographs (right).

Dashi
A DELICATELY AROMATIC, ALMOST CLEAR STOCK FROM JAPAN

The lightness and subtlety of Japanese cuisine is reflected in this extract of fish and seaweed. Unlike Western stocks, which usually need to simmer for a long time, dashi is ready after a few minutes' boiling, a completely fat-free liquid with a mild but distinctive taste. Kombu, a mild-tasting variety of dried seaweed is placed in a saucepan of cold water and heated so gently that as soon as the first bubbles appear on the surface of the water, the cooking process is over. The second step requires katsuobushi—shaved flakes of dried bonito, a fish similar to tuna. The clear seaweed stock is briefly brought to the boil with the dried fish flakes and absorbs their flavor. After it has been poured through a strainer lined with cheesecloth, it can be used as a base for soups, sauces, hot pots, and vegetable mixtures. The proportions of water, seaweed, and fish flakes are variable. The stock has a delicious taste when flavored, for example, with a few dried shiitake mushrooms. The step-by-step photographs (below) illustrate the method in detail.

Preparing dashi: To make 3½ cups stock, sponge off the white powder from ¾ ounce kombu with a damp cloth. Bring to a boil over 10–15 minutes in 4 cups water over a very low heat. When bubbles rise to the surface, check whether the seaweed is soft. If not, continue to cook for 1–2 minutes. Remove the kombu from the pan. Add 5 tablespoons cold water to the pan. Sprinkle 1 ounce bonito flakes into the pan and bring back to a boil. Remove from the heat. When the flakes have sunk to the bottom, pour the stock through a cheesecloth-lined strainer.

BAGNA CAUDA

This sauce from the Piedmont region of Italy is served hot and provides an aromatic "bath" for raw and cooked vegetables. Fennel, Belgian endive, radicchio, bell peppers, zucchini, and carrots, as well as cardoons, Jerusalem artichokes, celery, and almost any other vegetable in season may be used. As with many other regional dishes, the recipe varies from cook to cook. The basic recipe, consisting of the finest quality olive oil and butter, seasoned with garlic and anchovies, is often lightened with a little cream, milk, or red wine.

Serves 4–6
12 anchovy filets
⅞ cup extra virgin olive oil
6 cloves garlic, finely chopped
11 tablespoons chilled butter, diced, salt

Soak the anchovies in water for about 30 minutes. Pat dry and chop finely. Heat the olive oil over a low heat and add the garlic. Gradually beat in the butter, one piece at a time, until fully incorporated. Stir in the anchovies and season with salt. Keep the bagna cauda warm on a hot plate or in a bain marie. Do not allow the sauce to boil, or it will separate.

Tip: To regulate the temperature, stir a dash of red wine or milk into the sauce before putting it on the hot plate. The butter and oil mixture will then remain at a constant 212°F until the liquid has evaporated. In the hot sauce alone, the garlic could easily turn too dark and bitter. The sauce will separate if kept warm for any length of time, but this does not affect the taste.

Green sauces to accompany vegetables
CLASSICS OF MEDITERRANEAN CUISINE

Salsa verde from the Piedmont region of Italy is a typical summer sauce (far right). Served cold, it not only rounds out poached meats and cold fish or poultry, but also serves as a dip for vegetables cooked al dente or fried in batter. Ligurian pesto (right) is made from an incomparably harmonious quartet: basil, garlic, olive oil, and Parmesan cheese. This sauce can also be made in a food processor or blender.

SALSA VERDE

Serves 4–6
2 tablespoons red wine vinegar
salt, freshly ground white pepper
⅞ cup olive oil
2 shallots, 1 clove garlic
¾ cup each curly and flat leaf parsley leaves
¼ cup basil leaves
3 anchovy filets, 3 cornichons
1 tablespoon toasted pine nuts, 1 tablespoon capers

Stir together the vinegar, salt, and pepper until the salt dissolves. Add the olive oil. Finely chop or slice the remaining ingredients and add one at a time.

PESTO

Serves 4
1¼ cups pine nuts
3 cloves garlic, 1 teaspoon salt
11 cups basil leaves
⅔ cup freshly grated pecorino cheese
2 cups freshly grated Parmesan cheese
2¼ cups olive oil

Pound the pine nuts, peeled garlic, and salt to a smooth paste in a mortar with a pestle. Add the basil and pound it to a paste. Pour the mixture into a bowl and add the pecorino and Parmesan cheeses. Stir in the olive oil. Store in the refrigerator.

TIP: Pesto, covered with a layer of oil, will keep for several days in the refrigerator. However, the higher its moisture content, the more readily it turns moldy. Wash the basil leaves well in advance of making the pesto, so that they are completely dry. Aged, dry cheeses absorb a great deal of herb juices in the mortar, reducing the moisture content of the pesto and improving its keeping qualities.

RAMSON PESTO

Strong-flavored ramson leaves give this paste an assertive note. In any case, it is not to be confused with traditional pesto, which is prepared with basil and garlic.

(not illustrated)
Serves 4
1¼ cups pine nuts
1 teaspoon salt
5 cups ramson leaves
5 cups flat leaf parsley
⅔ cup freshly grated pecorino cheese
2⅓ cups freshly grated Parmesan cheese
2¼ cups olive oil

Pound the pine nuts and salt in a mortar with a pestle to a smooth paste. Add the ramson and parsley leaves and pound to a paste. Pour the mixture into a bowl and mix in the grated cheeses. Stir in the olive oil.

TOMATO SAUCE

(top)

Makes 2¼–2½ cups

1 large celery stalk

3 medium carrots

2¼ pounds tomatoes

1 shallot

½ clove garlic

2 tablespoons olive oil

1 sprig each rosemary, basil, and thyme

1 bay leaf, 1 clove, 3 allspice berries

10 white peppercorns, salt

1 tablespoon balsamic vinegar, ¼ cup white wine

Trim and finely slice the celery. Peel the carrots and slice finely. Dice the tomatoes and finely chop the shallot and garlic. Proceed as shown in the step-by-step photographs (left).

TIP: If no fragrant outdoor-grown tomatoes are available, it is better to use canned peeled tomatoes than greenhouse varieties, since the quality of the tomatoes makes or breaks this sauce.

Preparing a tomato sauce: Sauté the shallot and garlic in the oil until translucent, then add the carrots and celery and sauté briefly. Add the herbs, spices, and seasonings, then the diced tomatoes. Pour in the vinegar and white wine. Bring to a boil and cook for 15–20 minutes, until slightly reduced. Before serving, strain or purée coarsely. Reduce again if necessary.

PUMPKIN SAUCE

(center)

Serves 4

1¼ pounds pumpkin

1 shallot, 2 tablespoons butter

1 teaspoon curry powder

salt, freshly ground white pepper

½ cup white wine, ⅞ cup white port

1 cup vegetable stock (see page 154)

½ cup light cream, 1 tablespoon heavy cream

Peel and seed the pumpkin and dice the flesh. Finely chop the shallot. Proceed as illustrated in the step-by-step photographs (below).

TIP: Adding a chopped, tart apple to the mixture produces a delicious combination of flavors. The curry powder may then be omitted.

Melt the butter and sauté the shallot until translucent. Add the pumpkin and continue to sauté over a low heat. Sprinkle the curry powder into the pan and season to taste with salt and pepper.

Add the wine, port, and stock. Bring to a boil and cook until reduced by half. Stir in the light cream. Cook until the pumpkin is tender. Purée, strain, and swirl in the heavy cream just before serving.

Vegetable-based sauces

SUPERB ACCOMPANIMENTS TO FISH, MEAT, AND VEGETARIAN DISHES

Probably the most popular vegetable sauce in the world, tomato sauce is godfather to numerous variations. Tomatoes are cooked, sometimes in stock, always with herbs and seasonings. The mixture is then reduced and rubbed through a strainer. The sauces are lent body mainly by the pectin content of the ripened tomatoes. Early and greenhouse varieties often do not provide enough flavor and substance.

Remove the pan from the heat and add the grated horseradish. Set aside to allow the flavor to develop.

Rub through a strainer and season to taste. Reheat, but do not boil, or the horseradish may lose its flavor and become bitter. Fold in the heavy cream.

YELLOW BELL PEPPER SAUCE

This sauce can also be made with red or green bell peppers. A particularly attractive effect is achieved when the sauce is prepared in all three colors.

(not illustrated)
Serves 4
1 tablespoon butter
1 shallot, finely chopped, ½ clove garlic, finely chopped
1 pound yellow bell peppers, seeded and diced
1 sprig thyme, 1 bay leaf
salt, freshly ground white pepper
1⅔ cups sweet white wine
¼ cup white wine
⅔ cup vegetable stock (basic recipe, page 154)
¼ cup light cream

Prepare the sauce as illustrated (below).

Melt the butter and sauté the shallot and garlic until translucent. Add the bell peppers and herbs, and season with salt and pepper. Stir in the wine and stock.

Cook the vegetables over a low heat until tender. When the stock has reduced by half, add the cream, and continue cooking until the bell peppers are soft.

Purée the sauce with a hand-held blender. Rub through a fine strainer and season with salt and pepper to taste again, if necessary, before serving.

TIP: For a heartier sauce, a mixture of bell peppers and onions can be used. First sauté the onions, covered, over a low heat until soft. Continue with the remainder of the recipe. Seasoned generously with cayenne pepper, the bell pepper and onion sauce tastes delicious with vegetables such as pumpkin, chayote, and zucchini.

HORSERADISH SAUCE

Horseradish is both a seasoning and a vegetable and horseradish sauce complements roasts, boiled meat, or oily fish, and also goes well with vegetables, such as boiled potatoes.

(bottom)
Serves 4
1¼ cups vegetable stock (see page 154)
⅔ cup each milk and light cream
5 ounces horseradish root
2 slices white sandwich bread, crusts removed
salt, freshly ground white pepper
dash of lemon juice, 1 tablespoon heavy cream

Peel the horseradish and grate finely. Set aside 1 tablespoon to garnish. Cut the white bread into cubes. Proceed as described below.

TIP: Add the horseradish as soon as it has been grated, as its aroma and flavor quickly deteriorate.

Bring the vegetable stock to a boil, together with the milk and cream. Lower the heat and simmer gently for about 5 minutes. Add the bread cubes and cook briefly.

HOLLANDAISE SAUCE

Makes 1 cup
3/4 cup butter, 1 shallot
1 sprig each tarragon and parsley
1/2 bay leaf
4–6 white peppercorns
2 tablespoons white wine vinegar
2 tablespoons water, 8 tablespoons white wine
3 egg yolks
salt, cayenne pepper
dash of lemon juice

Heat the butter until the whey has separated out and almost entirely evaporated. When light brown spots form, remove the pan from the heat and cool slightly. The rest of the method is described in the step-by-step photographs (below).

VELOUTÉ

Makes about 3 cups
2 tablespoons butter
1 shallot, finely chopped
1/4 cup flour
2 1/4 cups vegetable stock (see page 154)
1 cup heavy cream
salt, freshly ground white pepper

This classic sauce goes with most vegetables. Depending on how you intend to use it, chicken or veal stock may be substituted for the vegetable stock. It is the length of cooking time which makes or breaks the quality of the velouté. If it is cooked too briefly, it will have a sticky, floury taste. The starch grains in the flour break down only after about 5–10 minutes' cooking time, producing a velvety texture. The method is described in the step-by-step photographs (below).

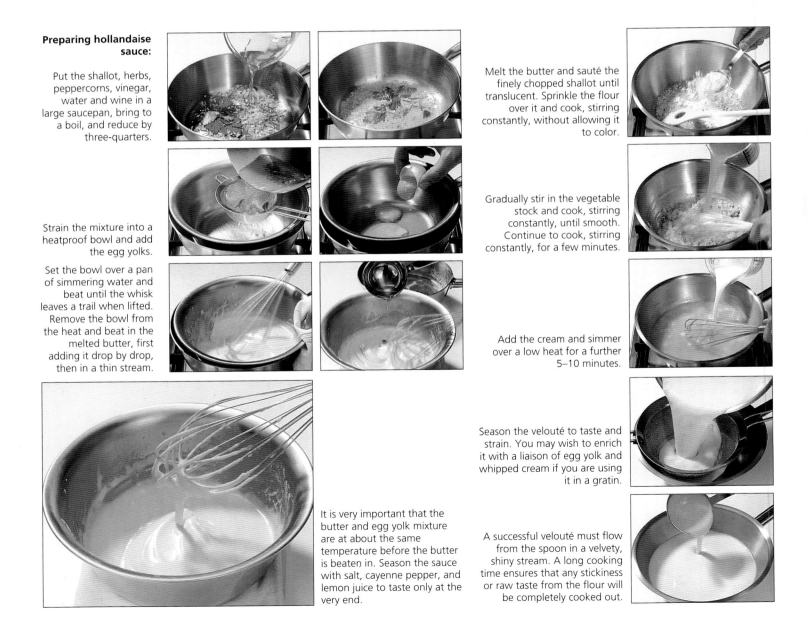

Preparing hollandaise sauce:

Put the shallot, herbs, peppercorns, vinegar, water and wine in a large saucepan, bring to a boil, and reduce by three-quarters.

Strain the mixture into a heatproof bowl and add the egg yolks.

Set the bowl over a pan of simmering water and beat until the whisk leaves a trail when lifted. Remove the bowl from the heat and beat in the melted butter, first adding it drop by drop, then in a thin stream.

It is very important that the butter and egg yolk mixture are at about the same temperature before the butter is beaten in. Season the sauce with salt, cayenne pepper, and lemon juice to taste only at the very end.

Melt the butter and sauté the finely chopped shallot until translucent. Sprinkle the flour over it and cook, stirring constantly, without allowing it to color.

Gradually stir in the vegetable stock and cook, stirring constantly, until smooth. Continue to cook, stirring constantly, for a few minutes.

Add the cream and simmer over a low heat for a further 5–10 minutes.

Season the velouté to taste and strain. You may wish to enrich it with a liaison of egg yolk and whipped cream if you are using it in a gratin.

A successful velouté must flow from the spoon in a velvety, shiny stream. A long cooking time ensures that any stickiness or raw taste from the flour will be completely cooked out.

Sauces to accompany vegetables

FOUR TRADITIONAL RECIPES TO ADD THE FINISHING TOUCH TO MANY DISHES

Velouté owes its velvety texture to a thoroughly cooked flour and butter mixture. The red wine and shallot butter is prepared with cold butter. Hollandaise sauce and sabayon get their airy consistency from being beaten with egg yolks. A sabayon (right) must be browned under the broiler at once or it will collapse.

RED WINE AND SHALLOT BUTTER

Makes about 1¼ cups
6 tablespoons chilled butter
½ cup finely chopped shallots
1 sprig thyme
½ cup red port
2¼ cups full-bodied red wine
salt, freshly ground white pepper
3 tablespoons beet juice (optional)

Melt 1½ teaspoons of the butter in a saucepan and sauté the shallots until translucent. Add the thyme, port, and red wine. Bring to a boil and reduce over a low heat until the shallot is only just covered with liquid. Meanwhile, dice the remaining butter. Remove the thyme from the pan and stir in the diced butter, one piece at a time. Do not allow the sauce to boil. Season with salt and pepper and stir in the beet juice, if using, just before serving.

To make the red wine and shallot butter, the wine, port, and diced shallots must boil until well reduced. The stronger-tasting and more aromatic the red wine, the more substantial the sauce. Beat in the chilled butter cubes to make a creamy emulsion. Beet juice gives a deeper color to the sauce, which can, however, fade if it is left standing too long or it is brought back to a boil.

SABAYON

Makes about 1 cup
1 bunch fresh herbs, such as cilantro or parsley
1 cup white wine
¼ cup chicken stock (see page 155)
1 shallot, finely chopped, 4–5 white peppercorns
3 egg yolks, salt, dash of lemon juice

A sabayon can be varied according to taste. The herbs, for example, can be replaced by other seasoning ingredients or stock. Flavorful accents can be lent by caraway, honey, and shallots, ginger and oranges or limes, mustard, horseradish, or beer. Put the herb leaves and stalks, the wine, stock, shallot and peppercorns in a saucepan and bring to a boil. Boil over a low heat until reduced by half. Strain into a heatproof bowl. Continue according to the step-by-step pictures (below).

Preparing a sabayon:

Add the egg yolks to the heatproof bowl and set over a pan of gently simmering water. Beat the mixture until the whisk leaves a trail when it is lifted.

Season to taste with salt and lemon juice. Add 1 tablespoon chopped fresh herbs, if desired. Pour the sabayon onto cooked vegetables and brown under the broiler.

Salads, appetizers, and cold soups

Understandably the great traditions of preparing salads, cold appetizers, and cold soups originated in countries with warm climates. It is no coincidence that the most important salad dressing in the world is vinaigrette, and that it is of French origin. The famous gazpacho, a chilled soup made from raw vegetables, comes from Spain. Dips and dressings are American inventions. Raw vegetables have a great deal to offer, and not only in terms of taste. Nutritionists advocate that we eat them at least once a day, since vegetables are at their healthiest served this way: heat- and light-sensitive vitamins and minerals are preserved, along with color, texture, and fiber.

SALAD OF WILD VEGETABLES: The ingredients for this salad of wild herbs and vegetables can be prepared after a country walk in the spring. Use whatever fresh, edible plants are available. For the example shown here, pick over, wash, and dry 7 ounces watercress, 3½ ounces ramson, 9 ounces dandelion leaves, and 3½ ounces sorrel, then combine them in a salad bowl. You could also add 3 ounces young nettle leaves, but take care. First place the nettle leaves between two dish cloths and roll over them carefully with a rolling pin to flatten the prickles. Prepare 2 ounces narrow-leafed plantain, ¾ ounce daisies, and 1½ ounces spoonwort and mix with the other herbs. To make the dressing, mix the juice of 1 lemon with salt, pepper and a pinch of sugar. Stir in 7 tablespoons sunflower oil, pour over the wild herbs, toss, and serve.

TOMATO VINAIGRETTE

Wash 1¼ pounds beefsteak tomatoes and dice the flesh. Sauté 1 diced shallot and ½ clove garlic in 4 tablespoons butter until translucent. Add the tomatoes, the leaves of 1 sprig of thyme, a pinch of salt, freshly ground black pepper, and ½ finely chopped fresh chile. Bring to a boil and reduce over a medium heat for 6–8 minutes. Rub the sauce through a strainer set over a bowl. Cool, then stir in 2 tablespoons red wine vinegar and 4 tablespoons olive oil. Add 1 tablespoon each diced tomato and snipped chives, and season with salt and pepper.

HERB DIP

Mix together ⅔ cup unsweetened yogurt and ⅔ cup crème fraîche or sour cream with a pinch of salt, freshly ground pepper, and the juice of ½ lemon. Wash and finely chop 3 cups fresh mixed herb leaves, such as chervil, tarragon, basil, parsley, watercress, sorrel, dill, and marjoram. Stir them into the dip and serve immediately.

TUNA DIP

Drain a 6-ounce can of tuna in oil and purée the fish in a blender or food processor. Transfer to a bowl and stir in 3 tablespoons mayonnaise until smooth. Chop 2 tablespoons capers and add to the tuna mixture, together with 1 tablespoon snipped chives. Season with salt and pepper.

Dressings, dips, and sauces

COMPLEMENTARY SAUCES FOR CRUDITES

Crudités are simply a raw vegetable platter: a selection of trimmed vegetables cut to the right size for dipping, arranged decoratively on a serving plate. Any raw vegetable that can be eaten with the fingers is suitable: celery stalks, hearts of lettuce, carrots, strips of bell pepper, cauliflower flowerets, cucumber sticks, and many more. Choose a vegetable, dunk it into one of the well-seasoned, thick dips and nibble away. This enjoyable and healthy way of serving vegetables as an hors d'oeuvre or as part of a cold buffet is very popular.

BLACK OLIVE DIP

Stir 3 tablespoons black olive paste (tapenade), together with 4 tablespoons lukewarm chicken stock until smooth. Mix in 3 tablespoons balsamic vinegar and 7 tablespoons olive oil. Season with freshly ground black pepper.

AVOCADO AND BASIL DIP

Halve and pit 2 soft, ripe avocados (about 7 ounces each) and scoop out the flesh with a spoon. Dice about 2 tablespoons of the flesh and finely purée the remainder with the juice of 1 lemon, ½ clove garlic, a pinch of salt, and freshly ground white pepper. Mix in the diced avocado and 1 tablespoon finely chopped basil. Adjust the seasoning to taste.

MAYONNAISE

Mayonnaise is the basis of many classic cold sauces, such as rémoulade, Chantilly, and tartar sauce. Mayonnaise is prepared as below.

Place 3 egg yolks in a bowl and, with a balloon whisk, beat together with a little mustard, a pinch of salt, freshly ground white pepper, and a dash of lemon juice.

Add ⅔ cup olive oil, drop by drop, beating constantly. It is important for all the ingredients to be at the same temperature—otherwise they will not bind smoothly.

Add a further 1⅓ cups olive oil in a continuous thin stream, still beating constantly.

Stir in 1 tablespoon warm water to stabilize the mixture. The finished mayonnaise should be of a semi-firm consistency.

Aïoli: This garlic mayonnaise is probably the best known of the cold Provençal sauces. It goes with both raw and cooked vegetables, and consists of the simplest variation of mayonnaise: 10 tablespoons mayonnaise, 2–3 crushed cloves garlic, and a pinch of cayenne pepper.

Radishes in contrasting red and white: A checkerboard pattern is cut deep into the radish (top). Large, jagged notches reveal the white (left). Cutting out narrow, vertical wedges at regular intervals gives radishes the appearance of Chinese lanterns (right). Carved radishes "bloom" when placed in ice water.

Cucumbers fanned out attractively. For each of these garnishes you need pieces of cucumber about 1¼–1½ inches long, which can be halved, slit, and notched in different ways. The large arabesque (top), the delicate rosette (right), and the flat, notched fan (left) were made in this manner.

Fresh garnishes from raw vegetables
ALL YOU NEED IS PLENTY OF TIME, A STEADY HAND, AND A SHARP KNIFE

Carved radishes and tomato roses were once the hallmark of haute cuisine, but then fell out of fashion. Today once again, perfectly carved garnishes are appearing on the dishes served by the world's best restaurants. This surely must owe much to the influence of the aesthetically aware cuisines of Asia.

Carving radishes:

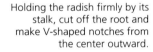

Holding the radish firmly by its stalk, cut off the root and make V-shaped notches from the center outward.

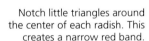

Notch little triangles around the center of each radish. This creates a narrow red band.

Alternatively, hold the radish by its stalk and cut a narrow lattice pattern to no more than half the depth of the root.

For Chinese lanterns, notch the red skin all around the radish to leave narrow, vertical strips.

Making cucumber garnishes:

Fans: Halve 1¼-inch long pieces of cucumber. Notch the peel. Cut the piece of cucumber crosswise into slices joined together on one side. Lay flat and fan out.

A continuation is the rosette: for this, cut off the peel in a ¼-inch thick strip from one side. Do not cut through completely on the other side.

Carefully bend apart the sections with your fingers and fold every second one in on itself toward the center.

Tomatoes: These can be carved to look like roses in full bloom—here in red and yellow—or like buds that have not yet opened. Roses are easy to make: they are rolled from the spiral-cut skin of a firm-fleshed tomato. The buds (see below), on the other hand, require more time, effort, and dexterity.

Scallions: These attractive, unusually shaped curls can be made fairly effortlessly from young scallions. As with the radishes, the carved scallions must be placed briefly in ice water to complete the garnish: only then do the stems curl into decorative rosettes.

Rosebuds:

Cut concentric wedges from the rounded portion of a tomato half so that they can be detached.

Cut the firm part of a scallion crosswise from the top downward. The deeper the cuts, the more the tops curl.

Cut a flap of skin as thinly as possible from the thicker side portions of the tomato and bend outward.

Fan out the individual wedges from bottom to top to form the pointed, bud-like shape.

Tomato roses:

Peel the tomato skin in a continuous spiral of even width—the longer the strip, the better.

Roll up the strip quite tightly with the shiny outer skin on the outside. With your fingers adjust to a rose shape.

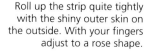

Raw vegetable salads taste better when their ingredients are sliced or shredded finely. However, they look less attractive than salads with ingredients left in larger pieces, so they will require a garnish. The carved radishes, cucumber fans, and young kohlrabi leaf work especially well against the pale background of the kohlrabi salad with a yogurt dressing.

Dandelion salad with walnut dressing: Wash and pat dry 5 cups each of blanched and green dandelion leaves. Dissolve a little salt in 3 tablespoons sherry vinegar. Season with pepper and stir in 5 tablespoons walnut oil. Blanch 2 tablespoons walnut kernels in a little milk, then skin, chop, and add to the dressing. Pour the dressing over the dandelion leaves and toss.

Spinach with sesame vinaigrette: Wash and dry 4½ cups young spinach. Dissolve a little salt in 3 tablespoons red rice vinegar, stir in 6 tablespoons sesame oil, and season with pepper and grated lemon rind to taste. Dry-fry 2 tablespoons hulled sesame seeds until golden brown and add to the vinaigrette. Pour the dressing over the spinach, toss, and serve.

Mâche salad with a potato dressing: Wash 1 pound mâche. For the dressing, thoroughly mash 1 small boiled potato and stir together with 7 tablespoons warm chicken stock, 4 teaspoons white wine vinegar, 4 teaspoons white wine, salt and pepper. Dice 1 small boiled potato and mix with the mâche. Pour the dressing over the salad while still lukewarm.

Belgian endive salad with pumpkin vinaigrette: Trim and wash 8 Belgian endives. Dissolve a little salt in 4 teaspoons white wine vinegar, stir in 3 tablespoons each sunflower oil and pumpkin seed oil, and season with freshly ground pepper. Dry-fry 1–2 tablespoons pumpkin seeds, chop coarsely, and add to the vinaigrette. Pour the vinaigrette over the Belgian endive.

Frisée salad with garlic lardons: Mix together 7 tablespoons olive oil, 3 tablespoons red wine vinegar, 1 crushed clove garlic, and ½ cup crisp-fried bacon strips. Season with salt and pepper. Prepare 2 heads of frisée, place in a bowl, pour the dressing on top, and toss. Cut 2 slices of white bread into cubes, fry in 4 tablespoons butter until golden, then sprinkle them on top.

Ice plant salad with Roquefort dressing: Wash 14 ounces ice plant. Rub ½ cup Roquefort cheese through a strainer, and stir with 4 tablespoons heavy cream and 3 tablespoons sour cream. Season with salt, pepper, and the juice of ½ lemon. Toss the ice plant in the dressing and sprinkle 1½ tablespoons snipped chives on top. You could substitute mâche for the ice plant.

Salads—fresh and leafy

IN ALL SHADES OF GREEN: SALADS WITH SOPHISTICATED DRESSINGS

Absolute freshness is essential for all salad greens and a complementary dressing rounds out the flavor. Dairy products form the basis of light, creamy dressings. Traditional vinaigrette requires only four ingredients: one part vinegar, three parts oil, and salt and pepper to taste. Flavored vinegars, lemon juice, and various oils help ring the changes. Herbs lend a special note, whether used individually or in combination. Mustard enhances flavor and digestibility, and acts as an emulsifier.

Watercress with raspberries: Trim 5½ cups watercress. Mix 1 tablespoon clear honey, salt and pepper to taste, and 4 teaspoons raspberry vinegar. Add 1–2 tablespoons lemon juice. Gradually stir in 4 tablespoons grapeseed oil. Mix together the watercress and 4 ounces bean sprouts. Pour the vinaigrette over the salad and garnish with ⅓ cup fresh raspberries.

Arugula salad with truffle vinaigrette: Wash 6 cups arugula. Mix 3 tablespoons bottled truffle juice with 4 teaspoons each red and white port in a saucepan and reduce by two-thirds. Cool, stir in 4 teaspoons balsamic vinegar, salt and pepper to taste, and 5 tablespoons soy oil. Slice 1 black truffle into strips, add to the vinaigrette, and use to dress the salad.

Fine mixed salad greens with guinea fowl eggs: Wash and dry the leaves of 1 head of frisée, 1 blanched dandelion plant, 1 head each of red and green cicorino, 5 ounces ice plant, 5 ounces mâche, 1 head of red crisphead lettuce, and 2 ounces trimmed and blanched buck's horn plantain (barba di frate). Cut into bite-size pieces and place in a large bowl. For the dressing, mix together 4 teaspoons sherry vinegar, the juice of ½ lemon, salt and freshly ground pepper to taste, and ½ teaspoon Dijon mustard. Gradually beat in 7 tablespoons olive oil until smooth and well blended. Pour the dressing over the salad greens and toss gently. Garnish with 4 guinea fowl eggs that have been boiled for 7 minutes, rinsed in cold water, shelled, and halved.

Radish salad with chive vinaigrette: Wash and thinly slice 14 ounces radishes. Season with salt and freshly ground pepper and let stand for 5 minutes. Blend 4 teaspoons white wine vinegar with 3 tablespoons sunflower oil. Add 1 tablespoon snipped chives. Pour the vinaigrette over the radishes and mix thoroughly to coat.

Carrot salad with orange dressing: Peel 1¼ pounds carrots and cut into matchstick strips. Mix together 3 tablespoons cider vinegar and 7 tablespoons orange juice and season with salt, a pinch of sugar, and freshly ground pepper. Stir 5 tablespoons sunflower oil into the dressing and pour over the salad. Peel 1 orange, cut into segments, and fold into the salad.

FAVA BEANS WITH PINZIMONIO: This Tuscan specialty is prepared by tossing 1½ cups shelled young green fava beans with pinzimonio, an Italian variation of vinaigrette. It is made with 1 tablespoon balsamic vinegar, salt and pepper to taste, and ¼ cup olive oil. In Tuscany, the beans are traditionally eaten raw, although they contain indigestible substances. This salad also tastes good with blanched beans.

Red cabbage salad with apple: Shred 1¼ pounds red cabbage. Add the juice of 1 orange and 1 lemon, 5 tablespoons red wine, and 3 tablespoons balsamic vinegar. Season with salt and pepper. Add ½ shredded apple and the blanched finely pared rind of 1 orange, cut into thin strips, and stir. Marinate for 1 hour. Mix in 7 tablespoons sunflower oil and ½ diced apple.

Cucumber salad with yogurt-dill dressing: Thinly slice a cucumber weighing about 1¼ pounds. Combine 5 tablespoons low-fat unsweetened yogurt, 5 tablespoons sour cream, salt and freshly ground pepper, the juice of ½ lemon and 1 teaspoon finely chopped dill. Pour the dressing evenly over the cucumber slices and garnish with dill sprigs.

"Waldorf" celery root salad: Cut 1¼ pounds celery root into matchstick strips and toss in the juice of ½ lemon. Peel and cut 1 apple into matchstick strips and mix with the celery. Mix together ¼ cup mayonnaise and 5 tablespoons crème fraîche or sour cream and season with salt and freshly ground pepper. Skin ½ cup walnuts and add to the salad with the dressing.

Bamboo shoot salad: Quarter 1 pound cooked bamboo shoots. Seed, dice, and blanch 1 red bell pepper. Mix 7 tablespoons heavy cream, 2 tablespoons creamed coconut, the juice and grated rind of ½ lime, a pinch of grated ginger, a pinch of crushed garlic, 1 teaspoon curry powder, and salt, pepper and a pinch of cayenne pepper. Pour on the dressing.

From raw and cooked ingredients
COLD VEGETABLES WITH SPICY SALAD DRESSINGS

Raw vegetables: the very phrase has a crunchy, health-conscious ring to it. Here we mean finely sliced, grated, or chopped raw vegetables, particularly those more usually served cooked. Raw vegetables as well as salad greens are often served before a meal instead of a traditional appetizer. Just what is a salad, then? The answer is anything that is tossed or drizzled with a dressing and served cold or lukewarm. It may contain raw or cooked vegetables, or a mixture of both. Sometimes it even slips into the role of a main course.

Avocado salad with yogurt-mint dressing: Halve 2 avocados and ease the flesh out of the shells. Slice 3 halves into fans and drizzle with lemon juice. Mix ⅔ cup unsweetened yogurt and 1 tablespoon chopped mint, season with salt, pepper, and lemon juice. Pour the dressing over the fans. Dice the remaining avocado. Garnish the fans with diced avocado and mint sprigs.

Removing avocado flesh from the shells: Halve the avocados and remove the pit. With the aid of a spoon, ease the avocado flesh from its shell. Immediately brush all over with a little lemon juice to stop it from going brown.

Lentil salad with vinaigrette: Soak ⅔ cup each red and green lentils separately for 3 hours in cold water. Boil separately until tender. Slice and blanch 4 ounces carrots, 2 ounces celery, and 4 ounces leeks. Mix 5 tablespoons soy oil, 2 tablespoons red wine vinegar, salt, pepper, and 1 tablespoon snipped chives. Mix the lentils and vegetables and toss in the vinaigrette .

Potato salad: Slice 1¼ pounds boiled potatoes. Put into a bowl and add 4 tablespoons lukewarm beef stock. Mix 3 tablespoons wine vinegar, ½ teaspoon mustard, salt and pepper to taste, and 5 tablespoons corn oil. Pour the dressing over the potatoes. Fry ⅓ cup diced bacon with 4 tablespoons finely chopped onion and fold into the salad, with 1 tablespoon chopped parsley.

Snow peas and Jerusalem artichoke salad: Mix the juice of 1 lime, the finely grated rind of ½ lime, 2 teaspoons red wine vinegar, 2 teaspoons clear honey, 4 tablespoons sunflower oil, and salt and pepper to taste. Peel 9 ounces cooked Jerusalem artichokes, slice, and sauté in peanut oil until light brown. Mix with 9 ounces blanched snow peas and toss in the vinaigrette.

Bean and artichoke salad: Halve 11 ounces cooked green beans. Cut 5 ounces cooked artichoke hearts into wedges. Mix 4 teaspoons sherry vinegar, 2 teaspoons balsamic vinegar, 2 teaspoons cream sherry, ½ teaspoon mustard, salt, sugar, and pepper to taste, 2 diced shallots, 4 teaspoons peanut oil and 4 teaspoons grapeseed oil. Pour the dressing over the vegetables.

Antipasti
UNBEATABLE ITALIAN APPETIZERS, MARINATED IN HERBS AND OIL

In Italy, antipasti are cold dishes served before the main course. Although ham, salami, and seafood predominate in some regions, herb-flavored preserved vegetables are also typical antipasti. These are always served at room temperature, never straight from the refrigerator. It is truly delightful to have several of these usually simple dishes to choose from. Just one antipasto does not make much of an impression—it is the choice that your guests will find stimulating. Vegetables cooked until just tender, fresh Mediterranean herbs, garlic to taste, and the best extra virgin olive oil—the recipe is as simple as that. The finer the oil, the more generously it can be used. Liberally coated with a delicate green, aromatic olive oil, blanched green beans and crushed garlic turn into an experience— and will keep fresh for several days in the refrigerator. Creative cooks take advantage of this principle and turn all kinds of vegetables into an Italian-inspired delight.

ARTICHOKES WITH TOMATOES

(above left)
Serves 4
6 medium globe artichokes
2 shallots, 4 tablespoons olive oil
½ cup white wine, ½ lemon
2 sprigs thyme, 1 sprig rosemary
1 bay leaf, 1½ cloves garlic, finely chopped
salt, 5 white peppercorns, freshly ground white pepper
2 beefsteak tomatoes, 4 teaspoons red wine vinegar

Trim and halve the artichokes and remove the chokes. Sauté the diced shallots in 1 tablespoon

Tomatoes with mozzarella—a dish as delicious as it is simple. Arrange slices of sun-ripened tomatoes and mozzarella cheese alternately on a serving plate. Sprinkle with a pinch of salt, a little black pepper, some fresh basil, and a few olives. Drizzle with good olive oil.

olive oil in a large saucepan. Add the wine, lemon juice, 6¼ cups water, 1 thyme sprig, the rosemary, bay leaf, ½ clove garlic, salt to taste, and the peppercorns. Bring to a boil, add the artichokes and cook for 15–20 minutes, until tender. Drain, reserving 1 tablespoon of the cooking liquid. Peel, seed, and dice the tomatoes. Cut up the artichokes and mix with the tomatoes. Mix the vinegar with the reserved cooking liquid, the leaves of the remaining thyme sprig, and salt and pepper to taste. Stir in the remaining garlic and oil. Pour the sauce over the drained artichokes and tomatoes and marinate for at least 30 minutes.

TIP: You can add 1 clove and 2 allspice berries to the stock for cooking the artichokes.

BELL PEPPERS WITH GARLIC

(center)
Serves 4
2 red, green, and yellow bell peppers
1–2 cloves garlic, 1 tablespoon thyme leaves
4 teaspoons balsamic vinegar
6 tablespoons olive oil
salt, freshly ground black pepper

Halve and core the bell peppers, then roast them in the oven or place under a preheated broiler, skin side up, until their skins blister. When cool enough to handle, peel, cut the flesh into large pieces, and place in a shallow dish. Thinly slice the garlic and mix with the thyme leaves, vinegar, and olive oil. Season generously with salt and pepper. Pour this mixture over the bell peppers and marinate for at least 30 minutes.

BEAN SALAD WITH ROSEMARY

(right)
Serves 4
1¼ pounds cooked or canned and drained white cannellini beans
1 teaspoon sliced fresh red chile
1 teaspoon finely chopped rosemary
2 tablespoons red wine vinegar
salt
freshly ground white pepper
pinch of crushed garlic
6 tablespoons olive oil

Mix together the beans, chile, and rosemary in a serving dish. Combine the vinegar with the salt, pepper, and crushed garlic. Beat in the oil and pour the dressing over the beans. Marinate for at least 1 hour, so that the flavors can develop fully.

TOMATO ASPIC

Makes 4 cups

3½ pounds beefsteak tomatoes

salt, 1 star anise

1 envelope unflavored gelatin

Cut the tomatoes into quarters and blend or process to a fine purée, together with a pinch of salt. Put the mixture into a jelly bag or tie in cheesecloth, suspended over a bowl and drain. Heat about ½ cup of the tomato liquid and steep the star anise in it for 5–10 minutes. Then, sprinkle the gelatin over the warm tomato liquid and leave to soften. Stir to dissolve completely. Add the gelatin to the cold tomato liquid in a continuous stream, stirring constantly. Refrigerate the mixture until it starts to set, but is not yet firm. Proceed according to your recipe; for example, use for vegetable molds, or as below, for a sophisticated aspic.

TIP: If the tomato aspic is poured into a shallow bowl while it is still liquid, this can be set over ice and stirred until the aspic reaches the desired consistency and temperature.

Obtaining raw tomato liquid: Place the fruit flesh in a jelly bag or a piece of cheesecloth and tie with kitchen string. Hang this bag over a bowl to collect the juice as it drips out. As this takes several hours, it is best to let the purée drain overnight.

For this aspic, blanched zucchini and carrot strips, halved quail eggs, lukewarm fried fillets of red mullet, and shrimp tails are arranged in a shallow bowl; semi-liquid gelatin is then poured over.

COLD AVOCADO SOUP

Serves 4

2 ripe avocados (about 7 ounces each)

juice of 1 lemon

1¼ cups buttermilk

⅔ cup chicken stock (see page 155)

salt

freshly ground white pepper

1 tablespoon green peppercorns in brine, rinsed and drained

1 medium eating apple

1½ teaspoons butter

2 tablespoons sugar

1 tablespoon crème fraîche or sour cream

Halve and pit the avocados. Ease the flesh out of the shells with a tablespoon and purée, together with the lemon juice, in a blender or food processor. Stir in the buttermilk and stock. Season with salt, white pepper, and the green peppercorns, and chill. For the garnish, peel, quarter, core, and thinly slice the apple. Trim each slice into a crescent shape. Melt the butter in a skillet and add the sugar and apple. Fry over a medium heat until the apple slices are slightly caramelized. Serve the soup in individual bowls, garnished with the hot apple crescents and a little crème fraîche or sour cream.

TIP: Do not leave the soup standing for too long, since in spite of the lemon juice, it will eventually lose its lovely delicate green color.

GAZPACHO

(background)

Serves 4

1¾ pounds tomatoes, 12 ounces cucumber

9 ounces red, 4 ounces green, and 7 ounces yellow
bell peppers

salt, 2 medium onions

1 clove garlic

4 slices white sandwich bread, crusts removed

7 tablespoons olive oil

freshly ground white pepper

dash of Tabasco sauce, 1 tablespoon balsamic vinegar

Finely dice the tomatoes. Peel the cucumber, scoop
out the seeds, and dice the flesh. Core, seed and
dice the bell peppers. Reserve about 4 tablespoons
of the diced vegetables in the refrigerator. Transfer
the remainder to a large bowl. Sprinkle a little salt
over them and set aside for several hours. Continue
as described in the step-by-step photographs (right).
Season the finished soup to taste with pepper,
Tabasco sauce, and balsamic vinegar. Before
serving, garnish with the reserved diced vegetables.

CHILLED CUCUMBER SOUP

(foreground)

Serves 4

2 pounds cucumbers

salt

1 cup unsweetened yogurt

2 tablespoons finely chopped fresh herbs

Peel the cucumbers. Scoop balls from half of
1 cucumber with a small melon baller and set aside.
Seed and slice the remaining cucumbers. Place the
seeds and cores in a strainer and press out and
reserve the juice. Place the cucumber slices in
a bowl, sprinkle with salt, and set aside
for 1 hour. Put the cucumber in a
food processor with the
reserved juice, and
process. Rub the mixture
through a coarse
strainer. Stir in the
yogurt and chill.
Garnish with the
cucumber balls and
fresh herbs.

Preparing gazpacho:

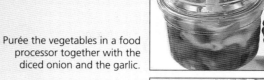

Purée the vegetables in a food
processor together with the
diced onion and the garlic.

Add the cubed white bread
and process until all the
ingredients are smooth.

Pour the vegetable and bread
mixture into a fine strainer and
rub through with a spatula.

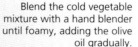

Blend the cold vegetable
mixture with a hand blender
until foamy, adding the olive
oil gradually.

Preparing each bell pepper mousse:
Melt 1½ teaspoons of the butter in a pan. Sauté the shallot and the bell peppers until the shallot is translucent.

Add the thyme, garlic, salt and pepper to taste, the wine and stock. Simmer, uncovered, over a low heat until most of the liquid has evaporated.

Purée the bell pepper mixture with a hand blender until uniformly smooth.

Vivid colors and attractive shapes make sophisticated vegetable-based hors d'oeuvre particularly tempting—especially when the garnish is right and the plate looks perfect. For uniform cone shapes from a light-textured mousse, dip a large spoon in hot water and pierce the mousse vertically with the tip. Rotate the spoon around its own axis and lift out the cone.

Rub the bell pepper purée through a fine strainer to remove the remainder of the skin and the seasonings.

Dice the remaining butter. Briefly heat the purée and gradually incorporate the diced butter with a hand blender.

Dissolve the gelatin in ½ cup water. Stir in the dissolved gelatin, adding it in a continuous stream. This is most easily done while the purée is still slightly warm.

Cool the purée. Add the lemon juice, and fold the cream into the purée. Pour into a bowl and smooth the surface.

Pour the individual purées into the bowl, chilling each layer for 10 minutes before adding the next. Cut out cone shapes using a spoon rinsed in hot water. Serve with cubes of tomato aspic (see page 174) and a chive vinaigrette.

Elegant hors d'oeuvre
TERRINES AND MOUSSES

TRICOLOR MOUSSE

Serves 4
For each color:
11 ounces bell peppers
1 shallot, 4½ teaspoons chilled butter
1 sprig thyme, pinch of crushed garlic
salt, freshly ground white pepper
3 tablespoons white wine, ½ cup chicken stock
⅓ envelope unflavored gelatin dash of lemon juice,
5 tablespoons heavy cream, stiffly whipped

Following this basic recipe, the mousse can be prepared in green, yellow, and red layers. Seed and finely dice the bell peppers. Dice the shallot and follow the step-by-step instructions (left).

VEGETABLE TERRINE

Serves 15 as an hors d'oeuvre

20 scallions, about 2¼ pounds pumpkin

30 green beans, 25 small carrots, 3 green kohlrabi

2 heads of broccoli, 4 leeks

For the mushroom cream:

1½ pounds white mushrooms, finely chopped

½ cup butter, 1 shallot, finely chopped

½ clove garlic, crushed

1 sprig each thyme and rosemary

½ bay leaf

salt, freshly ground black pepper

½ cup white wine, 3 cups heavy cream

1¼ cups milk, 1 envelope unflavored gelatin

Trim the scallions, beans, and broccoli. Peel and seed the pumpkin and slice the flesh. Peel the carrots. Halve the leeks. Peel and slice the kohlrabi. Cook all the vegetables separately in lightly salted boiling water until just tender. Drain and rinse in cold water. Sauté the mushrooms in butter, together with the shallot. Add the garlic, herbs, and seasoning. Add the white wine and reduce by half. Add the cream and milk and simmer until the mushrooms are tender. Strain into a clean pan, reserving the mushrooms. Return the cream and milk mixture to the heat, and reduce to 3 cups. Add the reserved mushrooms and purée with a hand blender until foamy. Dissolve the gelatin in ½ cup cold water. Add the gelatin in a continuous stream to the mushroom cream, stirring. Cool slightly, then follow the step-by-step instructions (far right).

ARTICHOKE MOUSSE WITH LOBSTER

Serves 4 as an hors d'oeuvre

1 lobster (about 1¼ pounds)

3 egg yolks

salt, freshly ground white pepper

1 tablespoon chicken stock (see page 155)

3 tablespoons butter, melted

1 envelope unflavored gelatin

1 cup artichoke purée (made from 6 artichoke hearts)

1 cooked artichoke heart, finely diced

2 tablespoons heavy cream, whipped

2 tablespoons crème fraîche or sour cream

dash of lime juice

1 cup caviar

radicchio di Treviso, mâche, frisée

Bring plenty of water to a rolling boil in a large saucepan and drop in the lobster. Bring back to a boil, then reduce the heat and cook for about 8 minutes, or until it has changed color. Lift out the lobster, rinse with cold water, and crack open. Cool, then remove the meat from the shell. Place the egg yolks, salt and pepper to taste, and the chicken stock in a heatproof bowl. Set the bowl over a pan of gently simmering water and beat until the whisk leaves a trail when lifted. Remove the bowl from the heat and slowly mix in the lukewarm melted butter. Soften the gelatin in ½ cup cold water for 3–5 minutes, until translucent. Add the gelatin to the egg yolk mixture in a continuous stream, stirring constantly. Stir in the artichoke purée and the diced artichoke heart. Fold in the whipped cream. Line a 2-cup mold with plastic wrap. Half-fill the mold with half the artichoke mousse. Cover with a layer of lobster meat and pour in the remaining mousse. Smooth the surface. Chill in the refrigerator until set, then turn out and cut into slices. Season the crème fraîche or sour cream with salt and lime juice. Serve the mousse, garnished with the flavored crème fraîche or sour cream, caviar, and salad greens.

VEGETABLE TERRINE: Line a terrine with plastic wrap and cover with blanched leek leaves. Layer the vegetables to produce a decorative cross-section when sliced, alternating with the mushroom cream. Fold the overlapping leek leaves over one another at the top. Chill for at least 2 hours, then turn out and cut into 15 slices. Serve the vegetable terrine on a pool of cold tomato sauce, decorated with a spiral of unsweetened yogurt.

Boiling, steaming, and poaching

THE RIGHT COOKING METHODS FOR THE MOST VARIED VEGETABLES—SUCCESS GUARANTEED

Boiling is such a common cooking method that in a number of languages the terms for cooking and for boiling are virtually synonymous. This section of the book deals with methods of cooking vegetables in or over water or another liquid. Because a watertight, flame-resistant vessel is needed for boiling foods, this simple cooking method was able to evolve only after people had learned how to fire clay, in other words, to make pottery. Just how long it then took until the first soup was bubbling over the fire in a fire-resistant clay pot we do not know. In any case, boiling evolved only long after roasting and barbecuing, some 10,000 years ago. Many cooking methods have evolved from this simple process, leading in each case, to particular results. It makes a significant difference whether a vegetable is cooked in a little or a lot of liquid, in a covered or uncovered pan, or in steam. The immense variety of shapes, colors, structures, and constituents of plant foods demands a range of cooking methods. Boiling in plenty of salted water is ideal for earthy tubers with a firm peel, whereas the color and texture of delicate leaf vegetables are best preserved by brief steaming. There are also vegetables, such as eggplant, which should never be poached, boiled, or steamed.

Cooking methods
WATER—AN ABSOLUTE NECESSITY

Whether you are poaching vegetables very briefly in boiling liquid, steaming them, or simmering them in a covered pan over a low heat in a little stock, water is the essential mediator between the cooking utensil and the vegetable, and its boiling temperature is one of the few reliable constants in cooking. When bubbles rise to the surface and the liquid seethes, there is no doubt that it has reached 212°F and is boiling. However, every rule has its exception: if the water is put under pressure, as in a pressure cooker, the boiling point rises to above 212°F, and the cooking time decreases. Conversely, at high altitudes, where the pressure is lower, water boils at a lower temperature, so the cooking time increases. The operative term here is cooking time, but there is disagreement about exactly what this should be. No one wants to eat vegetables that have been boiled to death, with all the nutrients and color cooked out of them. Equally, when, mainly to preserve their lovely color and shape, they are served half raw, aroma, flavor, and character are also sacrificed. As with so much else, the ideal lies somewhere in between the two extremes.

Boiling
THE CLASSIC METHOD— COOKING IN A BOILING LIQUID

Vegetables as different as broccoli, globe artichokes, and legumes are cooked in plenty of water, but for very different reasons. With broccoli, the aim is to preserve the delicate structure of the flowerets, while simultaneously cooking the tougher stalks and retaining the bright green color. Because of their bulky shape, artichokes need a large pan. If it is too small, the parts touching the side or base could cook more quickly and to a greater extent than the rest of the vegetable. Legumes, on the other hand, which have a very low moisture content, are not only meant to cook when they are boiled, but also to swell, even though most varieties of beans as well as dried peas are soaked in cold water before cooking and have already increased in size. The temperature is right when the surface of the water barely moves at all and only small bubbles rise to the surface. With legumes, the best results are obtained when neither salt nor acid is added to the cooking water. Salt increases the cooking time and acid makes the legumes tough; they should be added only after cooking. Herbs and aromatic vegetables on the other hand, can be added to the pan at the outset. In the case of very long cooking times, the food may first be cooked in water at a rolling boil, then over a medium to low heat, usually with a lid on in order to reduce energy consumption and prevent the water from boiling away too quickly. Admittedly, water-soluble vitamins, minerals, and trace elements will be lost with this method, although less so with unpeeled, whole vegetables, the skins of which stop nutrients from leaching out.

Broccoli flowerets are best cooked in boiling salted water in a large saucepan. The heat is distributed evenly where there is a large quantity of water, so that even the harder stalks cook in the minimum time.

Blanching
COOKED TO PERFECTION, OR UNTIL READY FOR FURTHER PREPARATION

With this method, trimmed vegetables—often cut up—are plunged for a few seconds to 2 minutes in a large quantity of water at a rolling boil, then lifted out, and cooled at once under cold running water or in ice water. Delicate spinach leaves will be cooked in a few seconds; carrot sticks or sliced cabbage should be boiled until only half done and ready for further treatment, such as deep-freezing. Vegetables are blanched because the shock of the heat is thought to deactivate their enzymes. Active proteins are sealed within cell walls in the whole plants and are released only when the vegetables are peeled and thinly sliced or finely diced. Enzymes set a number of undesirable processes in motion: the vegetable discolors, and flavor, vitamins, and texture decrease. Blanching stops enzyme activity, and quick cooling then prevents further cooking in the retained heat. It also preserves colors well. Depending on how finely the vegetables are cut up, nutrient loss is 10–40 percent. A second reason for blanching is that it makes bulky leaf vegetables supple and removes some of their water content. Leeks, cabbage, sorrel, and spinach are often blanched and used as wrappers for stuffings.

For blanching you need a large saucepan and a bowl of the same size or larger. The more water you have at a rolling boil in the pan, the less the temperature drops when the vegetables are added. This is particularly important with short blanching times, as for the spinach leaves and snow peas (above). Transferring the cooked vegetables to a bowl of ice water immediately arrests the cooking process.

Sliced or diced root vegetables, such as carrots, should be brought to a boil in as little water as possible and cooked over a low heat. In this way, both flavor and nutrients are preserved.

Poaching
THE SIMPLEST AND GENTLEST METHOD

This method is used for all sorts of vegetables, especially finely diced or sliced ones, because it preserves the majority of nutrients and flavor. The vegetable is brought to a boil in a minimum of water and cooked until done. Sometimes, no water is added to the saucepan beyond that which clings to the vegetable after washing. Pans with perfectly fitting lids are essential. Poaching achieves really good results, in terms of taste as well as nutrients, chiefly for diced or sliced turnips, carrots, kohlrabi, beets, and other tubers that are fairly rich in sugars and starch. The cooking liquid provides an extract-rich base for sauces, particularly when a seasoned liquid or stock is used in place of salted water. This is advantageous from a nutritional standpoint, since all the nutrients from the cooking water are reused. The drawback is that with larger quantities, the vegetables on the bottom may cook more quickly than those in the center, so that the color and texture of the former suffer and the food is unevenly cooked.

Tip: To preserve the color, texture, and flavor of broccoli and other green vegetables, cook uncovered, at least for the first few minutes. Although this entails cooking at maximum heat and "wasted" energy, the trade-off is that the chlorophyll—the bright green color—is preserved. With this method, the acids contained in the vegetable are driven off with the steam in the first 6–8 minutes of cooking. Otherwise, they react with the chlorophyll, causing the vegetable to turn unattractively gray. This is true whether you are cooking in a large or small amount of liquid.

Thoroughly wash and scrub the potatoes under cold running water. Choose potatoes of the same size so that they cook in the same time.

Place the potatoes in a large pan, pour in enough cold water to cover, and add salt. Cover with a lid.

Cooking in a covered pan
SAVE TIME AND ENERGY WHILE PRESERVING NUTRIENTS

This cooking method is particularly suitable for whole root vegetables and tubers that should be cooked slowly over a moderate heat to preserve their structure and nutrients. For example, when potatoes are cooked too quickly they tend to fall apart. With the relatively long cooking times required, a properly fitting lid helps to save energy. Leaving the vegetables whole and unpeeled helps stop vitamins, trace elements, and minerals from passing into the cooking water. Vegetables cooked whole also taste different. Their outer skins protect the volatile oils and organic acids responsible for imparting flavor. The potato is a good example of this: potatoes boiled in their skins have a stronger taste than peeled, boiled potatoes.

Bring the potatoes to a boil, then lower the heat so that the water is boiling gently.

Cook until the potatoes are completely tender. Test by inserting a sharp knife.

Cooking time varies from 18–30 minutes, depending on variety and size. As soon as the potatoes are done, pour off the water.

The skins of mealy potatoes tend to split open when they are cooked.

Potatoes boiled in their skins cook to perfection in plenty of water. Their skins help stop the nutrients from leaching out. It is a good idea to use a pan with a glass lid so that you can see the vegetables cooking without removing it.

Steaming
WITH AND WITHOUT PRESSURE

Steaming without pressure: Delicate vegetables can be steamed more gently in a perforated steamer over boiling salted water in a covered saucepan than under pressure. This is especially true for those that will cook in 10 minutes or less. It is almost impossible to estimate their cooking time in a pressure cooker. Delicate vegetables can be overcooked very quickly, but steamed without pressure they acquire a good texture and retain their fine flavor. Green vegetables lose some of their bright color, however. Cooking times are often longer than for poaching. Although a temperature of approximately 212°F is reached in the saucepan in both cases, foods cook more slowly in steam than when placed directly in liquid. To prevent the ingredients from coming into contact with the liquid, you will need a petal steamer which can be adjusted to fit any saucepan, or a special steamer insert. A properly fitting lid is particularly important.

Steaming under pressure: The pressure cooker, on the other hand, steams food under pressure, as its name indicates. Old models were not always adjustable, cooking everything at high pressure. Although they cooked quickly, vegetables lost their color, vitamins, and taste. With modern pressure cookers, the food can be cooked at lower pressures and temperatures. This leaves the structure, flavor, vitamins, and minerals largely intact. Depending on the vegetable, savings in time and energy can amount to 70 percent. Using a pressure cooker takes a bit of practice: they should never be filled beyond the level indicated in the instruction manual; otherwise there is a risk of scalding when the lid is removed. For the same reason, ingredients, such as legumes, that tend to swell or foam a great deal should reach no more than halfway up the cooker. Choose vegetables of the same size, or cut them into uniform pieces; otherwise, small pieces will already be overcooked by the time larger pieces are just done. Keep strictly to the cooking time; it is best to set the timer as soon as the valve indicates that the process is underway. When cooking delicate foods, do not cool the cooker in cold water, but reduce the cooking time slightly and wait until the pressure drops and the lid can be opened. This applies especially to potatoes cooked in their skins, which tend to split if subjected to abrupt cooling.

Cook beets before peeling to prevent them from losing all their juices. This method is also recommended for Jerusalem artichokes.

Cooking cauliflower in a pressure cooker:

Pour about 2 cups of liquid in the cooker. The cauliflower should not come into contact with the liquid.

Place the cauliflower in the steamer. Several steamers can be placed one above the other or side by side, depending on the type of cooker, provided that the different vegetables require the same cooking time.

Place the lid on top and lock. Heat to the lowest pressure. When the valve pops up, the cooking process has begun. Time carefully.

Let the steam escape completely and the pressure drop before opening the lid.

Preparing and cooking artichokes:

Snap off the stalk directly under the base of the head. This pulls tough fibers out of the artichoke heart.

Tear off the small tough leaves around the base of the stalk.

Trim the prickly tips of the leaves to an even length with a kitchen knife.

With firm, rounded, compact artichokes, cut off just the tips of the leaves. With loose, elongated varieties, cut off up to one-third.

With a large, sharp knife, even out the base of the stalk. This makes it easier to tie the artichoke.

A small plate or lid used as a weight keeps the artichokes submerged, allowing them to cook evenly.

Place a slice of lemon on the base of each stalk. Tie firmly crosswise with kitchen string.

To test whether the artichokes are ready, pull a leaf out of the center of one. If it comes away easily, the heart is tender. Lift out the artichokes and drain upside down thoroughly.

To prevent discoloration, place the prepared artichokes in water acidulated with lemon juice until required.

Twist out the light leaves from the center of the artichoke.

Do not cover the saucepan with a tight-fitting lid; otherwise the acids cannot escape and the vegetables will turn from green to gray.

Using a melon baller or small spoon, lift out the choke from the artichoke base.

ARTICHOKES IN VEGETABLE BUTTER

Serves 4

2 lemons, 4 large globe artichokes
salt, 2 tablespoons oil
For the vegetable butter:
2 medium carrots, 2 celery stalks
1 small leek, 1 shallot, 6 tablespoons chilled butter
⅔ cup white wine, ⅞ cup port
1 teaspoon white wine vinegar
freshly ground black pepper
1 teaspoon chopped tarragon

Cut 4 slices from 1 lemon and set aside. Squeeze the juice from the others. Tie the artichokes and lemon slices together as shown (left). Bring a large pan of salted water to a boil, add the lemon juice, oil, and artichokes and simmer for 15–20 minutes. Dice and blanch the carrots, celery, and leek. Slice the shallot and sauté in 2 tablespoons of the butter. Add the wine and port, bring to a boil, and cook until reduced by two thirds. Dice the remaining butter and beat it into the mixture, one piece at a time. Add the blanched vegetables and season with salt, pepper, and tarragon. Drain the artichokes and remove and discard the string and lemon slices. Hollow out the artichokes and divide the lukewarm vegetable butter among them.

Sophisticated vegetables cooked whole

ARTICHOKES AND ASPARAGUS COOKED TO PERFECTION

Not only are fine vegetables, such as asparagus and artichokes, traditionally cooked whole, they are also served and eaten whole, often with the fingers. Their true qualities, however, only shine fully when they are accompanied by a sauce.

Asparagus: variations on a theme

To make the most of these delicious spears, make a stock from the peel and trimmings and cook the asparagus in it. At the height of the asparagus season, when the same stock can be used several times, the flavor becomes concentrated and it can be used as the basis of thickened sauces and soups. In addition to the classic melted butter or hollandaise sauce, cold sauces and dressings, such as vinaigrette, are becoming increasingly popular.

ASPARAGUS WITH MOREL MUSHROOM CREAM

Serves 4
14 ounces each green and white asparagus
4 ounces fresh morel mushrooms
1 shallot, finely chopped
4 tablespoons butter, 7 tablespoons white wine
½ cup each milk and light cream
salt, freshly ground white pepper
½ lemon, ½ teaspoon sugar
1 tablespoon heavy cream

Peel the asparagus and wrap it in a damp cloth. Trim the mushrooms, reserving the trimmings. Sauté the shallot and the morel trimmings in 2 tablespoons of the butter. Add the white wine, bring to a boil, and reduce to about 2 tablespoons. Add the milk and cream, reduce to a creamy consistency, and strain. Season with salt, pepper, and a dash of lemon juice. Bring 11 cups of water to a boil with ½ teaspoon salt, the sugar, and a slice of lemon. Tie the asparagus in a bundle and cook in this liquid for 10–12 minutes. Sauté the morel mushrooms in the remaining butter. Season with salt and pepper and stir into the sauce, together with the heavy cream. Drain the asparagus. Cut off the lower third of the spears, dice, and add to the sauce. Serve the sauce with the asparagus spears.

TIP: To serve as illustrated, pour the morel mushroom cream into a puff pastry shell.

Boiled asparagus—a mouthwatering feast. The tender spears are among the few vegetables that can stand on their own as the focal point of a meal, turning meat into a thoroughly optional side dish. A sauce made from sautéed shallots and wine, reduced, and thickened with chilled butter, is ideal with a mountain of asparagus. Before serving the cooked spears, it is important to drain them thoroughly; otherwise the sauce will not coat them properly.

People are seldom able to eat their fill of fresh vegetables in fashionable restaurants (here, broccoli and cauliflower flowerets, kohlrabi "teardrops," and decoratively shaped zucchini slices), as nutritionists advise. Vegetables are often more a decorative garnish than a major item of the menu.

advisable to choose an equally robust vegetable. Besides classic sauces, such as hollandaise, velouté, or sabayon, and a bacon and onion mixture for stronger-tasting vegetables, the traditional knob of butter is still in first place when it comes to adding an extra touch. For Mediterranean vegetables, a drizzle of olive oil is a good addition at the last moment before serving. Dairy products can round out the flavor of boiled or poached vegetables. Light or heavy cream mixed with fresh herbs, goes well with almost any vegetable. Tangy dairy products, such as crème fraîche, sour cream, or unsweetened yogurt perfectly complement starchy vegetables, such as carrots, beets, corn, and peas, pleasantly counterbalancing their sweetish note. Vegetables sprinkled with toasted seeds and nuts not only taste good, but this also supplements their nutritional value. Even earthy-tasting vegetables, such as rutabaga and white cabbage, may benefit from the flavor of toasted sunflower or sesame seeds, peanuts, or cashews. Herbs, too, not only round out and enhance the taste of boiled vegetables, but also lend a decorative splash of green.

Boiled vegetables as a side dish
FRESH SEASONAL VEGETABLES: SIMPLE AND ATTRACTIVE

Boiled, steamed, or poached vegetables form the basis of a number of dishes which, served as an accompaniment, make a meal complete. Boiling is probably the most popular method of preparation, although it is frequently misused. All too often, the goodness is boiled out of vegetables, and flavor, color, and vitamins are lost. By following a few simple rules, you will be rewarded with the full flavor of tender green beans, delicate asparagus, or crisp baby corn. The vegetable side dish must not overpower the main dish. In addition, its flavor should complement the sauce, fish, or meat. With strong-tasting dishes, such as roasts or stews, it is

Asparagus with butter: The simplest of all asparagus dishes is also the most popular and delicate. The heartier green asparagus as well as the more delicate white spears are boiled and thoroughly drained, arranged on warm plates, and only then liberally coated with melted butter. The better the quality of the butter, the more delicious the dish.

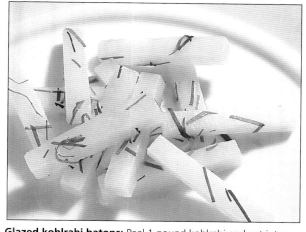

Glazed kohlrabi batons: Peel 1 pound kohlrabi and cut into batons. Cook in boiling salted water until tender, but still firm to the bite. Drain and sauté in 1½ teaspoons butter. Season to taste and add 2 tablespoons vegetable stock or kohlrabi cooking water. Reduce until the batons are coated with a glistening sauce. Stir in 1 teaspoon chopped parsley and serve.

Baby corn with tomato: Cook 11 ounces baby corn in boiling salted water until tender. Drain and rinse under cold water. Peel, seed, and dice 1 tomato. Melt 2 tablespoons butter in a pan and add the corn. Season with salt, sugar, and pepper. Add 4 tablespoons vegetable stock. Once the sauce has reduced, remove the corn, heat the tomato in the sauce, and serve.

Brussels sprouts with bacon: Trim 14 ounces Brussels sprouts and cut a cross in the base of each. Cook in boiling salted water until tender. Sauté 1 tablespoon each of diced bacon and finely chopped shallots in 1½ teaspoons butter. Drain the Brussels sprouts, add to the pan, and toss in the butter. Season with a pinch of salt, white pepper, and a pinch of nutmeg.

Cauliflower polonaise: Cut 2 pounds cauliflower into flowerets and cook in salted boiling water until tender. Melt 2 tablespoons butter in a pan and sauté ⅓ cup white bread crumbs until golden. Chop 1 hard-cooked egg and add to the pan, with 1 teaspoon chopped parsley and a pinch of salt. Drain the cauliflower and serve with the bread crumb mixture.

Glazed Swiss chard bundles: Peel 9 ounces Swiss chard stalks, cut into batons, and blanch. Cut 1 Swiss chard leaf into long, thin strips and blanch. Pile the batons into little bundles, tie together with the strips of leaf, and sauté in 2 tablespoons butter. Season with salt, add 4 tablespoons vegetable stock, and cook until reduced and the bundles are shiny with the glaze.

Spinach with garlic: Blanch 1¾ pounds trimmed spinach and rinse in cold water. Squeeze out as much moisture as possible with your hands. Sauté 1 finely diced shallot in 2 tablespoons butter. Add the spinach, season to taste with a pinch of chopped garlic, salt, freshly ground black pepper, and nutmeg, toss thoroughly, and serve.

Using a potato masher: Cook peeled potatoes in boiling salted water until tender. Drain, return to a low heat briefly to dry, and mash the potato pieces to a smooth purée.

Puréeing with a hand blender: Cook yellow split peas until very soft. Purée to a fine mush with a hand blender. Unhulled varieties will also need to be rubbed through a strainer.

Mealy potatoes are particularly good for mashing. Slightly waxy types are also suitable. Waxy early potatoes, however, retain too much moisture.

Adding the liquid: Heat a little milk, or a mixture of light cream and milk. Add butter to taste and melt in. Season with salt and mix into the potatoes, stirring gently.

Although starchy vegetables can be puréed on their own, they become smoother when butter or olive oil is added. Strain to remove peel and vegetable fibers.

Beat, but not too hard: Beat the potato purée with a whisk until light, but do not beat too hard or for too long, or it will become tough and sticky.

Light and creamy
TECHNIQUES FOR PURÉEING BOILED VEGETABLES

A smooth vegetable purée can serve as a side dish, thicken a sauce, or give body to a soup. According to type and the recipe, different techniques are used. The most important of these are shown here. Light mashed potatoes, for example, can be achieved only by hand, using a potato masher. Both a food processor and a hand blender make the purée tough and sticky, because they break down the cell walls of the potato, causing the starch to leak out. Beating the potatoes hard and heating them both reinforce the unpleasant effect still further. This, by the way, is true for all starchy tubers, such as Jerusalem artichokes, sweet potatoes, and yams.

This is how mashed potato should look: creamy and smooth. More liquid is required to achieve this consistency with mealy potatoes than with slightly waxy varieties.

CELERY ROOT PURÉE

Cooks often need a vegetable purée that is not too moist for coloring pasta dough or for terrines, savory puddings, and dumplings. In particular, young vegetables that are not yet fully ripe sometimes have too little dry matter. It is best to dice and cook them until very soft and press out all the water before puréeing, as described in the following step-by-step photographs.

Serves 4
14 ounces boiled celery root (about 1¼ pounds raw)
¾ cup chilled butter, diced
salt
freshly ground white pepper
butter, for greasing

Thinly sliced, tender, cooked carrots can be rubbed through a fine strainer with a ladle or wooden spoon.

Drying and puréeing:

Line a potato ricer with fine cheesecloth and spoon in the cooked, drained, and diced celery root.

Gently close the ricer several times to make room for more celery root. This allows you to work more efficiently.

Press until part of the vegetable juice has drained off. The puréed celery root can be used in many different recipes.

Alternatively, purée the freshly cooked hot celery root with the diced butter. Season and process to a smooth, creamy consistency.

The more liquid removed from the vegetables, the firmer the consistency of the purée.

CARROT TIMBALES

Serves 4
14 ounces carrot purée (1¼ pounds raw carrots)
8 egg yolks
salt
freshly ground white pepper

Preheat the oven to 350°F. Beat together the carrot purée and the egg yolks. Season with salt and pepper. Generously butter four timbale molds or ramekins. Fill with the carrot mixture to just under the rim. Gently tap the timbales on the counter to allow any air bubbles to escape, then place them in a roasting pan. Add sufficient hot water to come halfway up the sides and bake in the oven for about 20 minutes, or until a toothpick inserted in the center comes out clean. Note that the water should only simmer and not boil—otherwise the mixture will rise too much and be too full of holes. Invert the timbales onto plates and serve.

To make savory timbales from many types of vegetables—even from trimmings—mix the puréed vegetable with egg yolks, pour into molds, and cook in a water bath until just set.

BEET SAUCE

Serves 4–6

2¼ pounds beets
1 shallot, finely chopped
3 tablespoons chilled butter
salt, freshly ground white pepper
pinch of caraway seeds
1 tablespoon balsamic vinegar
¼ cup white wine
2¼ cups vegetable stock (see page 154)

Peel and slice the beets. Reserve about one third and process the remainder in an electric juicer or food processor. Sauté the shallot in 2 teaspoons of the butter. Add the reserved beet and sauté briefly. Season with salt, pepper and caraway seeds and add the balsamic vinegar, then the white wine and vegetable stock. Simmer over a low heat until tender. Reserve 2 tablespoons of the beet juice. Put the remainder in a pan, bring to a boil, and reduce to a very small amount. Dice the remaining butter and beat it into the juice, one piece at a time. Cool and chill. Purée the cooked beet mixture and rub through a strainer. While it is still hot, beat it vigorously into the chilled beet butter. Stir in the reserved juice just before serving.

TIP: This sauce goes just as well with vegetable dishes as with fish and meat. The vegetable stock may be replaced by a meat or fish stock.

FENNEL SAUCE

Serves 4–6

1 medium fennel bulb
4 tablespoons butter, 1 shallot, finely chopped
salt, freshly ground white pepper
½ teaspoon anisette
¼ cup white wine
2¼ cups vegetable stock (see page 154)
1 cup light cream, 1 tablespoon heavy cream

Trim the fennel, reserving the green fronds. Cut the bulb into thin slices and finely chop the fronds. Melt the butter in a pan and sauté the shallot until translucent. Add the fennel bulb, season with salt and pepper, and sauté briefly. Add the anisette and white wine. Pour in the vegetable stock and reduce by half over a low heat. Add the light cream and cook the fennel until tender. Purée finely, rub through a strainer, and fold in the heavy cream. Add the chopped fronds and season once more with salt and pepper to taste.

CHILLED LEEK AND POTATO SOUP

Combining potatoes and leeks is popular and guarantees a good result: a real warming winter soup. This recipe, a variation of classic Vichyssoise, proves that this combination is suitable for a summer meal.

Serves 4
¾ pound mealy potatoes
3 tablespoons butter
salt, freshly ground white pepper
¼ cup white wine
3 cups vegetable stock (see page 154)
1 medium leek
1 cup fresh herb leaves (parsley, chervil, tarragon, sorrel, dill)
1 teaspoon lemon juice
1 teaspoon balsamic vinegar
dash of Tabasco sauce
⅔ cup crème fraîche or sour cream

Peel, and slice the potatoes. Melt 2 tablespoons of the butter in a pan and sauté the potato slices. Season with salt and pepper and pour in the white wine. Add the vegetable stock and cook the potatoes over a low heat until tender. Meanwhile, halve the leek lengthwise, wash, and cut into thin slices. To make the herb butter, wash and dry the herbs, and strip the leaves from the stalks. Place in a blender or food processor with the remaining butter and process until smooth. Spread on a plate and chill. Add the leeks to the soup and cook for 10 minutes, then process in a food processor or blender. Add the chilled herb butter and process again. Strain the soup and season to taste with lemon juice, balsamic vinegar, and Tabasco sauce. Refrigerate the soup and serve well chilled, garnished with the crème fraîche or sour cream.

TIP: Lukewarm fried quail eggs, gravlax, smoked salmon, or caviar would make an elegant garnish.

Sauces and soups
THE BASIS FOR BOTH: A FINE VEGETABLE PURÉE

Vegetable sauces are the creations of modern-day cooks. A potato soup, on the other hand, served warm or cold, is one of the best-loved classics. With all variations, finely puréed and strained vegetables provide flavor, thickening, and character.

CREAM OF JERUSALEM ARTICHOKE SOUP

Jerusalem artichoke makes a very interesting alternative in vegetable cookery. Although not related to the globe artichoke, they have a slightly similar taste.

Serves 4
11 ounces Jerusalem artichoke purée (made from 1¼ pounds Jerusalem artichokes)
1⅔ cups vegetable stock (see page 154)
7 tablespoons milk
¼ cup light cream
salt
freshly ground white pepper
dash of lemon juice
2 tablespoons heavy cream
1 sprig of lemon balm

Bring the Jerusalem artichoke purée to a boil, together with the stock, milk, and light cream, and reduce to a creamy consistency. Season to taste with salt, pepper, and lemon juice and fold in the heavy cream. Garnish with lemon balm leaves.

Snow pea soup (far right) can be enriched with pan-fried fish or strips of poultry. Chopped herbs and diced tomatoes complement the **cream of Jerusalem artichoke soup** (right).

SNOW PEA SOUP

A snow pea purée is well suited to light soups or hors d'oeuvre. Because of their fine, delicate taste, snow peas can be successfully combined with many different ingredients.

Serves 4
14 ounces snow pea purée (made from 1¼ pounds snow peas)
1¼ cups chicken stock (see page 155)
⅔ cup chilled butter, diced
salt, sugar
freshly ground white pepper

Prepare the snow pea purée as described on the right. Bring to a boil with the chicken stock. Beat in the chilled butter, one piece at a time, with a hand blender or balloon whisk. Season the soup with salt, sugar, and pepper to taste and serve in warm soup bowls.

To make the snow pea purée, cook the pods until tender, purée in a food processor, and rub through a fine strainer with a spatula.

Cream soups
PURÉED VEGETABLES PROVIDE COLOR AND FLAVOR

A food processor and strainer are crucial tools here, since only an evenly blended and very fine purée of tender vegetables thickens the soup stock. Cream is often added to round out the taste.

CREAM OF PUMPKIN SOUP

(top)
Serves 4
2¼ pounds pumpkin, 2 shallots, 2 tablespoons butter
salt, freshly ground white pepper
cayenne pepper, curry powder
4 teaspoons white port, 5 tablespoons white wine
juice of ½ lime
2½ cups chicken or vegetable stock (see page 155 or 154)
1 cup heavy cream, 1 tablespoon crème fraîche or sour cream

Peel and seed the pumpkin and dice the flesh. Chop the shallots. Prepare as described in the step-by-step photographs (below). Before serving, garnish each portion with a swirl of crème fraîche or sour cream.

Sauté the shallots in the butter until translucent. Add the pumpkin and sauté briefly. Season to taste with salt, white pepper, cayenne pepper and curry powder, and add the port, white wine, and lime juice.

Bring to a boil and reduce by half. Add the stock and reduce by half again. Add the heavy cream and simmer until the pumpkin is tender. Purée and rub through a fine strainer.

Caviar croûtons are an unusual and luxurious garnish for soup. Cut or stamp out small rounds from white bread and fry in butter until golden brown. Cool and top with caviar.

CREAM OF SCORZONERA SOUP

(bottom)
Serves 4
3 tablespoons milk, 1 tablespoon lemon juice
3½ pounds scorzonera
2 shallots, finely chopped
5 tablespoons butter
salt, freshly ground white pepper
7 tablespoons white wine, juice of ½ lime
4 cups chicken or vegetable stock (see page 155 or 154)
2¼ cups heavy cream
1 small bunch chervil

Mix about 4 cups salted water with the milk and lemon juice in a bowl. Peel and dice the scorzonera and immediately put it into this mixture to prevent it from discoloring. Sauté the shallots in the butter until translucent. Add the drained scorzonera and salt and pepper to taste and sauté briefly. Add the wine and lime juice. Bring to a boil and reduce by half. Pour in the stock and cook until reduced by half, then add the cream. When the scorzonera is tender, purée the soup and rub through a strainer with the back of a wooden spoon. Adjust the seasoning, if necessary, and garnish with chervil.

TIP: Truffle gnocchi (potato gnocchi prepared with truffles) make a wonderful soup garnish.

ARUGULA SOUP

(center)
Serves 4
1 pound arugula
3 shallots, 6 tablespoons chilled butter
salt, freshly ground white pepper
7 tablespoons white wine
3½ cups chicken stock (see page 155)
1⅔ cups heavy cream

Pull the arugula leaves off the stalks, reserving the stalks, and set aside. Chop 2 shallots. Sauté the arugula stalks with the chopped shallots in 3 tablespoons of the butter until translucent. Season with salt and pepper and add the wine. Bring to a boil, reduce by half, then add the chicken stock. Reduce by half, then add the cream. Cook for 5 minutes and rub through a strainer. Blanch the arugula leaves, rinse in cold water, and squeeze dry. Finely chop the remaining shallot. Heat 1 teaspoon of the remaining butter and sauté the remaining shallot with the arugula leaves. Remove from the heat. Dice the remaining butter and beat it into the arugula mixture, one piece at a time. Chill in the refrigerator. Bring the soup to a boil again and beat in the arugula butter, one piece at a time, with a hand blender. Season and serve.

SPINACH ROULADE SOUP GARNISH

For the crêpe batter:
½ cup all-purpose flour
½ cup milk, 4 tablespoons water
salt, 2 egg yolks, lightly beaten
2 tablespoons butter, melted
1 teaspoon clarified butter
For the filling:
7 ounces spinach, 1 egg yolk
½ teaspoon all-purpose flour
salt, nutmeg
1 slice white sandwich bread, crusts removed

To make the crêpe batter, sift the flour into a bowl and beat in the milk and water. Season with the salt and beat in the egg yolks. Slowly stir in the melted butter, strain and let rest for 30 minutes. Fry 4 thin crêpes in the clarified butter, cut into squares, and set aside to cool on a sheet of plastic wrap. To make the filling, blanch the spinach, squeeze dry, and purée in a food processor with the remaining ingredients. Spread this mixture on the crêpes, roll them up, and wrap in plastic wrap. Tie the ends tightly with string and cook in hot, but not boiling, water for 15 minutes. Rinse briefly in cold water, remove the plastic wrap, and slice the roulades into rounds. Use to garnish hot soup while still warm.

SPINACH ROULADE: Purée the filling ingredients and spread onto the crêpes. A reliable method of rolling the crêpes is to place them on a piece of plastic wrap. Gently raise the plastic wrap on one side, and the roll virtually forms itself. To cook, wrap in plastic wrap and secure the ends tightly with string. After cooking, rinse with cold water, remove the plastic wrap, and slice the roll into rounds.

Peel and thinly slice the parsley root and shallots, then sauté in the butter. Season to taste, add the vermouth and wine, bring to a boil, and reduce by half. Add the stock and boil until the parsley root is tender.

Strain the parsley root stock and chill. To clarify, put the peeled parsley root and the peeled carrot, together with the beef, through a meat grinder.

Transfer this mixture to a large saucepan. Stir in the egg whites, followed by the remaining clarifying ingredients. Pour in the chilled parsley root stock.

Bring the stock to a boil, carefully stirring at the base of the pan. Lower the heat as soon as a white scum forms at the edge.

Once all the clarifying meat has risen to the surface, simmer the soup for a further 10 minutes over a low heat, then pour the consommé through a strainer lined with cheesecloth. Season once more to taste and serve in warm bowls.

Clarified with meat
A CLEAR BOUILLON OR THE BASIS FOR HEARTY SOUPS

Although preparing a consommé takes a lot of time and effort, the result is worth the trouble. This clear, highly aromatic and rich soup will always impress your guests. The soluble protein components of the beef not only bind the cloudy substances, they also fortify and harmonize the taste of the vegetable stock. An especially important requirement for preparation is a piece of clean cheesecloth. It should be rinsed in clean water and wrung out before use to remove any residual detergent which could spoil the fine aroma and flavor of the consommé.

PARSLEY ROOT CONSOMMÉ
Serves 4

2¼ pounds parsley roots, 2 shallots
3 tablespoons butter
sugar, salt, freshly ground white pepper
1⅔ cups dry white vermouth, ⅔ cup white wine
8 cups chicken stock (see page 155)
For clarifying the stock:
7 ounces parsley roots, 1 carrot
14 ounces beef knuckle, 5 egg whites, salt
½ caramelized onion (see page 155), unpeeled
1 bay leaf, 1 sprig of thyme, 1 clove
¼ clove garlic, 2 allspice berries
5 crushed ice cubes

Prepare the parsley root consommé as described in the step-by-step photographs (left).

Tip: A well-roasted onion half will give the consommé a golden-yellow color. Either place the cut surface of the onion on an electric burner or dry-roast it in a cast iron skillet until dark brown.

Poached quail eggs and strips of snow peas make a delightful garnish for consommé.

ASIAN VEGETABLE SOUP WITH A FISH GARNISH

This is a combination well worth trying—with dashi, the light vegetable and fish stock as a base, and exotic vegetables and fish as a "filler."

Serves 4
3 ounces lotus root
4 ounces yam
7 ounces scallions
2 ounces winter squash
1 teaspoon cornstarch
⅞ cup sunflower oil
¾ pound brill or sole fillets
3½ cups dashi (see page 156)
1 lemon grass stalk
1 small fresh chile
2 Japanese ginger flowers (about ¾ ounce each), halved
¼-inch piece fresh ginger root, cut into thin strips
¼ ounce chrysanthemum leaves
¾ cup finely chopped Chinese chives
salt, 1 lime

Peel the lotus root and yam and cut into slices. Trim and thinly slice the scallions. Cut the squash flesh into batons, sprinkle with the cornstarch, and sauté in sunflower oil. Cut the fish into bite-size pieces. Bring the dashi to a boil with the lemon grass, simmer briefly over a low heat, and strain into a clean pan. Halve, seed, and dice the chile and add to the stock. Add the lotus root, ginger flowers, and ginger root and simmer over a low heat for about 10 minutes. Add the yam and scallions and simmer for 5 minutes. Add the squash, chrysanthemum leaves, and Chinese chives. Remove the pan from the heat, season to taste with salt, and add the fish to the piping hot soup just before serving. Quarter the lime and hand with the soup, so that everyone can season his or her portion to taste.

TIP: The brill can be replaced by fillets of other delicate flatfish. It is important to cook the fish pieces in the hot broth without heating the stock any further. This preserves the flavor at its best and keeps the fish firm and juicy. If the soup bowls are well warmed beforehand, the hot broth may even be ladled straight into them over the uncooked fish.

MINESTRONE

Serves 4

2 large celery stalks, 4 medium carrots
2 medium waxy potatoes
7 ounces peas in their pods
4 ounces fresh white beans, such as cannellini
5 ounces cauliflower, 4 ounces zucchini
7 ounces leeks, 4 small tomatoes
2 tablespoons butter, 1 tablespoon olive oil
salt, freshly ground white pepper
8 cups chicken stock (see page 155)
¾ cup small pasta, such as stelline, ditalini, anellini
4 ounces pancetta or bacon
1 onion, 2 cloves garlic
1 tablespoon chopped parsley

Slice the celery, carrots and potatoes. Shell the peas and beans. Divide the cauliflower into flowerets. Slice the zucchini and leeks. Peel and seed the tomatoes and cut the flesh into strips. Heat the butter and olive oil in a large pan. Add the celery, carrots, potatoes, peas, beans, and cauliflower and season with salt and pepper. Sauté briefly, then add the chicken stock and bring to a boil. Add the pasta and cook for 5–8 minutes. Add the zucchini and leeks and simmer for 20 minutes. Meanwhile, chop the pancetta or bacon, onion, and garlic and sauté over medium heat until the onion is translucent. Add to the soup, with the tomato strips and parsley. Serve immediately.

Irish stew, made with cabbage and lamb, is a typical example of an oven-braised meat and vegetable dish.

Stews and soups
WHAT UNITES AND DIVIDES THESE REGIONAL SPECIALTIES

The earthier relatives of soups come in many guises: sometimes with plenty of braised meat and substantial enough to eat with a fork. One of the most famous soups in the world is probably the Italian "minestrone di verdure," which is made in an almost infinite number of regional variations. The simplest version is prepared as follows. Chopped and sliced vegetables are cooked in water, sometimes with garlic and herbs, and when the soup has been served, a few drops of olive oil are added to the bowls. This soup becomes more substantial when based on a stock. Rice may be substituted for the pasta to give the soup body. Similar dishes can be found throughout the world. They may be cheap and filling with plenty of starch, or aromatic and sophisticated with delicate-tasting vegetables. In Germany, such a varied vegetable soup was sometimes called "straight through the garden," to indicate that any vegetable was suitable. Scotch broth contains barley, in addition to lamb or mutton stock, turnips, carrots, and leeks. The national dish of Portugal is *caldo verde*, a green cabbage soup with potatoes and sausage. In Eastern Europe, earthy cabbage stews with beets often appear on the menu.

PROVENÇAL BEAN STEW

Green beans are surely one of the ideal vegetables for stews, particularly with lamb. Bean stews—with or without a substantial garnish—can be found in all countries and regions. In Provence, plenty of inexpensive pork belly is added, and the stew is seasoned strongly with fresh herbs.

Serves 6
2¼ pounds green beans
3 medium carrots
1¾ pounds waxy potatoes
1 onion, 1 clove garlic
2 celery stalks
4 tablespoons olive oil
1¼ pounds pork belly, diced
8 cups sieved tomatoes
2¼ cups vegetable stock (see page 154)
1 bay leaf, 1 sprig each of thyme, rosemary, basil, savory, and lavender
salt, freshly ground white pepper
1 tablespoon chopped parsley

Trim the beans. If necessary, string them, then cut into pieces. Peel and thinly slice the carrots, potatoes, onion, and garlic. Slice the celery. Heat the olive oil over a low heat and fry the pork until browned. Add the onion and garlic and sauté until translucent. Add the remaining vegetables and sauté briefly. Stir in the sieved tomatoes and the vegetable stock. Tie the herbs loosely together to make a bouquet garni and add to the pan. Simmer over a low heat for 15–20 minutes, then season with salt and pepper, and remove the bouquet garni. Sprinkle with the parsley before serving.

VEGETABLE STEW

This is a completely vegetarian dish, prepared with a vegetable stock.

Serves 4
3 medium carrots
½ red and yellow bell peppers
11 ounces small potatoes
5 ounces parsley roots or parsnips
4 ounces baby turnips, 1 large celery stalk
4 ounces green beans, 11 ounces peas in their pods
4 ounces zucchini, 7 ounces scallions
7 ounces broccoli, 3 tablespoons butter
salt, freshly ground white pepper
10½ cups vegetable stock (see page 154)

Peel the carrots, bell peppers, potatoes, parsley roots or parsnips, and turnips, and cut into equal-size pieces. Chop the celery. Trim the beans and halve or quarter them. Shell the peas. Cut the zucchini in half and then into slices. Trim and halve the scallions. Trim the broccoli and separate into flowerets. Melt the butter in saucepan and briefly sauté the prepared vegetables. Season with salt and pepper and pour in the stock. Simmer gently for 10–15 minutes, then serve at once.

Cut vegetables into pieces that will require about the same cooking time. After sautéing them in butter (top), add the stock (above) and cook briefly until the vegetables are tender, but still firm to the bite.

RISOTTO OF RADICCHIO DI TREVISO

A good risotto is moist. The grains of rice should be tender, but firm. This is easiest to achieve in a heavy-based saucepan, as it conducts heat evenly. Season sparingly to begin with, since the cheese and stock often provide enough salt.

(bottom)
Serves 4 as a side dish or 2 as a main dish
1 shallot
¼ clove garlic
3 tablespoons butter
1 cup risotto rice
salt
⅔ cup white wine
2¾ cups chicken stock (see page 155)
7 ounces radicchio di Treviso
¾ cup shaved or grated Parmesan cheese

Prepare the risotto as described in the step-by-step instructions (below).

There are over 40 varieties of Italian rice to choose from when making risotto, although not all of them are available in every country. Arborio rice (top) is a top-quality risotto rice and is widely exported. The brilliant white Carnaroli (above) absorbs very large amounts of liquid and is therefore highly regarded in Italy.

Finely dice the shallot and garlic and sauté in 2 tablespoons of the butter until translucent. Add the rice and cook, stirring constantly, until it is translucent. Add a pinch of salt.

Pour in the white wine. Cook, uncovered, until the liquid has reduced by half.

Simmer, uncovered, for about 15 minutes, stirring frequently and gently, gradually adding enough chicken stock just to cover the rice.

Add the sliced radicchio and heat briefly. Stir in the grated Parmesan and top with thin shavings of the remaining butter or more Parmesan cheese, if desired.

Rice and vegetables
JUICY AND TENDER—A CLASSY COMBINATION

Where rice grows, vegetables grow too. These ingredients, with or without meat, are combined in the world's kitchens into an infinite variety of dishes. A tempting idea for just such a dish comes from the Veneto region of Italy. Selected vegetables are combined with a good stock and the round grains of the local rice to create risotto. Fluffy long grain rice with glazed baby vegetables is also appealing. There is a difference between the two dishes. With risotto, the rice swells in the stock and is cooked with the vegetables, creating a creamy, moist dish. With the fluffy rice, the rice is boiled in salted water, while the vegetables are cooked separately in stock and a little sugar. Only when both are done are they mixed together.

GOBO RISOTTO

(left)

Serves 4 as a side dish, 2 as a main dish
2 tablespoons butter, 1 shallot, diced
1¼ pounds edible burdock root or scorzonera
1 cup risotto rice, ⅔ cup white wine
3¼ cups chicken stock (see page 155)
1 leek, ⅓ cup grated Parmesan cheese
2 tablespoons heavy cream, salt

Melt the butter and sauté the shallot. Slice the burdock root or scorzonera and add to the pan, with the rice. Sauté briefly, then add the wine and reduce by half. Simmer, stirring, for 15 minutes, gradually adding more stock as it is absorbed. Cut the light green part of the leek into strips, add to the pan, and cook until the rice is tender. Stir in the cheese and 1 tablespoon of the cream. Season and garnish with the remaining cream.

RICE WITH SPRING VEGETABLES

Serves 4 as a side dish
⅓ cup long grain rice
7 ounces green asparagus, 1 cup baby carrots with tops
5 ounces young turnips, 1 green kohlrabi
1 shallot, chopped, 3 tablespoons butter
2 teaspoons sugar
1½ cups vegetable stock (see page 154)
7 ounces scallions, thinly sliced
freshly ground white pepper

Cook the rice in lightly salted boiling water for 20 minutes. Cut the asparagus, carrots, turnips, and kohlrabi into bite-size pieces. Sauté the shallot in the butter until translucent. Stir in the sugar and add the asparagus, carrots, turnip, kohlrabi, and stock. Cook, uncovered, until the stock has almost evaporated and the vegetables are glossy. Add the scallions and cook for 3 minutes. Drain the rice, add to the vegetables and heat through together. Season to taste with freshly ground pepper.

Glazed vegetables with spring rice: instead of cooking the rice and vegetables together, as with risotto, the glazed vegetables are mixed with boiled rice after cooking.

WAKAME SOUP
WITH BAMBOO SHOOTS

Young, tender bamboo shoots are especially popular in Japan. This delicacy is available fresh only in the months of March and April. At about the same time, fresh wakame seaweed is also available.

4 ounces fresh wakame
12 ounces cooked bamboo shoots
¾ ounce bonito flakes
For the stock:
3½ cups dashi (see page 156)
7 tablespoons sake (Japanese rice wine)
3–4 tablespoons mirin (Japanese sweet rice wine)
2 tablespoons soy sauce, 1 tablespoon sugar, salt
⅔ cup sliced scallions, to garnish

Rinse the wakame and poach for 10–15 minutes in lightly salted water. Drain, trim, and slice into wide strips. Cut out the hard parts of the bamboo shoots, rinse, halve, and place in cold water. Tie the bonito flakes in a piece of cheesecloth. Put the dashi, sake, mirin, soy sauce, sugar, salt to taste, bamboo shoots, and bonito flakes in a large saucepan and bring to a boil. Lower the heat and simmer for 15 minutes. Remove the pan from the heat. Remove and discard the bonito flakes. Set the pan aside for 10 minutes, then return to the heat, add the wakame, and simmer for a further 5 minutes. Serve the soup, garnished with sliced scallions.

This is an original Japanese recipe, known as *Wakatake-ni*: a successful combination of two complementary vegetables—one crunchy, one tender.

Cooking with sea vegetables
A STAPLE FOOD IN JAPAN, A GOURMET TREND IN THE WEST

They all taste of the sea: mild, reddish-purple dulse and spinach-green sea lettuce from Atlantic and Pacific waters, thin brown haricot vert de mer or sea spaghetti from the coast of Brittany, and translucent green wakame which grows along the beaches of Japan. These sea vegetables, which are low in calories but extremely rich in nutrients, are so popular in Japan that underwater farms produce delicate varieties by the ton—yet they do not usually form the centerpiece of a meal, but rather dot the culinary "i" as a side dish. Most varieties do not taste salty, but are sprinkled with coarse salt for shipping. They should be rinsed in cold running water to remove it. Dried sea vegetables from Japan are also available and must be soaked before use. While soaking they absorb so much water that they expand to 4–7 times their dried volume. Dried seaweed may be cut up with a pair of scissors. Once soaked, it is best sliced with a sharp knife.

SEAWEED AND BELL PEPPER
WITH RICE

(top right)
Serves 4
5 ounces sea lettuce, ½ cup basmati rice
1 shallot, finely chopped, 3 tablespoons chilled butter
3½ cups dry white vermouth, 7 tablespoons white wine
⅞ cup light cream, dash of lemon juice
salt, freshly ground white pepper
1 small yellow bell pepper

Rinse the sea lettuce for 10–15 minutes, then blanch for 1–2 minutes. Drain and rinse in cold water. Remove the roots and cut the leaves into strips. Bring the rice to a boil in 1½ cups water. Simmer for 10 minutes and set aside. Sauté the shallot in 1½ teaspoons of the butter until translucent. Add the vermouth and wine, bring to a boil, and reduce until almost all the liquid has evaporated. Add the cream and simmer for 10 minutes. Peel and seed the bell pepper, cut into diamond shapes, blanch, and rinse in cold water. Season the sauce with lemon juice, salt, and pepper. Dice 2 teaspoons of the remaining butter and beat it into the sauce, one piece at a time. Remove the pan from the heat. Sauté the sea lettuce with the bell pepper in the remaining butter. Add the rice and sauce, bring briefly to a boil, season, and serve.

SEAWEED TAGLIATELLE

(center right)

Serves 4

5 ounces fresh sea spaghetti

4 egg yolks, salt

1 tablespoon olive oil, ½ cup cornstarch

1 cup all-purpose flour

For the sauce:

2 tablespoons sugar

2 tablespoons soy sauce

6 tablespoons white wine

½ fresh chile, finely sliced

grated rind of ½ lemon

dash of rice vinegar

⅞ cup light cream, freshly ground white pepper

1½ teaspoons butter, ⅓ cup pine nuts, toasted

Rinse the seaweed for 20 minutes, then rub until the brown outer layer comes off. Wash and blanch it for 1–2 minutes. Drain, rinse in cold water, and finely chop. Beat the egg yolks with a pinch of salt, and stir in the oil, one third of the seaweed, and the cornstarch. Knead in the flour to make a smooth dough. Let rest for 1 hour, then roll out with a pasta machine and cut into tagliatelle. To make the sauce, heat 2 tablespoons water with the sugar until a light caramel forms. Add the soy sauce and wine and reduce. Add the chile, lemon rind, vinegar, and cream. Cook until creamy, then season. Cook the tagliatelle in lightly salted boiling water until tender, then drain. Combine the tagliatelle, sauce and reserved seaweed. Serve sprinkled with pine nuts.

POACHED HALIBUT WITH DULSE

(bottom right)

Serves 4

4 ounces fresh dulse

2 shallots, 6 tablespoons chilled butter

½ teaspoon chopped fresh ginger root

1½ cups white wine; grated rind of 1 lime

1¼ pounds halibut fillet

salt, freshly ground white pepper

1 tablespoon chopped parsley

4 nasturtium flowers, to garnish

Rinse the dulse for 20 minutes. Blanch, rinse, squeeze dry, and chop. Slice 1 shallot and sauté in 1½ teaspoons butter. Add the ginger, 1 cup of the wine, and the lime rind and reduce by two thirds. Cut the fish into pieces and season. Chop the remaining shallot and sauté in 1 teaspoon butter. Add the fish and the remaining wine. Simmer until cooked. Dice the remaining butter and stir it into the sauce. Add the dulse and parsley and heat through. Serve garnished with the flowers.

Varieties of sea vegetables, such as dulse, sea lettuce, Irish moss, and sea spaghetti grow in the coastal waters of Britain, Ireland, and Northern France, where for many centuries they have formed part of regional cuisine.

Sweating and braising
COMBINED METHODS

The difference between dishes that have been sweated and those that have been braised is usually obvious from their appearance. The former tend to retain their original color, while braised dishes usually become darker. When vegetables are sweated, they exude juices and may become translucent. If they continue to be sweated over a moderate heat they turn slightly golden. It is only when vegetables are fried at a high temperature that they really brown. Sweated vegetables cook over a low heat in their own juices, which then become concentrated in the fat or oil. Braising requires a small amount of additional liquid, such as wine, beer, or stock.

RATATOUILLE: This specialty from the south of France is traditionally cooked by sweating the vegetables in olive oil. It can be made more of a braise, if desired. Trim and slice 1 medium eggplant and 4–6 zucchini. Core, seed, and coarsely dice 1 yellow, 1 green, and 1 red bell pepper. Peel, quarter, and seed 2 beefsteak tomatoes. Sauté briefly or fry 2 sliced onions and 1 crushed clove garlic in 2 tablespoons olive oil. Add the other prepared vegetables and sauté briefly or fry until lightly browned. Season with salt and pepper to taste and add ½ cup vegetable or chicken stock. Stir in ½ teaspoon each thyme leaves and rosemary. Cover and cook over a low heat until the vegetables are tender. Sprinkle with 1 tablespoon chopped fresh parsley and serve immediately.

International specialties
TRADITIONAL RECIPES FROM ITALY, FRANCE, AND HUNGARY

Many simple, inventive, and delicious vegetable dishes come from the unsung experts of country cooking. These cooks have always made the most of of good local ingredients.

ITALIAN: SPINACH WITH PINE NUTS

Serves 4
½ cup vin santo or other sweet, white wine
⅓ cup raisins, 2¼ pounds spinach
1 tablespoon olive oil
salt, freshly ground white pepper
grated nutmeg
4 tablespoons butter
⅔ cup sliced scallions
¼ clove garlic, crushed
3 anchovy fillets, finely chopped
½ cup pine nuts
1 tablespoon chopped parsley

Warm the wine and soak the raisins in it. Trim, wash and dry the spinach. Heat the olive oil in a skillet, add the spinach, and season with salt, pepper, and nutmeg to taste. Sweat until the spinach wilts, then strain. Melt the butter in a saucepan, and sauté the scallions and garlic until translucent. Add the anchovies and raisins. Cook until almost completely reduced, then add the spinach and cook for 5 minutes. Sprinkle with the pine nuts and parsley and serve immediately.

CLASSIC FRENCH: PEAS WITH LETTUCE

Serves 4
1¾ pounds peas in their pods
4 large shallots
⅔ cup diced bacon
2 tablespoons butter
1 tablespoon all-purpose flour
7 tablespoons white wine
7 tablespoons vegetable stock (see page 154)
salt
freshly ground white pepper
nutmeg
1 head lettuce
1 tablespoon chopped parsley

Shell the peas. Finely dice the shallots and sauté, together with the bacon, in the butter until they are translucent. Add the peas and sauté briefly. Sprinkle the flour into the pan and cook over a medium heat, stirring constantly, for 1 minute. Gradually stir in the white wine and vegetable stock. Season with salt, pepper, and nutmeg to taste and simmer over a low heat for about 10 minutes. Meanwhile, trim the lettuce, remove the outer leaves, and quarter the heart. Cut out the thick midribs from the outer leaves and slice the green portion into thin strips. When the peas are tender, add the lettuce hearts and strips and heat briefly. Adjust the seasoning, if necessary, and sprinkle with parsley before serving.

PROVENÇAL: BEANS WITH BLACK OLIVES

(foreground)
Serves 4
1¾ pounds green beans
6 shallots
1 lemon
2 tablespoons olive oil
salt
freshly ground white pepper
1 bay leaf
2 sprigs thyme
½ cup white wine
⅓ cup black olives
1 tablespoon finely chopped parsley
1 teaspoon finely chopped savory

Wash and trim the beans. Peel and quarter the shallots. Cut the lemon into wedges. Heat the oil in a saucepan and sauté the shallots over a low heat until translucent. Add the beans and lemon wedges, toss, and sauté briefly with the other ingredients. Add the salt, pepper, bay leaf, thyme, and wine. Cover and cook over a medium heat until the beans are tender, but still firm to the bite. Halve and pit the olives, add to the beans, and heat briefly. Sprinkle the beans with the chopped parsley and savory and serve immediately.

FROM HUNGARY: *LECSÓ WITH POTATOES*

(background)
Serves 4
2 small green bell peppers
2 small yellow bell peppers
9 ounces waxy potatoes
2 medium onions
2 tablespoons olive oil
⅔ cup diced bacon
1 tablespoon sweet Hungarian paprika
salt
1 cup beef stock
2 beefsteak tomatoes
1 teaspoon chopped thyme
1 teaspoon chopped rosemary

Core, seed, and slice the bell peppers. Peel and slice the potatoes and onions. Heat the oil in a large saucepan, add the bacon and the onions and sauté. Add the potatoes and bell peppers and sauté. Sprinkle in the paprika, season with salt, and stir in the stock. Simmer for 12 minutes. Peel, seed, and coarsely chop the tomatoes and add to the pan. Cook for a further 2–3 minutes. Sprinkle with the chopped herbs and serve immediately.

TIP: Highly spiced smoked sausage tastes good with this hearty vegetable mixture, and is often cooked with it from the outset. Typical are the garlic- and paprika-spiced Debrecen sausages, named after the Hungarian town of their origin.

Hot and spicy bean stews like this one are eaten throughout the Southwest of the United States. They are made from red or black beans, plenty of onions, garlic, and chile. This luxurious version also contains diced brisket, green beans, carrots, and tomatoes, but the dish is quite frequently wholly vegetarian, consisting of only legumes, chiles, and garlic.

BRAISED BOK CHOI

(top right)

Serves 4

1½ pounds bok choi
4 ounces buck's horn plantain (barba di frate) (optional)
2 shallots, 2 tablespoons butter
salt, freshly ground white pepper
4 tablespoons white wine
juice of ½ lime
7 tablespoons chicken stock (see page 154)
1 tablespoon sour cream

Separate the bok choi leaves and wash. Slice the stalks and cut the leaves into strips. Pull apart the buck's horn plantain, if using, and wash. Dice the shallots and sauté them in butter. Add the bok choi stalks, salt and pepper to taste, and the buck's horn plantain, if using, and sauté for 3 minutes. Add the wine and lime juice and reduce. Add the stock and braise briefly. Stir in the bok choi leaves, bring to a vigorous boil, stir in the sour cream, and serve.

VEGETABLE SPAGHETTI

Vegetable pasta: new kitchen gadgets from France and Japan make it possible. What could previously be made only in tiny quantities with a lemon zester can now be made in main-course amounts. Thread-thin "spaghetti" can be made from such vegetables as carrots, kohlrabi, black radishes, and zucchini.

Not a pasta dish with vegetables, but a brand new specialty: vegetables in the shape of spaghetti. Using a purpose-built tool, firm-fleshed vegetables are turned into whisker-thin long noodles. The advantage lies not only in the unusual appearance of the dish; cut finely like this, the vegetables are also cooked in a flash. It is important, however, not to leave the raw "spaghetti" standing for too long before cooking, as its large surface area could quickly lose vitamins and flavor.

(left)
Serves 4
2 medium carrots
4 ounces kohlrabi
4½ ounces black radishes
4½ ounces zucchini
2 tablespoons butter
salt, freshly ground white pepper
2 tablespoons white wine
3 tablespoons chicken stock (see page 154)

Wash and peel the carrots, kohlrabi, and radishes. Wash the zucchini. With a vegetable pasta maker, shape the vegetables into long spaghetti-like strips, as shown (left). Melt the butter in a saucepan and briefly sauté the vegetables. Season with salt and pepper. Pour over the white wine and stock and cook for 2–3 minutes. Adjust the seasoning and serve at once.

Interesting side dishes
ENRICHING THE MENU

Light vegetable dishes lend a different accent to classic meat, fish, poultry, and game dishes, as well as harmonizing brilliantly with vegetarian specialties.

OKRA WITH TOMATOES

(second left)

Serves 4

1¼ pounds okra

juice of 1 lemon, 2–3 beefsteak tomatoes

2 shallots, 2 tablespoons butter

salt, freshly ground white pepper

2 tablespoons vegetable stock (see page 154)

Trim the okra and place in a bowl of water acidulated with lemon juice. Peel, seed, and dice the tomatoes. Slice the shallots and sauté in butter until translucent. Add the okra, season with salt and pepper, and add the stock. Cook for 6 minutes, then add the tomatoes, bring to a boil, and serve.

BRAISED BROCCOLI RABE

(third left)

Serves 4

1½ pounds broccoli rabe, 2 shallots

3–4 small cloves garlic, 2 tablespoons olive oil

salt, freshly ground white pepper

3 tablespoons veal stock

2 slices white sandwich bread, cubed

2 tablespoons butter

⅔ cup thinly shaved Parmesan cheese

Wash and use only the tender leaves and young flowerets of the broccoli rabe. Thinly slice the shallots and push out into rings. Cut the garlic cloves into quarters. Sauté the shallots and garlic in the oil. Add the broccoli rabe and salt and pepper. Stir in the stock and cook over a low heat for 10 minutes. Fry the bread in butter until golden brown, then scatter it over the vegetables. Garnish with the shaved Parmesan before serving.

BRAISED CUCUMBER

(bottom left)

Serves 4

1 pound cucumbers

2 shallots, 4 tablespoons butter

salt, freshly ground white pepper, pinch of turmeric

1 cup dry white vermouth, 4 tablespoons white wine

1 teaspoon chopped dill, 1 tablespoon sour cream

Peel, halve, and seed the cucumbers. Cut the flesh into even-size pieces. Chop the shallots and sauté in butter until translucent. Add the cucumber, season with salt and pepper, and cook over a high heat. When the vegetables have released their juices, stir in the turmeric. Add the vermouth and wine, bring to a boil, then simmer for 10 minutes, until the liquid has almost completely evaporated. Stir in the dill, garnish with sour cream, and serve.

Trim the stalk tips of the okra to a point. Sauté in hot butter with the shallots for 6 minutes. Add the peeled diced beefsteak tomatoes.

The wide variety of vegetables available increases from day to day. The range changes with the seasons, making culinary variety more possible than ever before.

Preparing glazed onions:

Heat the butter in a skillet. Sprinkle in the sugar and brown slightly. Add the onions.

GLAZED WATER CHESTNUTS

Glazing is a superb way of making the most of the attractions of starchy, sweet vegetables. The simplest basic recipe, here illustrated using water chestnuts, consists of butter, sugar, salt and water. The liquid cooks the vegetables as it reduces. At the end of the cooking time the liquid has evaporated and the vegetables are tender and glossy. By replacing the water with stock, an even more intense, glossy glaze is obtained.

Cook, stirring constantly, until lightly colored. Add the stock.

Serves 4
11 ounces water chestnuts
2 tablespoons butter
2 teaspoons sugar, salt
1 cup water

Prepare the water chestnuts as described in the step-by-step photographs (left).

Lower the heat. Reduce the stock, stirring and tossing the onions frequently.

BROWN-GLAZED ONIONS

Pearl onions and small shallots, are suitable for glazing. They become sweet and juicy. Using a strong stock instead of water makes for a substantial glaze. The onions will then complement flavorful meat or fish dishes.

Cook for about 15 minutes over a low heat, then season the onions, and finish glazing them, stirring carefully.

Glazing water chestnuts: Heat the butter, sugar, and salt, add the peeled water chestnuts and sauté. Pour in enough water to half-cover and simmer without a lid. Add the remaining water, a little at a time, and reduce until the water chestnuts are a glossy golden brown. Serve at once.

Serves 4
1 pound small onions
2 tablespoons butter,
1½ tablespoons sugar
½ cup veal stock, salt

Peel the onions. Heat the butter, add the sugar, and cook until golden brown. Add the onions and sauté briefly, turning and stirring constantly. Add the stock and simmer over a low heat for about 15 minutes, until the onions are nicely glazed. Season with salt and serve.

Glazing
AN ATTRACTIVE WAY TO COOK STARCHY VEGETABLES

SWEET-AND-HOT BLACK RADISH
(top left)

Serves 4	
2¼ pounds black radishes	
1 cup sugar	
1¼ cups water	
2 small, fresh red chiles	

Cut or shave the radishes into thin strips. Bring the sugar and water to a boil, add the radishes, and cook over a low heat until the liquid has almost completely evaporated. Halve and seed the chiles, add to the pan, and cook for few minutes. Drain and rinse off the excess sugar with cold water.

TIP: Sweet-and-hot radish makes a tasty accompaniment for pan-fried fish or roast meat, but also goes well with salads. It will keep fresh for several days in the refrigerator.

SHALLOT CONFIT
(center left)

Serves 4	
12 ounces shallots	
1 tablespoon butter	
1 sprig thyme	
2¼ cups red wine	
½ cup red port	
1 cup rich veal stock	
salt, freshly ground white pepper	

Slice the shallots and sauté in the butter. Add the thyme, red wine, and port and reduce over a low heat until the liquid has almost completely evaporated. Pour in the veal stock and simmer until the shallots are tender and the stock is reduced by half. Season the confit with salt and pepper.

TIP: Shallot confit goes superbly with roast meat, liver, or pan-fried strong-flavored fish.

The shallot confit can be served with hearty dishes, in place of a sauce. Stored in a screwtop jar, it will keep for several days in the refrigerator.

GLAZED BABY CARROTS
(bottom left)

Serves 4	
2½ cups baby carrots	
2 tablespoons butter	
2 teaspoons sugar	
salt	
½ cup vegetable or chicken stock	

Peel and trim the carrots, leaving a little green at the top for decoration, if desired. Heat the butter with the sugar and salt in a saucepan. Sauté the carrots, turning frequently, until they are just beginning to color. Add the stock and cook until the liquid has evaporated and the carrots are glossy.

BRAISED CHAYOTE FANS

Like other members of the gourd family, the soft, white flesh of the pear-shaped chayote goes well with many spices, most typically cloves, allspice, ginger, and nutmeg. The fruit is cut into fan shapes or even-size slices so that it cooks evenly.

Serves 4
2 chayotes (about 11 ounces each)
5 tablespoons chilled butter, 1 shallot, thinly sliced
1 tablespoon sugar
salt, freshly ground white pepper
juice of ½ lemon, 7 tablespoons white wine
1⅔ cups chicken or vegetable stock (see pages 155 and 154)
¼ ounce Chinese chives, cut into strips

Prepare the chayote fans as illustrated in the following step-by-step photographs.

Peel the chayotes with a swivel-bladed vegetable peeler, removing any peel remaining in the depressions with a small knife. Halve the chayotes and remove the flat, soft pit.

Cut the chayote halves into fans, making many incisions close together, but leaving the pointed end uncut. Gently press the chayote halves flat.

Melt 1½ tablespoons of the butter in a shallow, flameproof casserole, and sauté the shallot until translucent. Sprinkle in the sugar and arrange the chayote fans on top.

Season the chayote fans generously with salt and white pepper. Add the lemon juice and wine and bring to a boil.

Add the stock, cover the casserole, and braise in a preheated oven at 350°F for 30–35 minutes.

Transfer the chayotes to a serving dish. Strain the stock into a saucepan and reduce to 5 tablespoons. Dice the remaining butter and stir into the sauce, one piece at a time. Pour the sauce over the chayotes and sprinkle with the Chinese chives.

BRAISED BELGIAN ENDIVE

Serves 4
1 shallot, diced, 5 tablespoons chilled butter
1 tablespoon sugar
4 Belgian endives, cut in half
salt, freshly ground white pepper
juice of 1 lemon, 5 tablespoons white wine
1 cup chicken stock (see page 155)
1 tomato, 1 cup chopped flat leaf parsley

Sauté the shallot in 2 tablespoons of the butter in a flameproof casserole until translucent. Sprinkle with sugar, then follow the step-by-step photographs. Braise in a preheated oven at 350°F for 20 minutes. Peel and dice the tomato. Transfer the Belgian endive to a serving dish. Strain the cooking liquid, dice the remaining butter, and stir it in. Stir the tomato and parsley into the sauce, pour over the Belgian endive, and serve.

Season the trimmed Belgian endive with salt and pepper and sauté briefly in 2 tablespoons of the butter. Add the lemon juice and wine.

Reduce the liquid slightly and add the chicken stock. Dot with 1 teaspoon of the remaining butter and cover the casserole.

BRAISED CELERY

Serves 4

1 small onion, 5 ounces carrots
2 tablespoons butter, 14 ounces celery
salt, freshly ground white pepper, juice of ½ lemon
¼ cup white wine, 1¼ cups light veal stock

Prepare as described below. Transfer the cooked celery to a serving dish. Purée the remaining mixture in a food processor, strain, and heat until creamy and reduced. Serve the celery with the sauce, garnished with celery leaves.

Slice the onion and carrot and sauté in butter in a flameproof casserole until the onion is translucent. Slice the celery, reserving the leaves to garnish. Add the celery to the casserole, season to taste, and add the lemon juice and wine.

Bring to a boil and add the veal stock. Cover and bake in a preheated oven at 350°F for 15–20 minutes.

FENNEL WITH BLACK OLIVES

Serves 4

2 fennel bulbs, 1 shallot, ¼ clove garlic
1 tablespoon olive oil
1 sprig each thyme and rosemary
1 bay leaf, salt, freshly ground black pepper
¼ cup white wine, 10 black olives
2¼ cups sieved tomatoes
1 tablespoon grated Parmesan cheese, to garnish

Prepare as shown below. Put the cooked fennel on a dish. Reduce the cooking liquid to make the sauce.

Trim and quarter the fennel bulbs, reserving the green fronds to garnish. Chop the shallot and garlic and sauté in the oil. Add the fennel quarters, thyme, rosemary, and bay leaf.

Season the vegetables with salt and pepper and add the wine.

Pit and slice the olives and add to the casserole. Cover the vegetables evenly with the sieved tomatoes. Cover and cook in a preheated oven at 350°F for about 35 minutes.

RED CABBAGE

(pictured below)

Serves 4

2½ pounds red cabbage, 1 apple

2 tablespoons red wine vinegar

salt, sugar

juice and grated rind of 1 orange

2 small onions, sliced

4 ounces goose or duck fat or lard

1½ cups red wine, 1 potato

For the spice mixture:

1 clove, 2 allspice berries

6–8 white peppercorns

4 juniper berries, 1 bay leaf

¼ cinnamon stick

Shred the cabbage into a large mixing bowl or saucepan. Core the apple, cut into thin segments, and add to the cabbage. Add the vinegar, salt, sugar, orange juice, and rind. Knead and leave for about 1 hour to macerate, as shown in the step-by-step photographs (below). In a large saucepan, sauté the onions in the fat until translucent. Add the cabbage and sauté briefly. Add the wine. Tie the spices in a piece of cheesecloth and add to the pan. Cook over a low heat for 15 minutes. Grate the potato, add to the pan, and cook for a further 15 minutes.

Mix together the cabbage, apple slices, vinegar, and bag of spices, crush lightly with your fist, and set aside for at least 1 hour to allow the flavors to mingle.

Sauté the onions in the fat in a large saucepan. Add the red cabbage and sauté well.

Add the red wine and the spices, tied up in a cheesecloth bag and hanging from the saucepan handle, so that they can be easily removed later.

Grate in a raw potato to thicken the mixture and continue braising the cabbage over a low heat for a further 10–15 minutes.

Traditional braised cabbage dishes
CAREFULLY PREPARED CLASSICS OF CENTRAL EUROPEAN HOME COOKING

White, red, and Savoy cabbages are well suited to braising, as this makes them very tender and digestible. In addition, the flavors of the typical spices, such as cloves, bay leaf, juniper berries, and caraway, are fully released only with prolonged cooking. Just how long a white or red cabbage dish should cook and whether it tastes better after reheating are matters of personal taste.

BAVARIAN-STYLE CABBAGE

Serves 4
2¼ pounds white cabbage
1 medium onion
½ cup diced bacon
3 tablespoons vegetable oil
salt
freshly ground white pepper
½ teaspoon caraway seeds
1 cup white wine
1 cup beef stock

Shred the cabbage. Peel and dice the onion. Sauté the onion and bacon in the oil until the onion is translucent. Add the cabbage, season with salt, pepper, and caraway seeds, and add the white wine and stock. Cover and braise for about 30 minutes.

CREAMY SAVOY CABBAGE

Serves 4
1¾ pounds Savoy cabbage
1 medium onion, finely chopped
½ cup diced bacon
2 tablespoons butter
salt
freshly ground white pepper
nutmeg
1¼ cups heavy cream

Halve the cabbage, cut out the stalk, and shred the leaves. Sauté the onion and bacon in the butter until the onion is translucent. Add the cabbage, season with salt, pepper, and nutmeg to taste, and cook briefly. Pour in the cream and reduce over a low heat until the mixture is creamy and the cabbage is tender.

Red cabbage with chestnuts as an accompaniment to roast quail with fried quail eggs (below). The red cabbage can be made more interesting by stirring in a little cranberry jelly toward the end of cooking, or by serving with glazed apples or chestnuts.

Stuffed vegetables

STUFFINGS FOR SCOOPED-OUT VEGETABLES, FILLINGS WRAPPED IN LEAVES

Fruiting vegetables of all sorts, such as tomatoes, squashes, and bell peppers, are natural containers for all kinds of fillings. This idea has been taken up worldwide, as the recipes in this chapter show. The idea of using cabbage, grape leaves, or other leaves as wrappings is widespread too. Stuffed cabbage, for example, is often thought to be typically East European, but from France to Greece to China there are innumerable dishes made with seasoned ground meat wrapped in white, red, Savoy, or Chinese cabbage leaves. Larger roots, bulbs, and tubers, such as potatoes, onions, and kohlrabi, can be scooped out, providing space for a filling. The flesh of the vegetable itself often forms the basis of the filling.

STUFFED TOMATOES: From 2¼ pounds beefsteak tomatoes select 4 attractive ones. Cut off their tops and scoop out the flesh. Peel, seed, and dice the remaining tomatoes. Blanch 7 ounces spinach, rinse in cold water, and squeeze out excess moisture. Peel and dice 1 medium onion and 1 clove garlic, then sauté in 1½ tablespoons olive oil until translucent. Add 10 pitted black olives and the spinach, and season to taste with salt and pepper. Sauté briefly and add the diced tomatoes. Stir in 1 cup finely diced mozzarella cheese. Stuff the tomato shells with the mixture and arrange in an ovenproof dish. Sprinkle with the finely grated crumbs from 2 slices of white bread, crusts removed, and 1 tablespoon finely chopped parsley. Drizzle 1 teaspoon olive oil over each tomato and cook in a preheated oven at 350°F for 10 minutes.

STUFFED ARTICHOKES

Serves 6 as a main course

6 large globe artichokes, juice of 2 lemons

5 ounces boneless pork loin

5 ounces boneless veal round

3 cups finely chopped mushrooms

2 tablespoons chopped parsley

1 tablespoon crème fraîche or sour cream

salt, freshly ground white pepper

18 paper-thin slices unsmoked bacon

2 tablespoons olive oil, 2 tablespoons butter

1¼ cups white wine

Break off the stalks of the artichokes, trim the leaves, loosen the chokes, and remove. Drizzle the heart and leaves with lemon juice to prevent discoloration. Blanch the artichokes in boiling salted water acidulated with lemon juice for 10 minutes and drain upside down. Finely dice the pork and veal. Mix together the pork, veal, mushrooms, parsley, crème fraîche or sour cream, and salt and pepper to taste. Fill the artichokes with this mixture, as shown in the step-by-step photographs (below). Transfer the artichokes to a casserole and braise in a preheated oven at 350°F for 60–80 minutes. Remove from the oven, remove and discard the string, and serve.

The filling: finely diced pork and veal, chopped mushrooms, parsley, and crème fraîche or sour cream.

Stuffing the artichokes:

Push the outer leaves to the side and spoon the stuffing into the hollow of the artichoke with a tablespoon.

Lay the thin strips of bacon crosswise over the top so that the stuffing is completely covered and protected from drying out during cooking.

Wrap trussing thread or kitchen string around the artichokes and knot tightly so that the bacon will not come away during cooking.

Stand the artichokes upright in a casserole with hot olive oil and butter. Pour in the wine.

Sophisticated fillings: artichokes and kohlrabi

SUCCULENT COMBINATIONS WITH MEAT

Not just pretty to look at: through braising, the flavors of filling and vegetable also mingle deliciously.

At one time, the artichoke was a vegetable with aristocratic associations and the symbol of a wealthy lifestyle. Even now, it is expensive, with the edible portion constituting only about 20 percent of the whole. However, less is more when it comes to this delicacy. An essential ingredient of French *haute cuisine*, it can be prepared in a countless variety of ways.

STUFFED YOUNG ARTICHOKES

For this Italian recipe it is best to use an elongated variety of globe artichoke with a small flowerhead, as the stuffing goes not only into the center, but also between the young, tender leaves.

Serves 4
8 young globe artichokes
juice of 1 lemon
3 cloves garlic
1 bunch parsley
½ cup diced pancetta or bacon
salt, freshly ground white pepper
½ cup olive oil, 2 tablespoons white wine

Break the artichoke heads from the stalks and remove the hard outer leaves. Cut off the top third of the heads and remove the chokes. Place the artichokes in water acidulated with lemon juice. Chop the garlic and parsley and mix with the pancetta or bacon. Transfer the artichokes to a shallow ovenproof dish, spread out the leaves, and stuff with the filling. Season with salt and pepper and drizzle with the olive oil. Sprinkle with the wine, cover, and braise in a preheated oven at 350°F for about 15 minutes.

STUFFED KOHLRABI

Serves 4 as a side dish, 2 as a main dish
4 kohlrabi (10 ounces each)
4 slices sandwich bread, 2 tablespoons butter
9 ounces ground beef
4 ounces chicken livers, ground
2 tablespoons chopped parsley
½ teaspoon each chopped thyme and marjoram
2 egg yolks, salt, pepper, 7 tablespoons brandy
1 onion, sliced, 7 tablespoons white wine
7 tablespoons chicken stock (see page 154)

Hollow out the kohlrabi, leaving a ¼-inch wall, and reserving the flesh. Blanch the shells in salted boiling water for 4 minutes. Cut the crusts from the bread, cube 3 slices, and brown them in 2 teaspoons butter. Mix the bread cubes, beef, chicken liver, half the parsley, the thyme, marjoram, and egg yolks. Season to taste and add the brandy. Fill the shells with this mixture. Finely grate the remaining bread and scatter the crumbs and the remaining parsley on top of the kohlrabi. Coarsely chop the reserved flesh. Melt the remaining butter in a flameproof casserole and sauté the onion with the kohlrabi flesh. Place the stuffed kohlrabi in the casserole and add the wine and stock. Cook in a preheated oven at 350°F for about 30 minutes.

Stuffed kohlrabi, here filled with a seasoned mixture of chicken liver, ground meat, and bread, can be served as a main course with a tomato sauce.

STUFFED EGGPLANT
Serves 4

| 4 medium eggplants |
| 2 medium onions, 1¼ pounds tomatoes |
| 3 tablespoons olive oil, 2 cloves garlic, crushed |
| salt, freshly ground black pepper |
| ¼ cinnamon stick, 1 bay leaf |
| 1 tablespoon chopped parsley |
| ½ cup chopped almonds |

Roast the eggplants in a preheated oven at 400°F for about 10 minutes, turning frequently. Pull off the skins, halve the eggplants lengthwise, carefully scoop out and reserve most of the flesh, leaving a ¾-inch thick shell. Slice the onions, and separate into rings. Peel, quarter, seed, and dice the tomatoes. Heat 2 teaspoons of the olive oil in a saucepan, and sauté the onions and garlic. Add the tomatoes. Season with salt and pepper, then add the cinnamon stick and bay leaf, and cook for 5 minutes. Coarsely dice the eggplant flesh, add to the saucepan, and cook for a further 5 minutes. Remove and discard the bay leaf and cinnamon stick. Add the parsley and almonds. Use this mixture to stuff the eggplant shells. Arrange the stuffed eggplants in an oiled casserole and drizzle with the remaining oil. Bake in a preheated oven at 350°F for 15–20 minutes, or until the eggplant shells are tender.

STUFFED BELL PEPPERS
Serves 4

| 1 cup couscous, 1 star anise |
| 4 yellow bell peppers |
| 3 green zucchini, 3 yellow zucchini |
| 1 small eggplant, 1 medium onion, ½ clove garlic |
| 2 medium tomatoes, 4 teaspoons olive oil |
| salt, freshly ground white pepper |
| 3 tablespoons white wine |
| 3 tablespoons chicken stock (see page 155) |
| For the sauce: |
| 1¼ pounds tomatoes, 1 onion, 2 tablespoons olive oil |
| 1 sprig thyme, 1 bay leaf |

Soak the couscous in 1 cup water for 15 minutes, drain, and steam with the star anise for 30 minutes. Sprinkle with 7 tablespoons water and simmer for a further 15 minutes. Cut the tops off the bell peppers and reserve. Core and seed the bell peppers. Coarsely chop the zucchini and eggplant, and finely chop the onion and garlic. Peel, seed, and dice the tomatoes. Sauté these vegetables in the oil and season. Add the wine and stock and cook until tender. Mix with the couscous and use to stuff the bell peppers. Replace the tops. To make the sauce, chop the tomatoes, and finely chop the onion. Sauté the onion in the oil. Put the bell peppers in an ovenproof dish, add the onion, tomatoes, thyme, and bay leaf, and bake in a preheated oven at 350°F for 25 minutes. Transfer the bell peppers to serving plates. Remove the herbs, purée the cooking liquid, strain, and season. Serve.

ONIONS STUFFED WITH RISOTTO

4 medium onions
⅔ cup diced pancetta or bacon
⅓ cup risotto rice
3 tablespoons butter, 1 cup white wine
1⅓ cups chicken stock (see page 155)
⅓ cup grated Parmesan cheese
1 teaspoon chopped thyme, 1 bay leaf

Peel the onions and cut a "lid" off the top of each. Scoop out the flesh, leaving a ¼-inch thick wall. Blanch briefly, rinse with cold water, and drain. Thinly slice the onion flesh and sauté, together with the diced pancetta or bacon and the rice, in half the butter until translucent. Add 7 tablespoons of the wine and simmer gently over a medium heat, gradually adding about 1 cup of the stock. Cook for 15 minutes. Stir in the Parmesan, thyme, and the remaining butter. Fill the onions with this mixture and place the "lids" on top. Arrange the onions in an ovenproof dish and add the remaining wine and stock, and the bay leaf. Cook in a preheated oven at 350°F for about 15 minutes, until tender.

STUFFED GOURDS WITH CURRY SAUCE

Serves 4
2 Chinese bitter melons or karelas (15 ounces each)
1 tablespoon salt
For the filling:
11 ounces salmon fillet
salt, freshly ground white pepper
1 cup light cream, chilled
1 tablespoon heavy cream
For the sauce:
2 shallots, diced, 2 tablespoons butter
2 teaspoons confectioners' sugar
1 teaspoon curry powder
¼ cup white wine, 1⅓ cups mirin (Japanese sweet rice wine)
1 tablespoon creamed coconut, 1 cup light cream
1 red bell pepper

Cut off both ends of the gourds and remove the cores with an apple corer. Sprinkle salt all over them and set aside for 20 minutes. Place the gourds in a bowl of hot water for 5 minutes, rinse with cold water, and drain. Finely dice 2 ounces of the salmon. Season the remaining salmon with salt and pepper, process in a food processor to a fine purée. With the motor still running, slowly pour in the light cream. Rub the mixture through a strainer, and fold in the heavy cream and the diced salmon. Fill the gourds as shown in the step-by-step photographs (right) and wrap in plastic wrap. Poach in gently simmering water (160–175°F) for about 20 minutes. Meanwhile, make the sauce. Sauté the shallots in the butter. Stir in the sugar and curry powder, then the wine and mirin. Stir in the coconut cream and reduce the liquid by three quarters. Add the cream and reduce until the sauce is creamy. Strain and keep warm. Peel, core, seed, and finely dice the bell pepper and add to the sauce. Unwrap the stuffed gourds, slice, and serve on a pool of sauce.

TIP: The sauce may be flavored with the finely grated rind of 1 lime, or with chile or ginger.

Filling the gourd: Use a pasty bag to pipe the salmon filling into the scooped-out gourd. Wrap the gourds in plastic wrap and tie the end securely.

STUFFED GRAPE LEAVES

These spicy packets, known as *dolmadakia*, are one of the classic Greek appetizers or *meze*. The tender grape leaves required for this dish are picked only in the spring and then preserved in brine.

Serves 4
2 medium onions, chopped
⅔ cup long grain rice, 3 tablespoons olive oil
salt, freshly ground white pepper
1 teaspoon sugar, ½ cup pine nuts
1 tablespoon chopped dill, 2 tablespoons chopped parsley
½ tablespoon finely chopped mint
15 grape leaves, juice of ½ lemon
¼ cup white wine, 2 tablespoons butter, melted

Prepare the filling and use to stuff 12 grape leaves as shown in the step-by-step photographs (left and below). Line the base of a casserole with the remaining leaves and place the rice packets on top. Add the lemon juice, wine, ½ cup water, and the melted butter. Season with salt. Cover and cook in a preheated oven at 350°F for 30–40 minutes.

TIP: Serve while still slightly warm on a lemon sabayon (see page 161), as shown (above right). They also taste superb cold, without a sauce.

To make the filling, sauté the diced onions and the rice in the oil. Season with salt, pepper, and sugar and add 7 tablespoons water. Simmer, covered, over a low heat for about 10 minutes.

Filling the grape leaves:

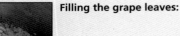

Transfer the just-cooked rice to a bowl, and mix with the pine nuts, dill, parsley, and mint.

Remove the stalks from the grape leaves. Place the leaves in a strainer and scald with boiling water, then rinse with cold water.

Lay 12 leaves face down on the counter and place a spoonful of the rice filling in the center of each.

Fold both sides of each leaf over the filling, roll up, and arrange in an ovenproof dish, seam side down.

STUFFED ZUCCHINI

All the numerous varieties are suitable for stuffing. In Greece this vegetable is served with a hearty rice and ground meat filling and a lemon sauce. In Italy, it is baked with a herb, bread crumb, and Parmesan filling. In the South of France, numerous variations with tomatoes, olives, and bay leaf are to be found. For a sophisticated hors d'oeuvre, a chicken or fish stuffing can be piped into scooped-out, blanched zucchini "tubes." In the following recipe, the zucchini are filled with a mixed vegetable and ham stuffing.

Serves 4
4 large zucchini
⅓ cup mushrooms
½ leek
2 medium carrots
3 ounces celery root
4 teaspoons butter
4 ounces ham
salt, freshly ground pepper
2 tablespoons chopped parsley
4 teaspoons olive oil

Wash the zucchini, halve them lengthwise, and remove the seeds with a melon baller. Trim and finely chop the mushrooms, leek, carrots, and celery root. Sauté in hot butter. Dice the ham and add to the pan of vegetables. Season with salt and pepper to taste and cook over a low heat until the vegetables are just tender. Stir in the parsley and spoon the filling into the zucchini halves. Oil an ovenproof dish, arrange the stuffed zucchini in it and drizzle with the remaining oil. Bake in a preheated oven at 350°F for about 10 minutes.

TIP: Yellow bell pepper sauce, (right) and other light vegetable sauces, go well with this.

strips of peel from the zucchini. Dice this peel and sauté in ½ teaspoon butter with 1 shallot. Season with salt, pepper, and nutmeg and add ¼ cup wine. Reduce slightly, add ¼ cup stock and cook until the vegetables are tender and almost dry. Stuff the flowers as shown in the step-by-step photographs (below). Melt the remaining butter in a flameproof casserole and sauté the remaining shallot until translucent. Add the zucchini flowers and season with salt and pepper. Pour in the remaining wine, reduce slightly, and add the remaining vegetable stock. Cover and cook the flowers in a preheated oven at 350°F for about 10 minutes.

STUFFED ZUCCHINI FLOWERS

The flowers look attractive served with red bell pepper sauce (below). This mixture may also be used for stuffing the larger pumpkin flowers.

Serves 2
4 zucchini flowers, 4–5 zucchini
2 tablespoons butter, salt, freshly ground pepper
2 shallots, diced, nutmeg
12 tablespoons white wine
12 tablespoons vegetable stock (see page 154)
2 egg yolks
3 slices white sandwich bread, crusts removed

Wash the flowers. With a sharp knife, pare off ¼-inch thick

Stuffing the zucchini flowers:

Carefully open the calyx of the zucchini flowers with your fingers and remove the pistil inside using a small knife, taking care not to damage the flower petals.

Dice the zucchini peel and sauté in butter with 1 diced shallot. Season, add the wine, and reduce.

Place the sautéed vegetables in a food processor while they are still warm and process to a smooth purée with the egg yolks and bread. Season to taste and let cool.

Using a pastry bag, pipe the cooled filling into the calyx of each flower.

Gently twist the petals of each flower to seal.

Cut the stem of each flower into a fan and flatten slightly.

CHINESE CABBAGE ROLLS

Serves 4

1 cup milk, ⅓ cup long grain rice

2 onions, chopped, 1 clove garlic, chopped

2 tablespoons butter

5 ounces each ground beef, pork, and lamb

⅓ cup finely diced bacon

3 tablespoons chopped parsley, ½ teaspoon oregano

2 egg yolks, salt, freshly ground pepper

12 Chinese cabbage leaves, 1 cup beef stock

Bring the milk to a boil with ½ cup water. Add the rice and cook for 20 minutes over a low heat. Sauté the onions and garlic, in 1½ teaspoons of the butter, then cool. Combine all the meat with the herbs, egg yolks, and the onion mixture and season with salt and pepper. Add the cooked rice. Blanch the cabbage leaves, rinse in cold water, and trim the leaf ribs flat. Spread out the leaves and season with salt and pepper. Divide the filling among the leaves, and roll them up. Grease an ovenproof dish with 1 teaspoon of the remaining butter, put the cabbage rolls in it, and add the stock. Dot the remaining butter over the top and bake in a preheated oven at 350°F for 35–40 minutes.

Making the cabbage rolls: Trim the thick leaf ribs flat. Place a portion of meat filling in the center of each leaf and roll up, continuing to tuck the sides in toward the center so that none of the stuffing can leak.

FISH IN SAVOY CABBAGE LEAVES

1¼ pounds white fish fillet

salt, freshly ground white pepper

⅔ cup heavy cream, chilled

1 medium carrot, 1 Savoy cabbage

For the chervil sauce:

1 small bunch chervil

1 shallot, 4 teaspoons butter

½ cup each white wine and fish stock

1 cup heavy cream, 4 teaspoons chilled butter

Cut 4 slices, about 4 ounces each, from the fish fillet. Dice the remaining fish and place in the freezer for a short while. Season the diced fish with

Appetizingly wrapped in leaves

A CABBAGE WRAPPING KEEPS MEAT AND FISH SUCCULENT

Delicate fish stuffings and fragile fillets of fish can be protected from the heat by wrapping them in cabbage leaves, but Swiss chard, bok choi, and large mustard-green leaves can also gently hold a filling together.

salt and pepper and process in food processor to a purée, gradually adding the cream. Rub through a strainer and chill in the refrigerator. Finely dice the carrot and blanch briefly in boiling water. Remove the outer 8–10 leaves of the cabbage, blanch briefly, rinse, and trim the leaf ribs flat. Remove the core from the remaining cabbage, shred the leaves, and blanch. Rinse in cold water and squeeze dry. Mix together the fish stuffing, carrots, and the shredded cabbage. Prepare the cabbage packets as shown in the step-by-step photographs (right) and refrigerate. To make the sauce, strip the chervil leaves from their stalks. Sauté the stalks, together with the diced shallots, in the butter. Add the white wine and the stock and reduce by three-quarters. Add the cream, reduce the sauce until thickened, then strain. Steam the fish packets for 8–10 minutes. Beat the chilled butter into the sauce, a little at a time, add the chervil leaves, and adjust the seasoning. Serve the fish packets on a pool of sauce.

BREAST OF PHEASANT ROULADE

Serves 4
1 pheasant (about 1¼ pounds), 3 ounces lean veal
salt, freshly ground white pepper
½ cup light cream, chilled
2 tablespoons heavy cream, whipped
7 tablespoons brandy
2 tablespoons chopped parsley, 2 tablespoons pistachios
3 ounces foie gras
1 white cabbage (about 2¼ pounds)

Cut off and skin the breast and legs of the pheasant. Remove the bones and sinews from the legs. Finely dice the leg meat, together with the veal. Chill in the refrigerator or freezer. Season with salt and pepper and process in a food processor to a purée, gradually adding the light cream. Rub through a strainer and fold in the whipped cream. Add the brandy, parsley, and pistachios and chill again. Cut the foie gras into 2 slices and season with salt and pepper. Fry briefly in a dry skillet, cool, and chill. Separate the cabbage leaves and remove the thick ribs. Blanch the leaves, rinse in cold water, and pat dry. Arrange the leaves in a large rectangle and spread the filling thinly on top. Place 1 pheasant breast portions on top. Spread with filling and top with the foie gras. Spread with filling and place the second breast portion on top. Wrap the leaves to form a packet and secure with toothpicks. Transfer to an ovenproof dish and bake in a preheated oven at 400°F for 18–20 minutes. Let rest for 2 minutes, remove the toothpicks, and cut into slices.

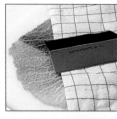

Fish in a Savoy cabbage jacket: Flatten the leaves, spread them with the filling, and place the fish slices on top. Roll up into a packet, sealing down the edges with filling.

Frying

VEGETABLES HOT OUT OF THE SKILLET, WOK, OR DEEP-FRYER

With these techniques, fat provides the heat for cooking. Unlike water, it can be heated to far above 212°F, so controlling the temperature is not so easy, but it is all the more important for the finished product. Butter, for example, elsewhere absolutely essential in haute cuisine, cannot be used for most frying, as it burns at around 248°F. Clarified butter, on the other hand, is more robust, and can take being heated up to 350°F. Even so, it is not suitable for deep-frying. When used for frying for half an hour or more, as can easily occur when potatoes and other vegetables are being deep-fried, it deteriorates in quality and tastes slightly burnt. It is better to use a neutral-tasting refined vegetable oil, even though this cannot provide the butter flavor. This can easily be remedied by adding a knob of butter to the dish shortly before serving, as in the recipe for rösti (opposite).

RÖSTI: Peel 1¾ pounds waxy potatoes, grate coarsely, and pat dry. Season with salt and freshly ground black pepper and divide into 4 portions. Melt 4 teaspoons clarified butter in a small skillet. Add one portion of potatoes, press down gently, and fry until golden brown on both sides. Top the rösti with 1 teaspoon fresh butter, let melt, and serve at once. Repeat for the other 3 portions.

BERNESE RÖSTI: Boil 1¾ pounds potatoes in their skins, drain, rinse with cold water, cover, and cool. Peel the potatoes, grate, and divide into 4 portions. For each portion, finely dice 1 thick slice bacon and fry in a skillet with 4 teaspoons clarified butter, until it has rendered all the fat. Add the grated potatoes, season with a pinch of salt and a little freshly ground white pepper, and fry until they have taken on some color. Drizzle with 1½ teaspoons heavy cream, flip the rösti over, and fry on the other side. Serve immediately and repeat for the other 3 portions.

Pan-fried vegetables

PATTIES AND CROQUETTES— WHOLE OR IN SLICES, WITH AND WITHOUT BREAD CRUMBS

A golden-brown crust brings out the best in many vegetables. Cooking at moderate temperatures, giving the pan the occasional shake or turning the vegetables from time to time, is the best way to achieve the desired even browning.

POTATO-ZUCCHINI PATTIES

Serves 4
14 ounces zucchini
1¼ pounds potatoes
salt, freshly ground white pepper
nutmeg
5 tablespoons clarified butter

Grate the zucchini. Peel the potatoes, grate, and squeeze out the moisture with your hands over a bowl to catch the liquid. Let the potato liquid stand until the starch has settled. Pour off the water and add the starch to the potatoes. Mix in the zucchini and season to taste with salt, pepper, and nutmeg. Heat the clarified butter in a skillet. Form 12 patties from the mixture, fry until golden brown.

Pan-fried young garlic is so mild-tasting that not only can it be used in small amounts as a seasoning, but it can also be served as a side dish like other vegetables. Bring 1 cup each of milk and water to the boil in a small pan. Add 7 ounces peeled young garlic cloves and simmer over a low heat for 5–8 minutes. Drain and rinse under cold running water. Pat the garlic dry, season with salt, dust with 1 tablespoon all-purpose flour, and pan-fry until golden brown in 1½ teaspoons clarified butter.

EGGPLANT WITH TOMATOES

Pan-frying in hot oil is an excellent way of preparing eggplant. To prevent the spongelike flesh from absorbing too much oil the slices should be sprinkled generously with salt and set aside for at least 15 minutes. Then pat dry with paper towels and fry. Fried eggplant should not be kept warm for any length of time, since it will soon lose its crispness and become greasy.

Serves 4
1¾ pounds eggplant
1¼ pounds beefsteak tomatoes
salt, freshly ground white pepper
1 tablespoon all-purpose flour, 4 tablespoons olive oil
1 sprig rosemary, ½ clove garlic, crushed
2 shallots, thinly sliced

Slice the eggplant into ½-inch thick slices and cut a crisscross pattern into them with a knife. Sprinkle with salt, leave in a colander for a short while, then rinse, and pat dry with paper towels. Peel, quarter, seed, and dice the tomatoes. Season the eggplant slices with salt and pepper, dust them with flour, and fry , a few at a time, in ¼ cup of the olive oil until golden brown. Turn the slices and add the rosemary. Heat the remaining oil in another skillet, add the crushed garlic and the shallots, and sauté until translucent. Add the tomatoes, season with salt and pepper, and sauté briefly. Serve the eggplant slices with the sautéed tomatoes.

FRIED CELERY ROOT PATTIES

Celery root must be boiled before coating with bread crumbs and frying. A sabayon with lemon thyme, as shown above, goes well with these crunchy patties.

Serves 4
2 small celery roots, weighing 1¼ pounds each
salt, 2 tablespoons lemon juice
freshly ground white pepper
1 bunch lemon thyme
1 tablespoon vegetable oil, ¼ cup all-purpose flour
1 egg, lightly beaten, 3½ cups fresh white bread crumbs
3 tablespoons clarified butter
1½ teaspoons butter
4 nasturtium flowers, to garnish

Peel the celery roots, slice each into 8 equal slices. Cook in boiling salted water acidulated with lemon juice. Rinse in cold water, pat dry, season with salt and pepper, and drizzle with oil. Strip a few lemon thyme leaves from their stalks. Stack the slices on top of one another, placing a few thyme leaves between them. Cover with plastic wrap and marinate for 20–30 minutes. Coat the celery root slices first in flour, then in beaten egg, and finally in bread crumbs, pressing these in firmly. Fry in clarified butter until golden brown. Pour off the clarified butter. Add the fresh butter to the pan, heat till foaming, and serve the celery root at once, garnished with the nasturtium flowers.

BEAN SPROUT AND CORN PATTIES: Lightly squeeze excess liquid from 11 ounces cooked or canned corn kernels. Process half the corn in a food processor to a fine purée and transfer to a bowl. Stir in 1 egg yolk, 1 teaspoon all-purpose flour, salt, pepper, a pinch of sugar, and 1 cup cornflakes. Add the whole corn kernels and 1 tablespoon chopped parsley and set aside to rest for 10 minutes. Mix in 6½ ounces bean sprouts, form into 16 small patties, and fry in 3 tablespoons clarified butter until golden.

Hot from the wok
QUICK AND CRUNCHY STIR-FRIED VEGETABLES

The Chinese invented the large, bowl-shaped wok and the technique of stir-frying. The secret of success is to cut the vegetables into pieces as even in size as possible. They are then kept in constant motion with a broad, flat wok scoop or spatula. This ensures that they cook evenly. It is especially important to cook the vegetables in small quantities, one type at a time. Add the slowest-cooking types first, so that they remain crunchy and retain as many nutrients as possible.

STIR-FRIED DAIKON
Serves 4

2 tablespoons peanut oil

1 scallion, thinly sliced

1 teaspoon finely chopped fresh ginger root

4 ounces ground pork

1¼ pounds daikon (mooli)

1 tablespoon Chinese rice wine, 1 cup beef stock

2 teaspoons sugar, 3 tablespoons soy sauce

1 tablespoon cilantro leaves, to garnish

Heat the oil in a preheated wok. Stir-fry the scallion and the ginger. Add the meat and stir-fry until browned. Add the daikon, prepared as shown in the step-by-step photographs (left), and stir-fry for 2 minutes. Add the wine, stock, sugar, and soy sauce. Reduce the heat and simmer until the daikon is tender and the liquid has almost completely evaporated. Garnish with the cilantro leaves.

STIR-FRIED BAMBOO SHOOTS AND ASPARAGUS WITH SQUID
Serves 4

11 ounces prepared squid

11 ounces green asparagus

6½ ounces cooked bamboo shoots

2 tablespoons peanut oil, grated rind of ½ lime

¼ teaspoon finely chopped fresh ginger root

salt, Szechuan pepper

1⅔ cups sweet rice wine

2 tablespoons chicken stock (see page 155)

Cut the squid into rings. Peel the asparagus, cut off the tips, and slice the stalks. Quarter the bamboo shoots. Heat the oil in a preheated wok. Stir-fry the lime rind and ginger briefly. Add the asparagus and stir-fry for 3–4 minutes. Add the squid and stir-fry for 2 minutes. Season with salt and Szechuan pepper. Add the bamboo shoots and stir-fry briefly. Add the wine and the stock, and simmer gently until the liquid has almost completely evaporated.

Preparing daikon: Remove the peel with an swivel-bladed vegetable peeler. Slice the daikon lengthwise first, then diagonally across into thin pieces.

Sweet-and-sour vegetables (right) are wonderful with Savoy cabbage crêpes, which are very attractive and easy to make. Briefly blanch and pat dry tender, medium-sized Savoy cabbage leaves. Prepare a crêpe batter (see page 193). Pour some batter into the pan, press a cabbage leaf into the moist surface of the batter, flip the crêpe over, and cook the other side.

SWEET-AND-SOUR VEGETABLES IN SAVOY CABBAGE CRÊPES

Serves 4

¹/₄ ounce dried tree ear mushrooms
4 ounces broccoli
2½ ounces each daikon, celery, and pumpkin
2 ounces snow peas, 1 red bell pepper
4 ounces scallions
2 tablespoons peanut oil
¼ teaspoon finely chopped fresh ginger root
½ clove garlic, thinly sliced, 1 teaspoon sugar
20 cashews, salt, freshly ground pepper
2 tablespoons soy sauce, dash of red rice vinegar
1 cup Chinese rice wine, ½ teaspoon cornstarch

Soak the tree ears in hot water for 15 minutes. Drain and squeeze out the moisture. Discard the stems, if any, and slice the tops. Cut all the vegetables into even-size pieces. Heat the oil in a preheated wok, and add the ginger, garlic, and sugar. Stir-fry briefly, then add the vegetables and cashews. Stir-fry the vegetables, season to taste, and add the soy sauce. Add the vinegar and wine and cook over a low heat until the vegetables are just tender. Mix together the cornstarch and 1 tablespoon water and stir into the wok and use to thicken the liquid. (See below left for Savoy cabbage crêpes.)

MUSTARD GREENS WITH SHRIMP

Serves 4

11 ounces raw shrimp, peeled and deveined
1¼ pounds mustard greens
3 tablespoons peanut oil, 1 clove garlic, finely chopped
½ teaspoon finely chopped fresh ginger root
1 tablespoon light soy sauce
1 tablespoon Chinese rice wine, five-spice powder
salt, 1 teaspoon cornstarch

Cut the mustard greens into bite-size pieces. Heat the oil in a preheated wok. Add the garlic and ginger, followed by the mustard greens, and stir-fry for 2 minutes. Combine 4 tablespoons water, the soy sauce, Chinese rice wine, a pinch of five-spice powder, and a pinch of salt and add to the wok. Reduce the heat, add the shrimp, and cook, stirring, for 1 minute. Cover and cook for a further 5 minutes. Mix together the cornstarch with 2 tablespoons water and use to thicken the liquid.

The essence of wok cookery: evenly diced or sliced ingredients which are cooked in a flash. The mustard greens are first halved, then their thick stalk is removed, and the leaves cut into thin strips.

When the oil is smoking hot add the garlic and ginger, then the mustard greens. Stir-fry for 2 minutes.

Add 4 tablespoons water, the Chinese rice wine, and the soy sauce. Continue to cook, stirring, over a low heat until the vegetables are tender, but still firm to the bite.

Add the shrimp to the cabbage and fry, stirring constantly, until they turn pink.

Potatoes: deep-fried and pan-fried
GOLDEN BROWN SPECIALTIES

Whether they are made from precooked or raw potatoes, the process remains the same: the potato is cooked in hot oil or fat. The heavier the pan used, the crunchier and more even the result.

POTATO CROQUETTES

Mash 1¼ pounds boiled mealy potatoes and mix with 2 egg yolks, 1½ teaspoons butter, 2 tablespoons crème fraîche or sour cream, salt and nutmeg to taste. Form the cooled mixture first into balls, then flatten into croquettes. Dip in beaten egg, then in bread crumbs. Make a lattice pattern with the back of a knife and fry in hot oil until golden. Drain and add a little butter to the pan at the end of cooking.

FRIED SMALL POTATOES—POMMES RISSOLÉES

Boil 2¼ pounds small new potatoes in their skins, then peel. Fry in 3 tablespoons oil until golden brown all over. Pour off the remaining oil, reduce the heat, add 4 teaspoons butter and heat until it foams, then season the potatoes with salt.

FRIED DICED POTATOES—POMMES CARRÉES

Cut 2¼ pounds peeled waxy potatoes into ¼-inch dice. Soak in cold water for 10 minutes. Pat dry, fry in oil until golden brown, and season with salt. Fresh herbs add an interesting touch to this dish.

POTATO DUMPLINGS—GNOCCHI

Mash 1¼ pounds boiled mealy potatoes. Stir in 2 egg yolks, 1½ teaspoons butter, 4 tablespoons cornstarch, ⅔ cup all-purpose flour, and salt and nutmeg to taste. Form the mixture into a roll, slice, and roll into balls. Make indentations with a fork and place the gnocchi on baking parchment sprinkled with flour. Cook in boiling salted water until they rise to the surface. Lift out the gnocchi with a slotted spoon, plunge into cold water, drain, and fry in fresh butter until golden brown.

Pan-fried golden brown potatoes (below): potato croquettes (bottom), Italian gnocchi (right), whole potatoes, precooked, then fried (left), and diced potatoes, fried uncooked (top).

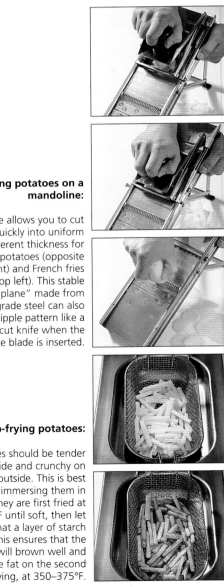

Slicing potatoes on a mandoline:

A mandoline allows you to cut potatoes quickly into uniform strips of different thickness for matchstick potatoes (opposite top right) and French fries (opposite top left). This stable vegetable "plane" made from high-grade steel can also create a ripple pattern like a crinkle-cut knife when the appropriate blade is inserted.

Deep-frying potatoes:

French fries should be tender on the inside and crunchy on the outside. This is best achieved by immersing them in oil twice. They are first fried at about 325°F until soft, then let cool, so that a layer of starch forms. This ensures that the potatoes will brown well and absorb little fat on the second and final frying, at 350–375°F.

French fries: This international dish is lifted out of the ordinary when mealy potatoes are cut into sticks and fried initially in fat at the low temperature of 325°F. This process is called blanching, even though it involves cooking in deep fat. The potatoes are then cooked until golden brown at 350°F.

Pommes allumettes (Matchstick potatoes): The potato sticks should be as thin as matches, as their name implies. Their small diameter means that blanching is not absolutely necessary, although it does make them crisper. As with all other types of fried potatoes, sprinkle with salt only just before serving.

TIP: It is advisable to cook moist potatoes (which tend to retain a lot of water) in their skins. After washing, bake the potatoes on a layer of coarse salt. Dry potato mixtures are the key to the success of many recipes.

Pommes pailles (Shoestring potatoes): Strips for these potatoes should measure at most ¹⁄₁₆ inch across and 2–2½ inches long. They turn out fine when cooked at a high temperature without blanching, because the thread-thin strips consist almost exclusively of crust and are cooked through and browned almost simultaneously.

Pommes gaufrettes: These wafer thin potato chips with a waffle pattern can be made only on a special mandoline. A rippled blade creates the grooves. The waffle pattern is achieved by turning the potato 90 degrees after each cut. Fry until golden brown in oil heated to 375°F.

Cylindrical croquettes: Drain 2¼ pounds boiled mealy potatoes, return to the saucepan, and reheat briefly to drive off the steam. Peel and mash. Mix with 4 egg yolks, 4 teaspoons butter, salt and nutmeg to taste. Form the mixture into finger-thick rolls and cool. Cut into 1½-inch long pieces, coat in flour, beaten egg, and bread crumbs, and deep-fry at 350°F.

Pommes dauphine: Make choux pastry from 1 cup water, 4 tablespoons butter, 1 cup all-purpose flour and 2–3 eggs. Mix this with 1¼ pounds croquette mixture (see left). Stamp out little dumplings and place on oiled baking parchment. Immerse in oil heated to 350°F with the paper side facing upward, then peel off the paper, and fry the potatoes until golden brown.

Potato pears: Prepare a croquette dough (see far left). Shape into pears and coat with bread crumbs. Decorate with a piece of spaghetti to make the stalk and a clove as the blossom, and deep-fry.

Serve the vegetables with a herb dip, or pass several different dips, such as basil, tuna, and olive, separately.

Deep-fried vegetables
A CRUNCHY BATTER CRUST KEEPS VEGETABLES MOIST

Their high water content makes most vegetables unsuitable for unadorned deep-frying, but if they are coated in batter or wrapped in some other covering they turn out quite delicious.

Preparing beer batter: Beat the egg yolks with the flour, salt, and beer. Rub through a strainer if lumps form. Let rest for 30 minutes. Finally, fold in the stiffly whisked egg whites. A variation is wine batter with saffron.

Mix the chopped and sliced vegetables with the lemon juice, oil, and herbs and marinate for 30 minutes.

Spear the vegetable pieces individually on a long fork, such as a fondue fork, and dip in the beer batter.

Allow the excess batter to drip briefly from the vegetables, then deep-fry until brown in oil heated to 350°F. Drain on paper towels.

VEGETABLES IN BEER BATTER

Serves 4
7 ounces each cauliflower and broccoli
1 kohlrabi
4 ounces each carrots, white and green asparagus, mushrooms, and snow peas
1 bunch scallions, juice of 1 lemon
2 tablespoons mixed chopped fresh herbs
4 tablespoons olive oil, salt, freshly ground pepper
10 sage leaves, 1 small bunch curly parsley
1½ teaspoons all-purpose flour
vegetable oil for deep-frying
For the beer batter:
4 eggs, 2¼ cups all-purpose flour, salt, 1 cup beer

Cut the vegetables into bite-size pieces. Blanch the cauliflower, broccoli, carrots, kohlrabi, and asparagus, rinse in cold water, and pat dry. Mix with the mushrooms, snow peas, and scallions. Mix the lemon juice, chopped herbs, and oil, and season to taste. Add to the vegetables and marinate for 30 minutes. Prepare the batter as illustrated in the step-by-step photographs (far left). Heat the oil in a deep-fryer to 350°F. Dip the vegetable pieces in the batter, let the excess batter drip off, and lower into the hot oil. Cook until golden brown, then lift out and drain. Hold the sage leaves by the stems, dip in the batter, and then fry. Dust the parsley with flour and fry.

SPRING ROLLS

The filling of this Chinese specialty is typically seasoned with cilantro and soy sauce. The vegetables used in this dish may be varied: the simplest recipes just contain strips of white cabbage and mung or soybean sprouts.

Serves 4
4 ounces snow peas
4 ounces carrots
5 ounces scallions
3 ounces celery
3 ounces Chinese cabbage
3 ounces shiitake mushrooms
4 ounces bean sprouts
4 tablespoons peanut oil
pinch of crushed garlic
salt, freshly ground white pepper
4 tablespoons soy sauce
1 tablespoon cornstarch
1 tablespoon chopped cilantro leaves
1 tablespoon all-purpose flour
8 spring roll skins
vegetable oil for deep-frying

Trim the vegetables and cut them into thin strips. Heat the peanut oil in a skillet or wok, then add the garlic and the vegetables and stir-fry. Season with salt and pepper and add the soy sauce. Mix the cornstarch with 2 tablespoons water and use to thicken the juices. Add the cilantro and set the filling aside to cool. Mix the flour with 1 tablespoon cold water, then gradually stir in 2–3 tablespoons hot water. Fill the spring roll skins as described in the step-by-step photographs (right), sealing them with the flour paste. Heat the oil in a deep-fryer to 350°F and lower in a few spring rolls at a time. Cook until golden brown, remove, and drain on paper towels.

TIP: The rolls may be filled, wrapped in damp cloths and refrigerated for 1–2 hours before frying. Hand round soy sauce separately as a dipping sauce.

Filling spring rolls:

Place the wrappers on a damp dish cloth and spoon a little of the cooked vegetable mixture close to one edge.

Fold over once. This is most easily done by raising the cloth slightly on one side.

Fold the top and bottom sides of the wrapper inward and brush all the edges with the flour paste to seal.

Lift up the cloth so that the roll forms itself. Gently press down all the edges again.

VEGETABLE QUICHES: For 4 servings you will need half the basic recipe for shortcrust pie dough (see page 236). For the filling, trim, dice, and blanch 4 ounces each zucchini and carrots, 1 red and 1 yellow bell pepper, and 5 ounces scallions, then drain. Cut 7 ounces broccoli into flowerets, blanch, and drain. Roll out the dough about ¼ inch thick and line four 4-inch quiche pans. Fill the dough shells with the vegetables and sprinkle with ½ cup grated Swiss cheese. Beat together 1 cup milk, ¼ cup heavy cream, 2 egg yolks and 2 eggs with salt, pepper, and grated nutmeg. Pour over the vegetables and bake in a preheated oven at 350°F for 25–30 minutes.

Baking

OVEN-COOKED VEGETABLE COMBINATIONS: QUICHES, PIZZAS, TERRINES, LASAGNE, STRUDELS, SOUFFLÉS, AND GRATINS

Crisp crusts and spicy, golden brown dishes are what this chapter is all about. The enticing smell of baking is one of the great delights of cooking. In the dry heat of the oven, protein particles and sugars or starches melt together into an unmistakable, mouthwatering combination. The process of browning creates a distinctive, intense flavor which goes superbly well with the juicy mildness of the interior of the vegetable dishes. Thus, the main charm of the simple southern Italian pizza lies in the contrast between its thin, crisp-baked crust and its juicy topping of tomatoes and cheese. The same is true for the spinach pie, a Greek specialty whose filling of vegetables and ewe's milk cheese is wrapped in well-browned pastry. All these dishes—whether French quiche, Italian pizza, or Greek vegetable pie—were originally by-products of the ancient art of breadmaking. The heat of the oven was used to create gratins: vegetable dishes warmed up in the oven and broiled or baked until crisp on top—a delicious meal to look forward to at the end of a day's work.

SHORTCRUST PIE DOUGH: BASIC RECIPE

This basic pie dough goes with almost any vegetable filling imaginable. Moreover, it can be prepared many hours in advance, covered in plastic wrap, and stored in the refrigerator until required.

Makes sufficient for a 10-inch pan
2¾ cups all-purpose flour
10 tablespoons chilled butter, diced
½ teaspoon salt, 3–4 tablespoons water
1 egg

Sift the flour onto the counter and put the butter on top. Rub the flour and butter together with your fingertips until the mixture resembles bread crumbs. Make a well in the center and add the salt, 3–4 tablespoons water, and the egg. Working quickly, knead with both hands to a smooth dough. Refrigerate, wrapped in plastic wrap, for at least 1 hour. Roll out on a lightly floured counter to a thickness of about ¼ inch. Lift the dough with the rolling pin and unroll over the pie pan you are using. Press the dough into the pan and cut off the excess with a knife.

Shortcrust pie dough: Rub the flour and butter together with your fingertips to the consistency of fine bread crumbs. Make a well in the center, add the salt, water, and egg, and quickly knead together into a smooth dough.

Form the dough into a smooth ball, wrap in plastic wrap, and refrigerate for 1–2 hours.

Roll out the dough on a floured counter to a uniform round about ¼ inch thick.

Lining the pan with the dough:

Lift the pie dough with the rolling pin, place over the pan, and unroll.

Crimp the edges of the pastry, using your fingers or a small ball of dough. Cut off excess pastry with a knife.

BACON AND ONION QUICHE

Serves 4
1½ pounds onions
7 thick slices bacon
4 teaspoons butter
7 tablespoons crème fraîche or heavy cream
1 cup milk, 5 eggs
salt, nutmeg, freshly ground white pepper
1 recipe basic shortcrust pie dough

Thinly slice the onions. Cut the bacon crosswise into thin strips and cook in a shallow skillet until the fat runs. Add the onions and sauté, then add the butter. Remove from the heat and cool slightly. Beat the crème fraîche or cream with the milk and eggs, then add the onion and bacon mixture and mix. Season with salt, nutmeg, and pepper to taste. Roll out the pastry and line a 10-inch quiche pan. Spoon in the filling and smooth the surface. Bake in a preheated oven at 400°F for about 45 minutes, until set and golden.

TRUFFLE AND LEEK TART

Serves 4
12 ounces frozen puff pastry, thawed
1¼ pounds leeks, 4 teaspoons butter
1½ tablespoons flour
1⅔ cups milk, 7 tablespoons heavy cream
salt, freshly ground white pepper, nutmeg
1–2 black truffles, 4 egg yolks
For glazing:
1 cup port
3 tablespoons each canned or bottled truffle juice and veal stock
pinch of cornstarch

Makes four 4-inch tartlets. Roll out the pastry ⅛ inch thick, cover with a clean cloth, and let rest. Line 4 tartlet pans with the pastry, leaving an extra ½ inch or so above the edges. Fill the pastry shells with crumpled foil and bake in a preheated oven at 400°F for 10–12 minutes. Discard the foil, cut off the surplus pastry, and cool the tartlet shells. Cut the leeks into strips and sauté in the butter. Stir in the flour and cook briefly, stirring constantly. Gradually stir in the milk and cream and simmer for 5–8 minutes. Season with salt, nutmeg, and pepper and remove from the heat. Peel the truffles, chop the peel, and add to the leeks, together with the egg yolks. Divide the mixture between the tartlet cases. Garnish with slices of truffle. Bake at 350°F for 12–14 minutes. Meanwhile, mix together the port, truffle juice, and veal stock in a saucepan and reduce by three-quarters. Thicken with the cornstarch and use to glaze the finished tartlets.

A simple but sophisticated variation consists in sprinkling the onion quiche with grated cheese three-quarters of the way through the cooking time, or topping the filling with a little finely chopped lovage.

Leek and onion quiche: These two vegetables are particularly well suited to baking and go superbly with cheese. It is therefore not surprising that quite a number of regional specialties make use of this combination with a savory egg custard, sometimes seasoned with paprika, pepper, or caraway seeds. Smoked bacon or ham adds a further piquant touch in many recipes, as in the best known, quiche Lorraine. Escoffier is said to have devised a combination with black truffles, similar to the little leek tarts shown here.

SPINACH PIE

This is a traditional vegetarian pastry from Greece with a filling of spinach and feta cheese.

Serves 4
4 cups all-purpose flour
2 cups whole-wheat flour
1½ ounces yeast, 1¼ cups water
2 eggs, salt
7 tablespoons olive oil
1 egg yolk, for glazing
butter, for greasing
For the filling:
4½ pounds spinach, 3 onions
2 cloves garlic, 1 bunch dill, finely chopped
2 cups diced feta cheese
freshly ground pepper, nutmeg

Sift together the two flours. Make a well in the center, crumble in the yeast and mix with tepid water. Cover with a little flour and leave for at least 15 minutes, until cracks develop in the surface. Add the eggs, 1 teaspoon salt, and ¼ cup of the oil and knead thoroughly. Put the dough into a bowl, cover and set aside in a warm place until it has doubled in size. For the filling, trim, wash, and dry the spinach. Peel and dice the onion and garlic and sauté in the remaining oil until translucent. Add the spinach leaves, season with salt, pepper, and nutmeg, and cook until the spinach has wilted. Drain in a colander and cool. Stir in the chopped dill and the feta cheese. Season with salt, pepper, and nutmeg. Knead the dough again. Roll out two-thirds and use to line a greased jelly roll pan. Prick the base at regular intervals with a fork and spread the spinach filling evenly over it. Roll out the remaining dough, cut into long strips, and arrange over the filling in a lattice pattern. Beat the egg yolk with 1 tablespoon water and brush over the pastry. Bake the pie in a preheated oven at 350°F for 40–50 minutes.

Pizza toppings
A SELECTION OF THE MOST VARIED COMBINATIONS

The classic—and simplest—pizza topping consists of peeled, seeded tomatoes, braised with garlic in olive oil to a thick purée, and seasoned with a pinch of oregano. Topped with mozzarella cheese, you have the simplest of all pizzas, but the light yeast dough naturally goes with many kinds of toppings. An interesting version (left): cooked artichoke hearts, onion rings, and black olives are arranged over the tomato purée with Gorgonzola melted on top. Another interesting version (left, second) is made with crème fraîche, scallions, German sausage, and marjoram, and does not need tomatoes. Shrimp, tomatoes, chopped garlic, and Fontina cheese are baked on a yeast dough (left, center). A lavish topping consisting of tomatoes, eggplant, zucchini, bell peppers, ham, anchovies, and Fontina cheese (bottom) is as appropriate as the combination consisting of red and yellow bell peppers, Italian salami, onions, olives, thyme, and Fontina cheese (below, right).

PIZZA DOUGH: BASIC RECIPE

Makes 2–3 pizzas or 20 mini-pizzas
2¾ cups all-purpose flour
¾ ounce fresh yeast
1 cup water
½ teaspoon salt
2 tablespoons olive oil

Prepare the dough as described in the step-by-step photographs (right) and leave to rise until approximately doubled in size. Knead thoroughly on a floured counter until elastic. Either divide the dough into 20 portions and roll out into mini-pizzas, as in the step-by-step photographs (below), or use to line 2–3 pizza pans. Bake in a preheated oven at 400°F for 12 minutes (mini-pizzas) or 12–15 minutes (large pizzas). Larger quantities are best baked on a cookie sheet.

Preparing pizza dough: Make a well in the flour. Crumble in the yeast and stir with the lukewarm water. Cover with a little flour and let stand until obvious cracks develop in the surface. Mix with the salt and oil.

Rolling out mini pizzas:

Thoroughly knead the dough on a floured counter until smooth and elastic.

Shape into two long logs. Mark out individual portions with a knife and cut the dough into pieces of equal size.

Making circular movements with your hand, shape each of the 20 pieces of yeast dough into a smooth ball.

Applying slight pressure, roll the dough balls into rounds of uniform thickness on a lightly floured surface.

Using your thumbs, create a slightly raised edge on each pizza. Prick each base several times with a fork and top with the chosen ingredients.

VEGETABLE STRUDEL

Serves 4
1¾ cup all-purpose flour
1 cup water, 7 tablespoons vegetable oil
For the filling:
3 medium carrots, 7 ounces kohlrabi
4 ounces each celery root and snow peas
5 ounces green beans
1¾ pounds peas in their pods
4 egg yolks, ½ tablespoon all-purpose flour
½ cup fresh bread crumbs
salt, freshly ground pepper, pinch of nutmeg
4 tablespoons butter, melted

Knead together the flour, water, and 1½ teaspoons oil into a smooth dough. Roll into a ball, put in an oiled bowl, and pour in the remaining oil. Cover with plastic wrap and let rest for 1 hour. Cut the carrots, kohlrabi, and celery root into batons. Blanch the snow peas, beans, and vegetable batons in boiling salted water, then rinse with cold water. Shell the peas and cook in boiling salted water until tender. Drain, process in a food processor, and rub through a strainer. Stir in the egg yolks, flour, and bread crumbs. Season with salt, pepper, and nutmeg. Drain the strudel dough and dust lightly with flour. Stretch on a cloth over the back of your hand until paper-thin. Fill as described in the step-by-step photographs (right) and bake in a preheated oven at 425°F for about 20 minutes.

Brush the strudel dough, stretched paper-thin, sparingly and evenly with half the melted butter.

Spread the pea purée in a strip about 2 inches wide and top with alternate rows of blanched vegetables.

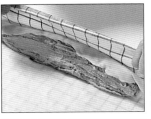

Lift up the cloth, raising the edge high enough to make the dough and filling form themselves into a roll.

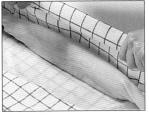

Roll up the strudel, place on a greased cookie sheet, and brush with the remaining melted butter.

KOHLRABI AND RED CHARD LASAGNE

(below right)

Serves 6–8

4 kohlrabi (about 9 ounces each)
6 tablespoons butter, salt, freshly ground white pepper
nutmeg, 1 tablespoon all-purpose flour
2¼ cups milk, 1 cup heavy cream
11 ounces tomatoes, 1¼ pounds red chard
2 shallots, 12 green lasagne sheets
1 teaspoon oil, 1¾ cups grated Swiss cheese
4 tablespoons sour cream
1 egg yolk, lightly beaten

Thinly slice the kohlrabi and cut the leaves into strips. Cook as shown in the photographs (below). Peel and seed the tomatoes and cut into strips. Separate the stalks of the chard from the leaves. Peel and cut the stalks into ¾-inch pieces. Remove the ribs from the leaves, slice the leaves into wide strips, and blanch. Put the kohlrabi in a bowl, cool, then mix with the chard. Bring a pan of salted water to a boil, add the oil, and cook the lasagne for 5 minutes, then rinse under cold water. Layer the ingredients in an ovenproof dish as shown. Mix the sour cream with the egg yolk and spread over the top. Bake in a preheated oven at 350°F for 40–45 minutes. Cut into squares to serve.

Sauté the kohlrabi in 2 tablespoons butter and season with salt, pepper, and nutmeg. Sprinkle with flour. Pour in the milk and cream and simmer for 10 minutes.

Peel and finely chop the shallots. Sauté the diced chard stalks with the shallots in 4 teaspoons butter.

Line a greased ovenproof dish with 3 cooked lasagne sheets and spread a third of the cooled vegetable mixture evenly over the top.

Top with a few strips of tomato and a third of the cheese. Continue layering the remaining vegetables, lasagne sheets, and cheese in exactly the same way.

LASAGNE WITH GREEN BEANS

(not shown)

Serves 6–8

11 ounces ground beef, 2 tablespoons vegetable oil
2 onions, chopped, 1 clove garlic, chopped
1 tablespoon tomato paste
7 ounces tomatoes, coarsely chopped
1 cup beef stock, leaves of 1 sprig thyme, 1 bay leaf
salt, freshly ground black pepper
12 plain lasagne sheets, 1¼ pounds green beans
2 cups grated Parmesan cheese
3 tablespoons butter, ¼ cup all-purpose flour
1⅔ cups milk, nutmeg

Fry the beef in 4 teaspoons of oil until brown. Add the onions and garlic and sauté. Add the tomato paste and fry until the mixture is almost dry. Add the tomatoes, stock, and herbs, season, and cook until nearly dry. Bring a pan of salted water to a boil, add the remaining oil, and cook the lasagne for 5 minutes, then rinse in cold water. Cook the beans in boiling salted water until tender, and rinse. Melt 4 teaspoons butter, stir in the flour and cook, stirring for 1 minute. Stir in the milk and simmer, stirring, for 15 minutes. Season and strain. Grease an ovenproof dish. Cover with a layer of lasagne sheets, a layer of beef, beans, sauce, and cheese. Layer until the ingredients are used, ending with pasta topped with the sauce and sprinkled with cheese. Bake in a preheated oven at 350°F for 40–45 minutes. Cut into squares to serve.

Both the vegetarian kohlrabi and red chard lasagne (shown here) and the bean and ground beef variant may be served as an hors d'oeuvre, appetizer, or main course dish, and will feed 4–8 accordingly.

Soufflés and terrines
LIGHT, AIRY DISHES BASED ON EGGS AND VEGETABLES

Eggs thicken, absorb liquid, aerate, support, and harmonize the flavors. Their role here is crucial: it is the lightening effect of the whisked egg whites that determines the success of a soufflé, for the heat of the oven causes the air bubbles to expand, raising the mixture high over the edge of the soufflé dish. In terrines, beaten eggs replace meat as a thickening agent, absorbing the moisture and ensuring a consistency that is easy to slice. Baking in a water bath guarantees gentle heat, and ensures that the delicate structure of the egg and vegetable combination is maintained. Otherwise, the egg mixture might rise so high that large bubbles could spoil the consistency of the dish. Classics such as artichoke, asparagus, and pumpkin soufflés also enjoy great popularity. Combined with eggs, more mundane ingredients, such as spinach and cheese, become delicacies.

SPINACH SOUFFLÉ
Serves 6–8

5 tablespoons butter, ¼ cup all-purpose flour
1 cup milk, 3 tablespoons heavy cream
salt, freshly ground white pepper
nutmeg, 5 eggs, separated
1¼ pounds spinach, 2 shallots
½ clove garlic, 4 teaspoons butter
4 ounces garlic chives
butter and bread crumbs, for the ramekins

Make a béchamel sauce as shown left. Season with salt, pepper, and nutmeg and cool. Beat the egg yolks and stir into the sauce. Blanch and rinse the spinach. Prepare the soufflé mixture as illustrated below. Grease 4 ramekin dishes with butter and coat with bread crumbs. Fill the dishes to about ⅛ inch below the top with the spinach mixture. Bake in a water bath in a preheated oven at 350°F for 20 minutes. Serve at once.

Preparing a béchamel sauce: Melt the butter and stir in the flour. Cook, stirring constantly, for 2 minutes. Gradually stir in the milk and simmer the sauce for 15 minutes. Add the cream and bring to a boil. Cool slightly and stir in the beaten egg yolks, a little at a time.

Preparing the soufflé mixture:

Wrap the blanched spinach in a dish cloth or piece of heavy cheesecloth and wring out thoroughly with your hands.

Place the spinach leaves on a board and chop with a large knife.

Sauté the diced shallots and garlic with the spinach in hot butter.

Stir into the béchamel sauce together with the snipped garlic chives.

Whisk the egg whites to stiff peaks and fold into the soufflé base with a wooden spoon or rubber spatula.

Trim the cauliflower, divide into flowerets, and cook in the milk and cream for about 8 minutes. Remove the cauliflower and reserve liquid.

Remove the hard stalks from the flowerets, return them to the cooking liquid, and cook until tender.

Purée the cauliflower stalks, together with their cooking liquid, and season with salt, pepper, and nutmeg.

Rub the puréed cauliflower, cream, and milk mixture through a fine strainer.

Beat together the eggs and the cauliflower mixture. The eggs ensure that the terrine will be easy to slice.

Line the terrine dish with foil, overlapping the sides, and grease with butter. Add the cauliflower and broccoli flowerets.

Cover the vegetables with the sauce. Seal the terrine by folding in the pieces of foil at either side.

CAULIFLOWER AND BROCCOLI TERRINE

Serves 4
14 ounces cauliflower
1 cup each milk and cream
salt, freshly ground white pepper, nutmeg
11 ounces broccoli, 3 eggs
¼ cup toasted slivered almonds
1½ teaspoons butter for greasing

Prepare the cauliflower as shown in the step-by-step photographs (far right). Cut the broccoli, into flowerets, blanch for 1 minute, and rinse in cold water. Line a terrine or loaf pan with aluminum foil and grease with butter. Fill the terrine or pan as shown in the step-by-step photographs (right). Bake in a water bath in a preheated oven at 350°F for 45 minutes. Test whether the terrine is set by inserting a toothpick; if it comes out clean, the dish is cooked. Turn out the finished terrine, garnish with the slivered almonds, and serve cut into slices.

POTATO GRATIN

GRATIN OF FENNEL

You can ring the changes with this classic dish. Often the potatoes are cooked in cream without any further seasonings apart from salt and pepper. Sometimes thyme, rosemary, and a generous amount of garlic lend a southern European touch to the potatoes. Dried mushrooms, such as morels or porcini, add a sophisticated note.

Gratin de pommes de terre à la Dauphinoise is the traditional and probably the best-known potato gratin. It makes an ideal accompaniment for lamb dishes and roasts.

Serves 4–6
2¼ pounds waxy potatoes
½ clove garlic
4 teaspoons butter
salt, freshly ground white pepper, nutmeg
1 cup grated Swiss cheese
2¼ cups milk, 1 cup heavy cream

Peel and thinly slice the potatoes. Rub the cut surface of the garlic clove over the inside of an ovenproof dish and grease the dish with 1½ teaspoons butter. Layer the potato slices in the dish, overlapping them like scales. Season each layer sparingly with salt and pepper. Finish by seasoning with nutmeg. Sprinkle the cheese over the top. Pour in the milk and cream, taking care that the liquid only just covers the potatoes and does not come too close to the top of the dish. Dot the potatoes with the remaining butter and bake at 350°F for 50–60 minutes, or until the potatoes are cooked and the top browned.

Not every vegetable can be cooked and gratinéed at the same time, like potatoes. Most are best blanched first in boiling salted water. In this way vegetables do not lose so much moisture, and their vivid colors are retained to a greater extent. A lightly bound sauce keeps the gratin moist.

Serves 4
4 medium fennel bulbs
2 small beefsteak tomatoes
3 tablespoons butter, 1 tablespoon flour
1 cup each milk and heavy cream
salt, freshly ground white pepper

Cut off the fennel stalks and reserve the fronds. Halve the bulbs. Blanch in boiling salted water for 3–4 minutes, then rinse in cold water, and drain. Peel, quarter, seed, and dice the tomatoes. Melt half the butter in a saucepan, add the flour, and cook, stirring constantly, for 2 minutes. Gradually add the milk and cream, stirring constantly. Simmer the sauce over a low heat for 10 minutes, stirring constantly. Season with salt and pepper and strain. Grease an ovenproof dish with the remaining butter. Slice the fennel halves and transfer to the prepared dish, together with the tomatoes. Chop the fennel fronds and scatter over the top. Season with salt and pepper and pour the sauce on top. Bake in a preheated oven at 350°F for 35–40 minutes, until golden brown.

Vegetables au gratin
SUCCULENT VEGETABLES WITH A GOLDEN BROWN CRUST

Although all the dishes here display golden brown crusts, these are achieved by entirely different methods. The potato gratin develops its well-browned surface over the course of long baking. With the fennel gratin, a combination of cooking methods is used—blanching and baking in a sauce. The asparagus and mixed vegetable gratins are broiled briefly.

MIXED VEGETABLE GRATIN

Serves 4
7 ounces new potatoes
salt, caraway seeds
7 ounces each baby carrots with green tops, broccoli, and green asparagus
11 ounces cauliflower, 9 ounces kohlrabi
4 teaspoons butter, sugar
½ cup vegetable stock (see page 154)
1 recipe hollandaise sauce (see page 160)

Cook the potatoes in boiling, salted water with a pinch of caraway seeds. Cut the remaining vegetables into bite-size pieces, blanch, rinse with cold water, and drain. Peel the potatoes. Melt the butter in a saucepan, add a pinch of salt and sugar, and sauté the vegetables. Add the stock and cook over a low heat until reduced and the vegetables are glazed. Transfer the potatoes and vegetables to a flameproof dish, pour on the hollandaise sauce, and broil lightly.

ASPARAGUS AU GRATIN

Serves 4
2¼ pounds white asparagus
1 shallot, finely chopped, 3 tablespoons butter
¼ cup white wine, 1 cup milk, 7 tablespoons cream
salt, sugar, ¼ lemon
2 egg yolks, 2 tablespoons heavy cream
9 ounces peeled cooked shrimp
chervil, to garnish

Peel the asparagus, cut off two-thirds of the stems, and set aside for the sauce. To make the sauce, melt 1 tablespoon butter in a saucepan and sauté the shallot. Add the asparagus stems, sauté, then add the wine. Add the milk and light cream and cook the stems until tender. Purée the mixture in a food processor and rub through a strainer. Bring a pan of lightly salted water to a boil and add the remaining butter, a pinch of sugar, and the lemon. Add the asparagus tips and cook until just tender. Mix the egg yolks with the heavy cream and fold into the sauce. Heat the sauce, beating constantly, until creamy. Arrange the asparagus with the shrimp on flameproof serving plates and add the sauce. Brown under the broiler until the shrimp are warm. Garnish with fresh chervil.

VEGETABLE-STUFFED POTATOES

Serves 6. Wash 7 medium baking potatoes. Wrap in aluminum foil and bake at 350°F for about 40 minutes or until cooked through. Meanwhile, core, seed, peel and dice 1 red, 1 green, and 1 yellow bell pepper. Peel and dice 2 tomatoes. Remove the cooked potatoes from the foil. Scoop out the flesh from 6 of the potatoes, leaving only a thin shell in place. Mash the potato flesh and rub through a strainer or put through a ricer or food mill. Peel and dice the remaining potato and add, together with the diced vegetables, to the purée. Mix in 1 egg yolk and a pinch of nutmeg and season with salt and pepper. Beat 1 egg white until it forms stiff peaks and fold into the mixture. Spoon the mixture into the potato shells. Sprinkle with ½ cup grated Swiss cheese and a few thyme leaves. Bake in a preheated oven at 400°F for 10 minutes, until golden brown on top.

FOIL-BAKED POTATOES WITH CAVIAR

Serves 6. Wash 6 medium baking potatoes. Wrap in aluminum foil and bake at 350°F for about 40 minutes, or until cooked through. Remove the potatoes from the foil, cut a cross in the top of each, and squeeze open. Serve each potato with 1 tablespoon crème fraîche or sour cream and 2 tablespoons caviar.

TRUFFLE POTATOES

Serves 6. Place 8 medium baking potatoes on a cookie sheet covered with a layer of salt about ¼–½ inch thick, and bake in a preheated oven at 350°F for 40 minutes. Cut a "lid" from 6 of the potatoes and scoop out the flesh, leaving an ⅛ -inch thick shell. Peel the remaining potatoes. Rub all the potato flesh through a strainer or put it through a ricer or food mill. Mix the mashed potatoes with 2 tablespoons heavy cream, 2 egg yolks, 2 tablespoons butter, ⅔ cup grated Parmesan cheese, and 1 ounce finely diced truffles. Season with salt and pepper and pipe decoratively into the potato shells. Dot with 1½ teaspoons butter and bake for 10 minutes at 350°F to brown the top.

Oven-baked vegetables

THEIR OWN SKIN—OR FOIL—PROTECTS THEM FROM DRYING OUT WHEN COOKED

Potatoes, onions, and garlic, not to mention beets and other tubers, develop a special taste when baked in the dry heat of the oven, as the skin of the vegetable—and in some cases an additional covering of aluminum foil—effectively seals in both flavor and moisture. The result is the pure, unadulterated taste of the vegetable.

BAKED ONIONS

Serves 6. Place 6 medium onions, unpeeled, in an ovenproof dish. Pour in enough water to come halfway up the onions. Bake in a preheated oven at 350°F for 1–1½ hours. Peel and serve the soft flesh with salt, pepper, and a pat of butter.

TIP: Baked onions are very tasty served with freshly toasted bread as an appetizer or an accompaniment to charcoal broiled dishes.

GARLIC BAKED IN RED WINE

Serves 6. Place 6 fresh heads of young garlic, weighing 2–2½ ounces each, in a flameproof dish. Pour in 2¼ cups red wine and tuck in 2 sprigs each of thyme and rosemary. Bring to a boil, then transfer to a preheated oven and bake at 350°F for about 30 minutes. Break the heads apart and separate the cloves. Squeeze out the soft flesh and eat with a little salt straight from the skin. Alternatively, serve as a purée with fried meats, or broiled fish or meat.

Glossary of cookery terms

Aspic: A savory gelatin containing vegetables, fish, or meat.

Béchamel sauce: A basic white sauce consisting of flour sautéed in butter to which milk and/or cream are added.

Bind: To thicken sauces and soups.

Blanch: To cook vegetables briefly in boiling salted water to eliminate unpleasant flavors and impurities, or to facilitate removal of the skin or peel.

Blend: To purée finely, creating an emulsion and a light texture.

Bouquet garni: A bunch of herbs, vegetables, or spices tied together and used to flavor stocks and sauces.

Braise: To cook food by first lightly browning in fat or oil, then cooking in a covered saucepan or casserole in a small amount of liquid.

Caramel: Sugar, including the natural sugar in vegetables, which has been browned by heating.

Casserole: An ovenproof, sometimes flameproof, cooking dish with a lid, made of earthenware, glass, or metal. Also, the food cooked in such a dish, usually slow-cooked in the oven.

Cheesecloth: Coarse cloth for straining sauces and soups—and for draining cheese.

Chiffonade: Thin strips of lettuce or other leaves.

Clarify: To bind and remove all murky substances from soups, juices, gelatins, etc. with the help of egg whites or finely ground meat or fish. Also, to remove the milk solids from heated butter to make a cooking fat that can be heated to a relatively high temperature without burning.

Confit: Preserved foods, such as goose, or a conserve of slow-cooked onions, shallots, or other vegetables.

Crinkle-cut knife: A grooved knife for cutting vegetables decoratively.

Deep-fry: To cook food until golden brown in hot fat or oil deep enough to cover.

Defat: To skim off excess fat from sauces and soups. When the food is chilled, the congealed layer of fat can be easily removed. When it is hot, a skimmer can be run carefully under the layer of fat to trap and remove it. Alternatively, paper towels may be placed on the surface to absorb it.

Essence: Heavily reduced vegetable, meat, fish or poultry stock with a concentrated flavor.

Farce, forcemeat: A filling of meat, fish, shellfish, vegetables, etc. that is put through the meat grinder or blended, bound with cream or eggs, and seasoned with herbs or spices. The texture may be lightened with the addition of white bread crumbs. It can be used as a stuffing, or made into dumplings and served as a side dish or soup garnish.

Foam: To blend briefly to create a head of foam and volume; also applied to butter, in the sense of heating it without letting it color.

Garnish: To decorate dishes with edible ingredients that harmonize with the food in shape and color.

Glaze: To give foods a glossy surface, by adding sugar or by applying a coating of beaten egg or milk before baking.

Gratin: Dish covered in a sauce, cheese, or breadcrumbs, and baked or broiled to produce a crust.

Hollandaise sauce: An emulsion of butter and egg yolks which forms the basis of numerous variations.

Julienne: Any ingredient cut into extremely thin strips.

Liaison: Egg yolk beaten with cream and stirred into soups and sauces to thicken them, or other thickeners.

Mandoline: A kitchen gadget made from high-grade steel which is used to cut wafer-thin slices, julienne strips, and potato waffles. Plastic mandolines are also available.

Marinade: A liquid containing herbs and spices which is used to season, preserve, and tenderize meat and fish.

Marinate: To steep or soak in a marinade.

Mirepoix: Finely diced root vegetables, onions, possibly lean bacon, lightly roasted or browned in fat, sometimes with herbs and bay leaf, used to season soups, stews, and sauces.

Mousse: A light mixture made from fish, seafood, meat, poultry, or vegetables (savory) or fruit or chocolate (sweet) blended with cream and/or eggs and sometimes gelatin.

Pan-fry: To cook vegetables, eggs, meat, and fish in a fairly small amount of fat or oil in a pan or skillet.

Pastry bag: A conical bag into which puréed or smooth foods are spooned, to be piped out as a decoration or garnish.

Poach: To cook a food slowly in simmering liquid at just below boiling point. This method is particularly suitable for delicate foods such as fish, eggs, and poultry.

Purée: To blend raw or cooked foods until smooth, using a hand blender, potato masher, blender, or food processor.

Quiche: A savory tart with an egg filling, such as quiche Lorraine (with bacon and cream).

Reduction: A vigorously boiled and reduced liquid with an intense flavor.

Refresh: To run or pour cold water over food or immerse it in ice water to prevent it sticking together (rice, pasta), to permit the easy shelling of boiled eggs, or to arrest the cooking process (vegetables).

Render: To fry bacon until the fat runs and the meat is golden brown.

Risotto: Round-grain rice sautéed in butter or olive oil, cooked in stock and/or white wine, generally mixed with butter and grated Parmesan cheese.

Roast: To cook vegetables, meat, or fish in the oven with the addition of fat or oil.

Roux: Flour cooked in butter as a basis for thickened soups and sauces.

Sabayon: A warm or cold sauce made in both a sweet and a savory version.

Sauté: To cook food briefly in fat.

Simmer: To cook at just under boiling point.

Steam: To cook above boiling water or other liquid in the steam created, without the food coming into contact with the liquid.

Stock: A liquid concentrate, obtained by boiling or stewing, foods, which serves as the basis of soups and sauces.

Strain: To pour, rub, or press a liquid or blended mixture through a fine strainer or cheesecloth.

Sweat: To cook gently in a little fat or oil, without additional liquid, so that the juices from the vegetables become concentrated.

Terrine dish: Ovenproof porcelain or stoneware dish.

Thicken with butter: To blend with chilled butter in order to bind or give body to a sauce.

Timbales: Cup-shaped molds of high-grade steel.

Velouté: A basic rich white sauce made of egg yolks, cream, and stock.

Zester: A special knife for cutting paper-thin julienne. Particularly suitable for citrus fruits, as it removes only the top layer of rind (the zest).

Index
Vegetable encyclopedia

Index
Practical guidelines and recipes

References

Autorenkollektiv [Writers' collective]: *Lebensmittel-Lexikon*, Leipzig, 1981.

Bärtels, A.: *Farbatlas Tropenpflanzen*, Stuttgart, 1989.

Baumeister, W., and Menzel-Tettenborn, H.: *Das große illustrierte Pflanzenbuch*, Bertelsmann Lexikon, Gütersloh, 1968.

Belitz, H.-D. and Grosch, W.: *Lehrbuch der Lebensmittelchemie*, Berlin, 1982.

Bissell, F.: *Sainsbury's Book of Food*, London, 1989.

Brücher, H.: *Die sieben Säulen der Welternährung*, Frankfurt, 1982; *Tropische Nutzpflanzen. Ursprung, Evolution und Domestikation*, Berlin, 1977.

Buishand, T., Houwing, H.P. and Jansen, K.: Groenten uit alle windstreken. Eeen geïllustreerde gids, met beschrijvingen en anwijzingen voor het gebruik van ruim 400 Soorten en rassen, Amsterdam, 1986.

Bundessortenamt: *Beschreibende Sortenliste für Fruchtgemüse, Blattgemüse*, Hanover, 1987; *Beschreibende Sortenliste für Gemüse-Hülsenfrüchte*, Hanover, 1987; *Beschreibende Sortenliste für Kartoffeln*, Hanover, 1990.

Campbell, S.: *Geheimnisse des Küchengartens*, Frankfurt, 1984.

Dahlen, M. and Phillipps, K.: A *Popular Guide to Chinese Vegetables*, Singapore, 1985.

Dassler, E.: *Warenkunde für den Fruchthandel. Südfrüchte, Obst und Gemüse nach Herkünften und Sorten*, Berlin, Hamburg, 1969.

De Balie, X. N.: *Exotische Groenten. Recepten uit De Antillen, China, Indonesië, Marokko, Suriname en Turkije*, Amsterdam, 1988.

Deutsche Gesellschaft für Ernährung: *Ernährungsberichte*, Frankfurt, 1984 and 1988.

Deutsche Gesellschaft für Hauswirtschaft: *Lebensmittelverarbeitung im Haushalt*, Stuttgart, 1984.

Encke, F., Buchheim, G. and Seybold, S.: *Zander. Handwörterbuch der Pflanzennamen*, 13th edition, Stuttgart, 1984.

FAO: *Production Yearbook*, Vol. 43, Rome, 1989.

Franke, W.: *Nutzpflanzenkunde*, 4th edition, Stuttgart, 1989.

Fritz, D. and Stolz, W.: *Gemüsebau. Handbuch des Erwerbsgärtners*, 9th edition, Stuttgart, 1989.

Fruchthandel: Internationale Fachzeitschrift für den gesamten Handel mit Früchten und Gemüse, Trockenfrüchten, Obst- und Gemüsekonserven, Kartoffeln und Blumen. Düsseldorf, issues from 1988–91.

Goetz, R.: *Kochen mit Meeresgemüse*, Berlin, 1986

Gemeinsamer Sortenkatalog für Gemüsearten. Anhang zum Amtsblatt der Europäischen Gemeinschaft, 16th complete edition, 33rd year, Luxembourg 1990.

Gemüse: Spezialblatt für den Feld- und Intensivgemüsebau, Stuttgart and Munich, issues from 1988–91.

Hartmann, H.D.: *Spargel*, Stuttgart, 1989.

Keller, F.; Lüthi, J. and Röthlisberger, K.:*100 Gemüse*, 1st edition, Zollikofen, 1986.

Krug, H.: *Gemüseproduktion. Ein Lehr- und Nachschlagewerk für Studium und Praxis*, Berlin and Hamburg, 1986.

Kunz, B.: *Grundriß der Lebensmittel-Mikrobiologie*, Hamburg, 1988.

Lang, R.-M.: *Feine und seltene Gemüse*, Stuttgart, 1986.

Liebster, G.: *Warenkunde Obst & Gemüse*, Vols. 1 and 2. Düsseldorf, 1988 and 1990.

Mansfeld, R.: *Verzeichnis landwirtschaftlicher und gärtnerischer Kulturpflanzen*, Vols. 1–4, publ. by Schultze-Motel, J., Berlin, 1986.

McGee, H.: *The Science and Lore of the Kitchen*, London, 1986.

Mennel, St.: *Die Kultivierung des Appetits*, Frankfurt, 1988.

National Academy of Sciences: *Tropical Legumes: Resources for the Future*, Washington, 1979.

Puseglove, J. W.: *Tropical Crops. Monocotyledons & Dicotyledons*, Vol. 1 and 2, London, 1988 and 1991.

Rehm, S. (Publ.): Handbuch der Landwirtschaft und Ernährung in den Entwicklungsländern. Vol. 4: *Spezieller Pflanzenbau in den Tropen und Subtropen*, 2nd edition, Stuttgart, 1989.

Rehm, S. and Espig, E.: *Die Kulturpflanzen der Tropen und Subtropen. Anbau, wirtschaftliche Bedeutung, Verwertung*. 2nd edition, Stuttgart, 1984.

Rinzler, C. A.: *Food facts*, London 1987.

Stegemann, H. and Schnick, D.: *Index 1985 Europäischer Kartoffelsorten. Mitteilungen aus der Biologischen Bundesanstalt für Land- und Forstwirtschaft*. Berlin, 1985.

Stein, S.: *Gemüse aus Großmutters Garten*, Munich, 1989.

Teubner Edition: Das große Buch der Exoten. Obst aus den Tropen und Subtropen., Füssen, 1990.

Tindall, H. D.: *Vegetables in the Tropics*, London, 1988.

Wirths, W.: *Lebensmittel in ernährungsphysiologischer Sicht*, Paderborn, 1985.

Picture credits:

p. 26, 2 photographs, p. 27, 2 photographs, p. 28, 1 photograph: Hans-Georg Levin; p. 29, 3 photographs: Pampus Associates, Utrecht; p. 30, 1 photograph: Prof. Dr. Jochen Alkämper, Gießen; p. 30, 1 photograph, p. 31, 1 photograph: Hans-Georg Levin; p. 32, 1 photograph, p. 36, 1 photograph: Pampus Associates, Utrecht; p. 42, 1 photograph: Hans-Georg Levin; p. 46, 1 photograph: Sopexa, Düsseldorf; p. 51, 1 photograph, p. 54, 1 photograph: Hans-Georg Levin; p. 59, 1 photograph: Willemse, the Netherlands; p. 65, 1 photograph, p. 70, 2 photographs, p. 71, 2 photographs: Hans-Georg Levin; p. 71, 1 photograph: Bumann; p. 72, 1 photograph: Hans-Georg Levin; p. 73, 2 photographs: Pampus Associates; p. 80, 1 photograph: Rondini, taken from *100 Gemüse*, Verlag Landwirtschaftliche Lehrmittelzentrale, Länggasse 79, 3052, Zollikofen; p. 83, 1 photograph, p. 90, 2 photographs, p. 92, 1 photograph: Hans-Georg Levin; p. 95, 1 photograph: Margit Fröhle; p. 98, 1 photograph, p. 99, 4 photographs: Hans-Georg Levin; p. 105, 1 photograph: Ulrike Lindner, Lehr- und Versuchsanstalt für Gartenbau, Auweiler; p. 117, 1 photograph: Margit Fröhle; p. 122, 2 photographs: Hans-Georg Levin.

Acknowledgments:

The authors and publishers wish to thank all those who have contributed to this book with their advice, help and expertise, especially:

Centro Bambù Italia, Mr Eberts, Mr Reis, Carasco; CBT, Headquarters for Fruit and Vegetable Auctions in the Netherlands, Ms Boekestein, Zoetermeer; Centre Français du Commerce Exterieur, Bernhard Neff, Frankfurt am Main; I.C.E. (Istituto nazionale per il commercio estero), Mr Paparella, Florence; I.C.E., Dr. Mario Russo, Verona; I.C.E., Dr. Leonardo Laganella, Frankfurt am Main; Institut für Obst- und Weinbau der Universität Hohenheim, Felix Lippert; International Fruits Bangkok Co. Ltd., Wanchai Lerdpongdee; Internationale Frucht-Import-Gesellschaft Weichert & Co., Mr Heuer, Hamburg; Japan-Import, Fujita Iacs Deutschland GmbH, Ms Fujita, Düsseldorf; Prof. Kosiyachinda, Bangkok; Fa. R. Laczek, Manfred Henke, Großmarkthalle Frankfurt am Main; Lehrstuhl für Gemüsebau der TU Weihenstephan, Mr Hongbin Zhang, Mr Krischke; Proexpo Hamburg, Jorge Riaño ; Prof. Dr. Sigmund Rehm, Institut für Pflanzenbau und Tierhygiene in den Tropen und Subtropen der Universität Göttingen; Schweizer Zentralstelle für Gemüsebau, Jörg Lüthi, Oeschberg; Sopexa, Förderungsgemeinschaft für französische Landwirtschaftserzeugnisse, Düsseldorf; Topinambur-Saatzucht, Mr Marquardt, Müden-Örtze; Prof. Dr. Wonneberger, FH Osnabrück/ Fachbereich Gartenbau.